Wholly
Unraveled

Wholly Unraveled

a Memoir

Keele Burgin

Little
a

Published by Little A, New York

www.apub.com

Amazon, the Amazon logo, and Little A are trademarks of Amazon.com, Inc., or its affiliates.

ISBN-13: 9781542042604 (hardcover)
ISBN-10: 1542042607 (hardcover)
ISBN-13: 9781542042628 (paperback)
ISBN-10: 1542042623 (paperback)

Cover design by Philip Pascuzzo

Printed in the United States of America

First edition

To Noah, Liam, and Greyson
Your strength, insight, and unwavering love have
taught me that I may just be worthy after all. Thank
you for teaching me the real meaning of family.

AUTHOR'S NOTE

My birth name is Kathleen. In this book, that's how I refer to myself. I've reconstructed my story and the dialogue from my memory. I've changed the names and identifying characteristics of many of the people to provide anonymity and protect privacy.

PROLOGUE

Winter, 1994: Remote Ontario, Canada

The only food I had was the three pieces of brown bread—which tasted of the outdoor oven where they had been made—and a cookie I'd stolen.

I had twenty-two hours before I could leave, and I needed to make one stolen cookie, two cigarettes, some stale brown bread, and a half gallon of water go the distance with me. I had to get the woodstove going, which meant I needed to force myself to go out into the blizzard to collect wood before it got dark, so I wouldn't freeze to death.

White was all I could see outside, but somehow it began to emulate every color of the rainbow as I stared out the old wood-framed window. Even the thousands of evergreens that surrounded my cabin were shades of white.

I looked at the Bible sitting on the tiny nightstand by the twin bed. It was the only book within a five-mile radius, and all I could think of was how much I wanted to use it for kindling. I asked myself if it would be just to spite my father or to test God, to see if He really would strike me down as I had been taught He would.

The gun snuck into my consciousness, as it had a thousand times before, and it was as if it had happened yesterday. I cowered inside that forgotten cabin. I was not a little girl anymore; yet I felt like a little girl in a grown-up body. I thought of the bathtub all those years ago and wondered if I would have been better off if I had allowed that to be the end of my life.

PART ONE

break (verb):

to separate into pieces as a result of a blow, shock, or strain

CHAPTER 1

Fall, 1980

I walked out of Alexander's, our local penny candy store, with a paper bag full of candy. All my favorites were in there: Bit-O-Honey, ZotZ, Tootsie Rolls, and some Swedish Fish. I loved Swedish Fish, but really I bought them in case I ran into my sister: Mary loved them too, and they'd come in handy as a bribe in case she caught me with the candy and threatened to tell Mom and Dad.

Mary and I were the two youngest in what was affectionately referred to as a set of Irish triplets. My oldest sister, Margaret Jr.—or Maggie, as we called her—was fourteen; Mary was thirteen; and I was twelve. Rachel, our little sister, was seven; she was my favorite. And then there was Ricky; he was three.

I started walking east down Third Avenue toward the ocean and home. Spring Lake, New Jersey, was a tiny town on the ocean, and I knew every grain of sand there. I felt panicked and powerful at the same time with this bag in my hand. If my mom was driving home, she would see the bag, and there could be big consequences.

I continued down my beloved street with the old-growth trees and stately homes, twirling my sun-bleached blond hair, which fell halfway down my back. I was always pleasantly surprised that I still had hair, given that I twirled it nonstop. I loved what the sun did to my body in the summer: my Irish skin took on more color from the days spent on the pristine beach across the street from my house. My face was oval-shaped, with a high forehead. I thought my eyes were too big for my face, but Shirley, our nanny, always shut down this self-criticism. She said my eyes were born from the sea and held the same magic that enabled the ocean to change from blue to green at any given moment.

I glanced down at my brand-new Levi's. They were bright red and fabulous. Mr. Cameli, the owner of the Camel's Eye, told me they had just gotten them in that morning, and I was the first to try them on. I was in love in an instant. My mom had sent me into town to buy a new version of what I already had, but that was ridiculous. Why would I need four pairs of the exact same blue jeans? I had already given two of the pairs to my best friend, Grace; she didn't get new clothes as often as I did, because her family didn't have a lot of extra money. I got new jeans. She got love.

I looked down at my red jeans and was happy with my decision to wear them out of the store. I had charged them to my mother's account, and now, even if my parents didn't let me keep them, they would have to pay for them.

As I rounded the corner by the lake, just three manicured blocks from my house on the ocean, I heard Grace's voice coming from the park.

"Kath-LEEN!"

"GRACE!" I screamed out.

We started to run toward each other from either side of the wooden bridge that spanned the lake. We were so alike on the inside but virtually opposite on the outside. Grace's brown hair fell almost to her shoulders with a curl, her eyes were the most opulent brown, and she had a figure that promised to be voluptuous in a few years. We met in the middle of the bridge, suspended over the water. I swatted Grace's sleeve with an inward chuckle. It was the pink Izod shirt that I had given her last week, and I was so happy she had something new to wear today. I was also relieved that I didn't have the same one on; I had another exactly like it in my shirt drawer at home. Besides, it would have clashed with my new jeans.

"Hey, you! How was your first day at the forbidden . . . I mean, public school? All those evil people running around doing evil things!" I joked.

"Yeah, totally. I was turned into a vampire in four different classes today," Grace said as she reached down into my bag of candy, pulled out an orange-flavored ZotZ, and began to tear open the wrapper. She looked down at my bright red legs. "I love your jeans! Where did those come from? I bet your mom hasn't seen those yet, huh?"

"Nope, but there's a *chance* she'll let me keep them." Grace lifted her eyebrow doubtfully as she bit into the candy. "Mary bought blue chinos last week, and Mom didn't say a word about them," I added. "Ya never know with my family."

"Well, I guess if they don't let you keep them, then you can give them to me!" she said, playfully. "I'd turn some heads at school with those. No more nasty uniforms!"

"Oh yeah, school. How was it?" I was so jealous that she had been allowed to transfer from St. Catharine's to Mountz, the public school.

"I am so glad I transferred! No escorts down the hall to your next class, and there's a real cafeteria: no more eating at desks in silence," Grace replied. "It's an open campus, so kids are allowed to come and go if we want . . ." Her voice trailed off, and I could tell she felt a little bad about telling me these things, knowing I would never be allowed to go to public school.

"It sounds like the freest place on earth," I said, smiling, trying to hide my envy. "I got recess taken away today for pushing up the sleeves of my blazer. Sister Dorothy Ann said I was out of dress code." I let my shoulders slump.

I looked right at Grace to see if she had missed me as much as I had missed her today. This was the first time we had been in different schools since kindergarten, and I was lonely without her.

She popped another ZotZ into her mouth and leaned in to cover me with her signature hug. Looking over her shoulder, I saw one of Grace's older sisters ascend the bridge to meet us.

"Hey, Kathleen," Grace's sister Patty said. "Want to grab some pizza with us? I was just about to take Grace for some grub at Tulio's."

Before I could answer, I saw my mom walking up the wooden bridge behind Grace and Patty. She wore her thin smile as she got closer to us, her frame petite, her posture perfect, and her clothes precisely ironed. I scanned her face and saw her left eye twitching ever so slightly. That meant trouble. I threw the bag of candy at Grace, my hands flying downward in a futile attempt to cover my jeans, which had just gone from fabulous to a real liability.

"Hello, girls," Mom said when she reached our gathering. She began to twirl her opal earring as she waited for our response. The moment of silence stretched across the bridge to both shores of the lake. She must have just come from the hairdresser: her frosted hair was perfectly mounted on her head, with just the right blend of blond to make it believable, as she was not really allowed to color her hair.

I felt my body shifting from one foot to the other as I tried to stand as tall as I could. "H-hi, Mom," I stuttered.

"Kathleen. Patty . . . Grace. How is your mother today? I think of her often when I receive the daily Eucharist. Please tell her so when you get home."

I watched in gratitude as Grace showed ownership of the candy bag by pulling out several pieces and eating them in plain sight of my mother.

"Time to go home, Kathleen. Please follow me to the car. Now," she said, her false smile still plastered on her face.

Grace and I exchanged glances as I turned to walk down the bridge behind my mother. Her eyes mirrored my worried look.

We both got in the car. I sat in the back seat on the passenger's side so I could see my mother's eyes if she turned around. Once we were tucked away from the world in the station wagon, she began in her low-pitched frown of a voice. She didn't start the car; she just sat looking straight ahead.

"Did I send you to town to play with Grace?"

"No."

"No what, Kathleen?"

"No, Mom."

"Did I send you to buy trashy red jeans?"

"No, Mom."

"Did anyone else see you? Anyone at all?"

"No, Mom, just Mr. Cameli," I lied.

"As soon as I pull this car into our driveway, you will get out, do your chores, and then go upstairs and stand outside our bedroom door to wait for your father to get home from work." She continued to speak in a low register; it sounded as if she were talking to herself. "Do not change those jeans: I want him to see them on you."

"No, Mom . . . please." My voice was shaking, and I could feel my heartbeat in my toes. "We can just take them back to the store. We don't need to tell Dad. Please, Mom."

"That's enough, Kathleen."

"But Mary bought those blue ones last week . . ." I was holding back my tears, trying to be strong.

My mom interrupted in her monotone voice. "That is different, Kathleen; now stop it."

From what I could tell by looking at her in the rearview mirror, the twitching under her eye had begun to subside. She took the keys out of her plain but expensive camel-colored pocketbook, which was on the passenger's seat, and held them for a moment before putting them in the ignition. She clicked her blinker light to go left—even though there wasn't a car to be seen—then checked her mirrors on both sides and carefully eased out onto Warren Avenue.

She tilted her head, leaning it against the driver's-side window, and began to steer the car with her knee, using one hand to play with her hair while the other lay idle in her lap. Sometimes when my mom drove, she looked younger. If there were more than two kids in the car, or if my dad was with us, she didn't, but times like now she was in her own world, humming "Bridge over Troubled Water." She looked like she was enjoying being in charge of something all her own, even if it was just a station wagon.

I began to play a game I called my somewhere-else place. I pretended to be in the car with my mom headed to Six Flags, just the two of us, to ride the roller coaster over and over again. I told myself that there would be no consequence for these jeans and that, really, my mom liked them. I kept it going, telling myself that my palms were sweating from excitement, not fear. I watched as my mom played her own somewhere-else game. I tried to imagine what she was picturing in her perfect place, where most everything was different from how it really was.

I would ask my mother about her childhood—what she was like when she was my age. She always seemed exhausted by the question; there was a perfect shroud of secrecy around her childhood. According to my mother, she had an idyllic childhood—despite my grandmother being put into a special hospital when my mother was seven and the fact that she was fourteen before she saw my grandmother again. She repeated the same stories every time I asked: they said the rosary every morning at five thirty; they didn't have a lot of money, but they had a lot of love; and my grandfather was a fireman and got a desk job after his stroke. That was it. My dad said they ruined her brain. My mother was the eldest of two and the only girl, so the cooking, cleaning, and laundry fell to her while my grandfather went to the firehouse. He had arthritis and had suffered two strokes by the time my mother was my age. A wonderful childhood indeed. My grandmother was staying with us now. She acted kind of strange sometimes, like she wasn't really where her body was. I didn't think she liked me.

My mom shuffled in her seat, correcting her posture, and straight-lined her smile as she sped up. She took the left turn onto Ocean Avenue a little too fast, the tires protesting as they squeaked onto our quiet street. She turned up the Christian radio station. I needed to come up with a plan to get out of this red-jean jam I was in.

One minute later we pulled up in front of our house. Maggie, Mary, and Rachel were in the front yard with tennis racquets in their hands. Jeremy, our tennis coach, was pulling out of the driveway after dropping them off from practice at the tennis courts. He gave a quick wave to my mom; she returned a proper wave.

I looked up at the only home I had ever known. It was an 1870s Victorian bed-and-breakfast that my parents had turned into our family home. *There must be a place I can hide in there,* I thought.

I stayed in the car a few seconds longer than my mom, who popped out like a cannonball and headed across the front lawn. I wasn't in a hurry to get to my dreaded post and wait for the punishment for having five minutes of girl time and red pants.

"Did your father call while I was gone?" my mom asked as she parted my sisters, who had stopped to greet her, and headed to the side door. She kept walking inside as Maggie yelled the answer across the lawn: "Dad is going to be home for dinner, but he didn't say what time!" As my mother disappeared into the house, I climbed out of the station wagon and made my way slowly toward the side door.

"Ha. Nice pants, Kath. I bet you're headed upstairs," Mary blurted out once she knew my mom was out of hearing range. "Have fun!"

"Love you too, Mary. Jerk!" I said. I purposefully brushed her shoulder as I passed my sisters and kept walking up the flower-lined driveway to the side door.

"Kath, I cleaned our room while you were out today. Mom let me," Rachel called after me.

She was so innocent. "Cleaning our room" meant Mom let her take anything she wanted of mine and call it her own. It was my parents' insurance policy to prevent me from getting tied to "worldly" things— things outside the Catholic world.

I waited outside my parents' bedroom for over an hour. I stood up straight as I had been taught: no slouching and no leaning on the wall for support. I couldn't stop thinking of my father's face, his voice, and my absolute powerlessness to stave off the impending punishment. How bad would this one be? I had been beaten for less than red jeans, but that was the problem: I just never knew what would be a big deal and what I could do without suffering the consequences.

Recently, my dad had forbade me to go outside for a day. I snuck out and rode my bike to Mike's Pizza in Belmar with Sean, the boy I had a crush on. We were eating our slices at a table by the beach when my dad's Cadillac pulled up. He ordered a slice, came and sat with us, ate, and didn't say a word. Then he got back in his car and drove in the direction of home. I shook from my toes to my skull when I walked back into my house. He never said a word about it.

I spent the time wondering why my family couldn't be like Grace's. She was allowed to hang out at the park, explore the beach, eat candy, and wear whatever color jeans she wanted. Hers was a big family too, but normal. They loved, they fought, they listened to the radio and each other, and they had differing opinions. In my family there was no radio (well, no non-Christian radio), no candy, no TV, no red jeans, and no individuality: we were a collective that moved as one. Whenever and wherever my dad said was law.

My body tightened, and the knot in my gut grew as my thoughts went back to my dad's pattern of punishment. I began to twirl my hair furiously. My muscles were knotting around each other, and I needed to go to the bathroom. The week before, I had peed in my pants when he hit me. He thought I'd done it on purpose and made me pull my pants down and bend over so he could hit me again.

I left my post and ran to the bathroom that separated Maggie's room from Mary's just a short way down the hall. I didn't bother to wipe myself or flush; I pulled my red jeans up and ran back to the ornate wooden door that separated me from my parents' room just in time to hear my dad's silver Cadillac pull into the driveway.

I counted the steps as he walked up to the side porch, up the green wooden steps, and in through the grand entrance, a huge covered porch with a hammock that had been tucked away in the corner for another day. He had all his shoes made in New York City and told us that shoes were a statement of who you were in the world. His shoes made his steps loud and powerful. I heard him announcing his presence downstairs and hoped that he was in a good mood.

"Margaret, I'm home." His voice was commanding; it brought you to him no matter where you were, and he knew that. It helped that his six-foot-two frame was thick and masculine and every bit intimidating.

"Coming, Richard. Coming, hon," my mom said as she quickly made her way from the enormous wraparound sunroom to the formal living room. "Here, let me take your briefcase. How was your day?" she asked.

I could picture her taking his briefcase and putting it by the antique coatrack with the mirror while willing all of us to come running to greet our father, which was the nightly drill. I heard three more sets of feet scurrying to meet him at the door, but mine wouldn't move.

"Hi, Dad," my sisters said, almost in unison.

"How was your day? Did your case go well?" Maggie squeaked out.

"I will tell you about it at dinner. Go back to your homework, girls. Where is Kathleen?"

All of my sisters fled; no one wanted to answer that question.

My mother spoke slowly and carefully in a hushed voice. When my mom's whispering stopped, my arm hairs stood on end. The thundering footsteps made their way up the ornate wooden staircase, and I heard his voice echo through the hallway.

"Those jeans better not be slut red."

He reached the top of the stairs quicker than I thought he could. My hand flew to my mouth to stifle the sound I didn't mean to make.

"Asking for it again, Kathleen? Get in here," he said as he whisked by me without a look.

"Yes, Dad," I said as I followed him into the bedroom.

He moved around to the far side of the Victorian bed and began to undo his tie. Behind him, through the wood-framed glass doors that led to the balcony, I could see the ocean waves crashing on the slick black jetty. I tried to get to my somewhere-else place. A safe place. I was willing myself to believe in the magic that would transport me anywhere else in the world. I watched his eyes run up and down my body.

"What did you say to me?"

"'Yes, Dad.' I said 'Yes, Dad.'" I could feel my lower lip trembling.

I blinked, and when I opened my eyes he was coming toward me, his suit perfectly tailored, his striped tie in one hand. His face was a mixture of anger and strange happiness. I had a desire to beg for his forgiveness.

"I'm sorry, Dad . . ." His left hand landed squarely on my cheek-bone, and I staggered to keep my body upright.

"Go to the woodpile, pick out a stick, and bring it to me."

I touched my face. There was blood from where his wedding ring had cut my cheek. My dad was walking into the bathroom still holding his tie, and I wanted to see his eyes. "Get moving," he said.

I ran down the long hallway to the back staircase, grateful to be putting distance between my father and me but confused and terrified at my mission. A *stick*? I ran past Mary's room, Maggie's room, the blue guest room. The house had gone silent.

I held on to the wood railing and headed down the dark, cold back staircase that was once the servants' stairway when the house was a bed-and-breakfast. It was pitch-black, but I knew to count nine steps on the red shag rug, turn left, and count eight more so I didn't have to stop and turn on the little overhead chandelier. I ran into the den, with its dark colors and limited light, through the heavy swinging wood door, and into the kitchen. I was sure to find someone in the kitchen—hopefully Shirley—but it was completely empty, with only the fire crackling in the corner.

I was too scared to run into the baking kitchen or the wraparound sunroom or alcove; my punishment would be worse if I were found to have wandered off course. I needed to stay focused on my route to the woodpile. I made my way out the back door and down the concrete steps two at a time to the side of the house. Maybe someone would be waiting for me. There it was, the five-foot-high woodpile. I stood in front of it, alone.

I had a strange feeling of numbness; it covered me from my toes to my forehead. I wanted to faint. I listened for the sounds of my father following me: nothing. I reminded myself of what I was there for: I needed to pick a stick. I had no idea what stick would be acceptable to my father. I wasn't sure what he'd use it for.

I began to search through the woodpile. I pretended that the stick would be used in the tree house I desperately wanted him to build for me. I picked up wood at a frantic pace. Too small, too big, too much bark, too scary to think about, too many splinters on one side, too small again. And then I found it: a medium-sized stick, definitely a weapon and sturdy enough to be in my tree house. It had a curved knot on one side of the gold-colored wood, and very little bark. I felt the other side, and it felt smoother than the others—safer. I took a really good look at it, almost trying to talk to it, to ask it to be kind no matter what my dad did with it.

How long had I been searching? I could feel my blood pulsing in my brain. I had lost track of time, avoiding the ascent back to my parents' room. My father was not a patient man, so I began to sprint back, my stick in hand.

I ran up the front staircase, one hand on the cool wood of the banister, giving up on trying to find anyone to save me.

My dad was waiting when I turned in to the bedroom. He was standing on the blue carpet with his back to me. He opened the screen door to the balcony. I could hear the ocean and smell the salt air. Then he turned to me with no expression on his face and what looked like no patience in his body as he switched his weight from one leg to the other.

I looked in his hazel eyes, hoping he would think, *You are flesh of my flesh,* which he had made us memorize from the Bible.

My heart beat unsteadily as he moved toward me again, slower this time.

"Open your mouth," he said as he ripped the stick out of my hand, leaving splinters in my palm.

"What?" I tried to hold the tears in the spaces behind my eyes, but I felt them leaking down my cheeks.

"OPEN YOUR MOUTH!" He was towering over me, and I trembled as I opened my mouth.

"Stick out your tongue," he demanded. I did as he asked. "Farther." His voice used all the oxygen in the room.

I stuck my tongue out as far as possible. I kept my eyes focused on his and I caught the wildness in him as I felt his hand brace against my shoulder and push me into the wall behind me. He took aim, raising the stick, and my body began to shake uncontrollably. He tightened his grip on my shoulder and paused with the stick in the air above his head. I looked him in the eye to steady myself against his anger so that I wouldn't faint.

My tongue involuntarily escaped to the inside of my mouth, and he screamed, "NOW!"

I stuck out my tongue again and braced myself. My breath was raspy and rapid.

"Do you know the rules in this house?"

"Yesth, Dad," I said as best I could with my tongue sticking out.

"DO YOU KNOW GOD'S RULES IN THIS HOUSE?" His voice made my clothes shake.

"Yesth, Dad." I kept looking him in the eye.

"Put your tongue out farther, so help me, God."

I saw the stick coming down toward me. His eyes were focused on my tongue, and he was holding my shoulder steady against the wood-paneled wall because of my trembling.

Just before the stick descended, he let go of my shoulder and grabbed my left wrist. I turned my head away, biting my tongue a little as I smashed my teeth together, bracing for impact. As my eyes closed, he whaled on the tender skin of my forearm with the stick. I landed on the floor in the fetal position. I screamed. The pain echoed throughout my body, and I fought for consciousness as I rolled from side to side, trying to move away from him.

"Get up. Don't be so dramatic." I sensed he regretted his decision to switch targets at the last minute. "Go help your mother with dinner," he said.

I flinched as he stepped over me and headed downstairs with even more confidence than when he'd come up.

I could feel a trickle of warm blood seeping from my forearm. My brain felt like it had nails moving around in it, and my mouth was dry. I kicked my foot out, shutting the door to the bedroom in hopes of having a second's warning if he were to come back for another round.

I lifted my head until I could see the digital clock on my mom's side of the bed. I gave myself five full minutes before I put one hand on the carpet and pushed myself up to a standing position. I glued my tongue to the roof of my mouth with a strange sense of gratitude that it wasn't bleeding too, and I held my bleeding forearm with my right hand. I walked around the bed, past the balcony, and into my parents' bathroom. I washed my forearm gently before preparing to head downstairs, where my family would have reappeared, ready to have dinner.

CHAPTER 2

As I left the bathroom, I noticed the stick he had just hit me with on the bed next to his black leather wallet. I was careful not to touch the stick as I picked up his wallet, took out two hundred-dollar bills, and stuck them in my pocket before walking around the bed and opening the bedroom door.

I hadn't heard my mom give the call to come downstairs to help with dinner, so I headed down the hallway to change my clothes in hopes of changing my existence. I frantically moved my tongue around the inside of my mouth to try to forget the pain on my forearm as I walked down the long hallway to my room. I went to work dulling the inner pain that was swelling in my heart too, and I allowed myself to believe that no one from my family saw me go to the woodpile.

I walked into my bathroom, the cold hexagonal white tiles chilling my feet. I took the money out of my pocket and stared at it. Benjamin Franklin's face looked ugly and preoccupied. I ripped the first bill in half and then half again. My breath was caught in my chest as I began to rip the bills into tiny pieces and throw them in the toilet. The first bits of money floated on the surface until I flushed the toilet with my toes and watched the pieces swirl around the bowl before disappearing. I wanted to give it to Shirley, but I knew she wouldn't accept it. I finished ripping the money up, flushed the toilet again, washed my hands, smiled into the mirror to see if my satisfaction was believable, and walked into my bedroom.

"I set the dinner table for you," Rachel said, from deep under her covers. "Mom looked kind of mad when she realized you didn't do it before you went upstairs. I hope I did it right so you don't get in more trouble."

"Thanks. I'm sure you did a great job," I said.

"I'm sorry I took your stuff today. I put it all back and told Mom that I didn't want it," she said.

I walked to her bed and sat down on the edge. She had her green blankie up as close as it could get to her face, and she was circling the soft fabric on the bottom with her thumb and middle finger.

For her own good, I hoped Rachel was more like Maggie and Mary; they never got hit. Maggie was always too busy praying, though I didn't know why Mary hadn't been hit. I must do something to deserve it, but I didn't know what it was.

"Are you OK? That looks like it really hurts." Rachel pulled back a bit from me to look at my forearm.

"It doesn't hurt; it just feels kind of numb," I lied, doing the best I could to cover the drying blood.

"Will you play school with me?" she asked as she began to twirl her hair.

"Of course. Come on." I gently tucked her hair behind her ear; she needed to break that habit she'd gotten from me. I pulled the covers off her. She jumped from the bed, her blankie left behind on the pillow, and scanned the room for the chalk we used to write on the wallpaper.

"I don't know anybody who is allowed to write on their wallpaper. Do you?" Rachel asked.

"We are," I said, then pulled her hair up in a clip so she couldn't twirl it.

"Can we leave the wallpaper like it is when we redo our room? I want to make it like a ship's room, with the beds built into the wall and our desks right below them so it looks like the desks are holding up the bed. We could have curtains across our two beds and lights and everything," Rachel said.

"Dinner!" Mary's voice came up from the front staircase.

I headed to the closet where we kept our more formal clothes. Our grandmother was having dinner with us that evening, and she demanded that we all dress our best for the meal. For Rachel I picked out a pink flowery dress with green vines, some socks with lace that folded down on the ankle, and her black patent leather Mary Janes.

I laid the outfit on the bed and helped her out of her tennis clothes and into the dress, which buttoned in the back.

"Perfect, Rachel. You look adorable. Now go greet Grandmother; she's probably in the alcove. I'll meet you downstairs soon. Go down the back steps so you don't disturb Dad if he's in his room. OK?"

She took my hand and looked at me with her beautiful brown eyes. She was silent for a moment, and I bent down and hugged her. "Love ya," she said, and headed out the door and down the back staircase.

I went back to our closet to create my outfit, less frilly but still dressy. I picked the light blue slacks with the side pockets, a white collared shirt that smelled of Shirley's iron, a white cardigan, and my penny loafers without socks, since my pants covered them. I pulled my shirt over my head and winced when it hit my wrist. I was more careful putting my cardigan on, and I went to the bathroom and wrapped toilet paper around my wrist, carefully tucking it under the cardigan and shirt in case it started to bleed again.

I folded the red jeans and hid them under my bed to give to Grace the next day. I kicked my somewhere-else game into gear—the one in which I pretended I was numb so I couldn't feel pain—and walked down the back staircase, this time stopping to turn the light on overhead. I practiced my smile with every step.

"Hi, Shirley," I said as I rounded the corner from the den to the kitchen.

"Miss Kathleen, how are you, sweet girl?" She placed the last log on the fire, closed the screen with one hand, and started to walk across the kitchen to me.

Her body was well worn from her thirty-seven years; her tired and scarred brown skin told of her abusive childhood and hard labor. The ever-present redness in her eyes made me sure that my tears were safe. I couldn't take my eyes off her; my feet stayed planted on the wood floor, and I felt the somewhere-else game harder to concentrate on as she got closer. The tears freed themselves to stream down my cheeks, one after precious one.

I watched her walk past the kitchen table and pantry and around the Italian-granite island and china cabinet, closing the glass door along the way. She never lost eye contact with me. She came to my corner, and as she struggled to bend down on one knee with the tiniest squeak escaping her lips, she placed one hand on the ground for support and the other on my face. Her hands felt rough on my skin and so soft in my heart, it made me cry harder.

"You are strong as an ox, Miss Kathleen; don't you forget that, girl. You strong: keep your head up. Got it?" she said.

I nodded as she took her tea towel from the pocket of her pressed white apron and wiped the tears from my cheeks.

"Get me that there pot and get it full of hot water, little Ox. We gotta get this dinner on the table for your grandmother; you know how she like it just so. You'll help me for a minute."

I filled the copper pot from the special temperature spout in the center of the granite island sink and put it on the burner. I looked at Shirley to get the high sign that I was allowed to turn the burner on. She gave me the flick of the wrist, which was her OK, and we shared a smile.

"Get in there and be proper with your grandmother, now, Ox. Go on—you can't stay in here with me, you know that. Go," she said.

I grabbed the serving tray from the counter and opened the china cabinet Shirley had just closed. I took out one Lenox dinner plate, one salad plate, a Waterford water and wineglass, and the appropriate silverware and napkin, and I placed them on the tray. I glanced at Shirley and saw her smile.

"Miss Kathleen, you are a lovely girl. You know that is never gonna happen. I just can't sit down with y'all for a meal; it doesn't work that way," she said.

"Let's just try it again," I said, as I leaned into the swinging wood door that separated the kitchen from dining room, with the tray in hand. I set the place setting with the precision I had been taught, every fork just so, the water glass placed two inches to the right of the wineglass. I finished the setting arrangement and went out the double French doors to the living room to join my family.

My father had his wing chair turned so his back was to the group gathered by the roaring fireplace. He was flipping through his record collection with one hand and holding his black coffee in the other. He turned when he heard the swinging door and then turned right back around to the music selection.

My mother stood at attention next to my grandmother, explaining her new upholstery choice with her body completely still, one hand at her side and the other in her mouth between words to bite her cuticles. Her voice had a subtle shake to it, with a childish tone of uncertainty.

I walked to my grandmother first. "Hello, Grandmother." I stood waiting for her to acknowledge me. Her body reminded me of a statue at the museum with the red rope around it so you can't get too close. Her tailored suit was impeccably wrapped around her petite frame, and her face was expressionless. She glanced down without looking at me and then looked back at my mother.

"Continue, Margaret," she said.

"Do you like it, Mother?" Mom asked.

There was too much silence between sentences with Grandmother; I fought not to fill in the gap. Maggie, Mary, Rachel, and I stood and stared at my mother, careful not to look in the direction of Grandmother as she let the words catch up to her.

"Well, Margaret, it doesn't matter whether I like it or not—you have chosen the color and now you must live with it. You don't waste money to redo this sort of thing. It is a bit drab; I would have thought you'd want to make it a cheerier place."

Grandmother took Rachel's hand in hers and then moved past my mother and toward the alcove at the far end of the living room. Rachel gave me a look that made me want to save her, but she was my grandmother's favorite and that was something that could help in the long run, at least with my mom.

Mom sat down in her newly upholstered chair, running her hand up and down the armrest.

"I love this shade of green, Mom; it's my favorite. It always puts me in a better mood," I said, trying to find her eyes.

Shirley came into the living room and said, "Dinner is ready, Mrs. Flanagan. Would you like me to have Mr. Flanagan and the girls be seated?" she asked.

"Yes, Shirley. Thank you." My mother stood, smoothed her suede skirt, and walked briskly into the dining room.

"Mr. Flanagan, sir, Mrs. Flanagan would like to serve dinner now," she said to my father.

"On my way, Shirley. This should be fun. Another day at the crazy house with Margaret's mom," my dad said, loud enough for all to hear.

My grandmother tightened her hold on Rachel's hand, straightened her back, and quickened her pace to the alcove. Maggie and Mary followed behind them.

My dad turned off the music and walked from his spot by the big picture windows that overlooked the ocean and made his way toward the fireplace, where I was standing, watching him. His smile was almost crooked, and his eyes looked to be a brighter hazel than they had been an hour ago. He ran one hand through his dark hair while the other jiggled coins in the front pocket of his khakis. He walked casually, as if he were being entertained by his very own existence.

I realized that he was deliberately coming toward me, and I froze, my wrists buried under my armpits for safekeeping. I reminded myself that he usually didn't hit me in front of the family, but as I watched him walk, I looked behind me to see if I could turn around and run and make it look natural. Before I could move, he was standing over me. I looked into his eyes, left to right.

"Come on, kiddo, let's have some dinner." He tousled my hair and nudged me toward the dining room. My body went taut, and I worked to loosen it as he kept one hand in my hair and the other draped on my shoulder.

"I have been riding Beau hard, and I think this weekend may be the time Beau beats your Lady. She's fast all right, but the reason you win is because you ride her bareback. Lots less weight."

My dad and I shared the love of horses. He treated Beau like an object. Lady was my friend. We kept them at a barn just a couple of miles inland. I often walked there to be with Lady. I had beaten my dad in every single horse race we had ever had—me on Lady, my dad on his horse, Beau. It was the only victory I had ever had over my dad. I would become one with Lady as we sailed through the open fields and jumped the fences and the creek by the barn, the leaves from the trees smacking my legs and the air tasting colder the faster we went. I was surprised that my dad didn't hit me after I won, but he never did.

My grandmother stood up from the couch where she had been sitting with my sisters in the alcove. A noise came out of her mouth that was half-human and half–wounded animal, and it was cut short with an inward breath. Her body froze and her hands went rigid, fingers spread in front of her. Her mouth was open, but there was no sound, and her eyes looked like someone whose life had just been taken away.

Rachel ran to the dining room and hid behind me. Mary moved more slowly toward the dining room and away from Grandmother.

Maggie stayed right where she was on the couch where my grandmother had just been. She was hugging her legs into her chest and rocking back and forth, mumbling something about God's mercy.

"Here we go . . . ," my dad said without turning to look at Grandmother. He chuckled as my mom ran past him to get to her mother.

"Jesus, Jesus, Jesus . . . Jesus, Jesus, Jesus . . . everyone is safe, Mom. We are all right here. Safe. Everyone is safe. You are safe," my mom's litany began as she gently brought Grandmother back to reality. Maggie got off the couch and started moving toward my mom, making the sign of the cross on her body over and over again. She joined in on the "Jesus" chant—louder, then softer, then louder again. Rachel slid her hand into mine, and we watched them.

"Let's eat," my dad said to Shirley.

My mother rubbed Grandmother's back as Maggie chanted the litany, and slowly Grandmother's blue eyes came back into focus. Her arms released their tension and fell to the sides of her body, and she began to walk to the dining room without a sound. My mother and sister followed in silence.

"Shirley," my father yelled, "let's eat!"

Shirley appeared from the kitchen with a water pitcher and a bottle of red wine in her hands while everyone took their seats around the dining room table.

My grandmother walked slowly into the dining room, past her chair, and to the left of the fireplace next to the grandfather clock, then stopped. She reached her right hand out and touched the striped red velvet wallpaper. She raised her left hand and placed it on top of her right. Her hands went up the soft wallpaper in slow motion and then down with an even slower motion, and then she put her face on the wall and held it there.

Mom walked to the wall and stood next to her. "It's beautiful wall-paper, isn't it, Mom? Come sit down; it's time to eat. We're having your favorite meal, salmon and risotto." She gently touched my grand-mother's shoulders and led her to her chair on the opposite side of the grandfather clock, the seat farthest away from my father. Grandmother inched her way to her seat, searching my mother's face for a name.

Shirley poured the wine and water and placed the bottle and pitcher on the side table behind my father. She came around next to my seat and, with a wink and a beautiful smile, quietly gathered up the place setting I had laid out for her. I would have rather had dinner with Shirley than anyone else in the world, and her smile told me she knew that.

Shirley left the dining room and came back with a beautiful array of salmon and risotto, prepared exactly as Grandmother preferred. Shirley's body may have been large, but she could blend right into the woodwork when grown-ups were around. She could serve you dinner, pour you water, and push your chair closer to the table without you knowing she was there.

There was a sort of protection in the fact that my grandmother would have these episodes of panic, because I knew the attention would be on her instead of me. So I settled into my chair with a greater sense of security than I had had five minutes earlier.

Grandmother lifted her head and looked around the room at us, and we knew that was our cue.

"Maggie, you start," Mom said, "quickly . . ."

"Hi, Grandmother, it's Maggie. I like when you read me books."

"Grandmother, it's Mary. You smell good today."

"It's ridiculous that we do this every time, Margaret," my dad said. He took a bite of salmon and leaned back in his chair.

"Now, Kathleen, please . . . ," Mom said.

"I'm Kathleen. I like chocolate chip mint ice cream, even though you don't."

My mom then took over, asking Grandmother questions, then answering them herself to move the conversation along.

I stared at Grandmother, wondering if I could catch a glimpse of sanity as she methodically wiped her mouth after every bite of food. Always left to right, pause, and place napkin on lap. Bite. Pause. Wipe mouth left to right, pause, and place napkin on lap.

"Rachel, please tell all of us about tennis today. What did you work on with your coach?" Mom asked.

"Um, backhand and serving, Mom. Mary got in trouble for not paying attention, and Maggie said she would rather be praying."

"Good, sweetie, that's great." Mom was staring at Grandmother, who had stopped the eating routine and moved on to drink water and wine. Sip water. Stop. Wipe mouth from left to right. Stop. Sip wine. Stop. Wipe mouth from left to right. Stop.

"Mary, how was your lesson?" Mom asked.

"Great, Mom; perfect, really," Mary said.

"Mother, would you like some more water? Shirley?" Mom turned her head toward the swinging door. Shirley took great care filling Grandmother's glass of water. She poured love as she poured the water, setting the pitcher down with precision.

Sometimes I would count to see how long it took Grandmother to come to her senses.

"Shirley, this salmon is impeccable. Where did you get the recipe?" Grandmother began to eat without the napkin routine. She picked up her fork and knife, moved her food around her plate, and urged the food onto her fork and into her mouth. She shifted in her chair and looked around the room with clear eyes.

"From Ms. Flanagan, ma'am. She's a very good cook," Shirley said.

"Oh, Shirley, you know I think that all black people should be sent back to Africa, but you can stay," my mom said without looking at her.

"Rachel, good girl, eating all of your dinner," Grandmother said. "How about you and I go to Jean Louise's Homemade Candies tomorrow after school? We'll get you some chocolate-covered strawberries."

"Can we have dessert tonight?" Rachel asked.

"No, no dessert tonight," Mom said. "I want you girls to clean the kitchen, since Shirley is leaving early, and do your homework. Grandmother and I are going to sit on the sunporch. Richard, will you join us?"

"Maybe, Margaret, we'll see," Dad said. "Girls, get moving on the dishes. Don't give me any reason to come in there tonight."

The four of us stood and began to scramble toward our respective jobs in silence.

I came through the swinging doors with an armful of dishes. I saw Mary from a unique angle: she was at the sink, scrubbing pots. Because she couldn't see me looking at her, I stopped to study her. She was heavier than me—not fat necessarily, just heavy in her body. She didn't have much in the way of eyebrows or many eyelashes, and what she did have were so blond, you couldn't see them. Her eyes were set far back in her head. Her hair was darker and straighter than mine. She turned from the sink and looked straight at me as if she had caught me red-handed. I noticed the sadness in the way she moved her body, as if her body didn't fit her. I tried to pinpoint when our outright hatred of each other had begun, but nothing specific came to mind. It just felt like it was always in the room.

"What are you doing, loser? Move it. I need the rest of the pots," she said.

I set the pan of salmon down next to her at the sink and decided not to say anything. Her hatred of herself was enough; I didn't need to add to it.

I finished my chores in silence and waited. It was crazy making that we all had to stay in the kitchen until it was spotless, regardless of who was taking forever to finish on purpose.

"Do you do that just to bug us? I could wash that pot in twenty seconds. Come on," I said to Mary, unable to hold it in any longer.

She slowed down even more, and I wanted to grab the S.O.S pad from her hand and get that pot clean, but she just smiled and moved slower than ever.

I looked around the newly remodeled kitchen and was proud of my mom. It was a work of art. The kitchen was enormous, yet there was a coziness to it that I really appreciated; it was a room I wanted to be in. A large built-in eating area in the far corner of the kitchen housed a rectangular wooden table where we ate dinner if we weren't in the formal dining room. The booth-style seating was inviting, with custom royal-blue leather cushions that fit perfectly into both corners of the seating area, held there with ornamental nails. It had a slanted shingled roof above the table that made it feel separate from the rest of the kitchen. The roof had a wooden molding around the base, and my mom had had the builders use the same shingles that were on the outside roof.

Instead of giving Mary the satisfaction of seeing me wait, I hopped off the stool I'd been sitting on, grabbed an orange out of the oversized and overflowing lime-green fruit bowl, and threw it to the top of the shingled roof above the kitchen table.

"You are dead meat if Dad walks in," Mary said as she quickened her pot-washing pace.

"Shut up and do the dishes, slowpoke."

The orange bounded down over the shingles, popped up after hitting one particular shingle, and landed again about midway down the roof. It rolled and hit the molding at the end, which made me back up several feet to catch it.

"I want to do it." Rachel was behind me, ready for her turn. I checked to make sure all the kitchen doors were closed and handed her the orange. She threw it to the top, and it began spraying juice in every direction as it made its way toward us, split in three places. We caught it together and laughed as I buffered our fall to the floor.

"Get another one," Rachel squealed. Rachel threw the orange, and we watched as it got stuck in the molding around the roof. I moved around the counter to grab the stool just as my dad walked in to inspect the kitchen.

"Dad," I said, frozen in place.

"Let's move it. Kathleen, take your grandmother upstairs to Maggie's room; Maggie, help Rachel with her homework; and, Mary, finish up in here." He glanced at the orange and added, "Mary, get up there and get that orange off the roof." Then he turned and left the kitchen.

I wished I had a rulebook for this family. Red jeans, no. Food fight, OK. But I knew those rules could be the opposite tomorrow, so I just moved on. Rachel jumped on my back for a ride over to Maggie for homework time.

"Do you think they're watching?" Grandmother asked my mom as she pulled her turtleneck higher than it should go.

"Mother . . . um, no." My mom looked around the room as if she weren't convinced and then took my grandmother's hand and placed it in mine. "Kathleen, take your grandmother upstairs to bed." Grandmother took her hand out of mine and walked to the stairs, looking over her shoulder every few steps.

I walked behind Grandmother as she took her time walking up the front staircase, her posture in the extreme upright position and her hand gripping the railing.

"Grandmother, would you like me to get you some water to put by your bed?" I wondered if she heard me or if the voices inside her were just drowning me out. "Grandmother?"

At the top of the stairs, she stopped at the linen closet, turned the light on, and counted out five slate-colored towels. Then she turned and headed through Maggie's room to the bathroom.

I hid behind the sheer white curtains by the twin brass beds to watch her. I wondered why Grandmother wanted to stay in here instead of in one of the guest rooms on the third floor with the Egyptian cotton sheets, cashmere blankets, and claw-foot soaker tubs. Maybe she didn't want to be alone, or maybe it was because Maggie's room was closest to the stairs, meaning she could get out quick if something went wrong.

I always had so many questions for her when she came to visit, but I never asked them.

I watched her narrow face and frightened blue eyes staring into the mirror above the antique sink. She squinted and looked closely at herself, then took one step backward and looked into the mirror again. Her eyes shone brighter, and I heard her exhale. She was smiling into the mirror; her face dropped the tension, and her pursed lips relaxed into a true smile. Her body looked lucid and vulnerable as she stopped just shy of a curtsy. She stepped forward again, close to the mirror, and pulled a porcelain bowl from her bag and set it by the sink.

She wore a wig. It was all teased up like a hive, to keep others from getting into her head. She was aware that we knew she wore it, but there was some weird code of silence around the wig, as if it kept all her secrets, and if you asked about it, it would instantly turn into a swarm of bees large enough to kill you.

I pulled the curtains to the side of my body and watched her take it off. She started from the back and released the set number of bobby pins as if they were her friends. She held each one of them for more than a second and counted them individually before putting them into the white porcelain bowl next to Maggie's sink. She pulled the wig off and stood perfectly still as she stared into the mirror. Her natural hair was flat against her head, and she moved both hands to touch her hair, which was still pinned up with more bobby pins. When the last bobby pin was laid to rest in the porcelain bowl, I could see her as she'd been in her youth.

Her natural hair underneath that godforsaken wig was like a silk carpet that she unwrapped from its packaging. Her long white-gray hair trailed behind her like a novel, one I would never have the privilege of reading because she would not publish it. Oh, what I would do to get my hands on that book. It would have explained something to me, given me a reason for my lack of mothering. It would have given me empathy and a place to go when I desperately needed to understand why I didn't have a mother of plenty, just a mother of sorts.

I stood up and slowly walked past the bathroom, watching Grandmother brush her hair as I passed without being noticed. The house was quiet, with the exception of the sounds of Mary practicing scales on the piano one story below me. I walked down the hall and took a left up the wooden staircase that led to the third floor. It was off-limits to the kids, and it was my favorite place in our house. Each of the four guest rooms had expensive and untouched décor and a private porch. I went straight down the hall, past the first three bedrooms and the small door to the attic, and came to my favorite room.

I opened the white wooden door with its original glass doorknob and went straight past the bed and dresser and out onto the smallest of the balconies that overlooked the Atlantic Ocean. The screen door creaked when I pushed it open. I tasted the salty air and felt moisture in my eyes. I made my way to the corner of the balcony, pulled myself up onto the six-inch-wide ledge of the railing, and sat with my back against the wooden shingles of the house.

I stared at the ocean. The waves were speaking to one another. They crashed into the beach with strength and moved out with a gentler force, taking part of the beach back out to sea with them. I waited as the waves once again became my confidants. I watched long enough to be sure my sadness would be safe. I wanted the waves to tell me that I belonged and give me the rope I needed to stay alive. I pulled my knees up to my chest, wrapped my arms around them, and allowed the tears to run steadily down my face. My voice was faint as it mixed with the salty air.

"I won't let him break me," I said, gently holding my wrist. "I won't let him win." My tears rolled into my mouth and mixed with my words.

I felt the waves listening in a way that made me believe in God— not my father's God, but someone with a presence of love and a tenderness that overwhelmed me. I looked at the full moon hovering over the ocean, and it seemed to be lighting the waves with reverence. A breeze kicked up, and I caught my body as it swayed, feeling a sense of endlessness. I stood up on the narrow ledge of the railing, took a moment to steady myself, and walked to the end perfectly balanced, my arms outstretched on either side, careful not to look down at the ground three stories below me. I was suspended in the air above the earth, and my special power was peace.

CHAPTER 3

Two days later, my sisters and I ran to pile into my mom's green station wagon with wood panels on the side. It was parked out in front of our house. We all wanted the third-row seat because it faced opposite everyone else's, and my sisters and I played games with the cars behind us as my dad drove. The week before, on the way to the General Community Gathering (GCG), Mary and I had broken the record for how many drivers behind us we could make give us the peace sign with their fingers. Our new record was thirty-three. Not bad for an hour-and-a-half drive on a Sunday afternoon. We wanted to beat that record today.

I was the first one to the car, with Maggie and Mary in a close race for second. The green leather in the back was sticky, and as I jumped in, I saw a half-eaten pouch of Pop Rocks stuck below the seat. As I yanked them out to see if they were in eating condition, Mary crashed in on top of me and won the second spot in the third row. We settled into our seats and began the wrestling match over the stale Pop Rocks.

Our mother stood on the sidewalk next to the car, waiting for my father before she would get into the passenger's seat.

I heard the sound of a loud vehicle coming down Ocean Avenue, and I raised my head to see a very out-of-place red-white-and-blue-striped bus veering to our side of the street and then parking in front of our house.

When I saw my dad sitting in the driver's seat, my eyes went directly to my mother. Her face had turned a pale green, and her lips were making a crooked smile as her eyes got moist. She took her purse, which she always held in her right hand, and swung it onto her shoulder, just staring at the bus. Mary and I climbed all over each other to get out of the station wagon as fast as we could.

I ran to my mom, took her hand, and led her to the multicolored bus. She walked without bending her knees, and I let go when we got to the open door. I ran up the fluorescent orange steps to join my sisters inside the long cavern.

"What do ya think of our new bus, kids? Pretty cool, right?" my dad said.

"Richard . . . what . . . ?" Mom said as she slowly stepped up into the bus and my dad closed the door behind her.

There were no actual bus seats inside; it was filled with couches, love seats, and funky chairs that were all nailed to the floor. The theme seemed to be *The Jetsons* meets a Haight-Ashbury coffee shop.

It still had the steel bars to hold on to above where the seats used to be, and they now looked like monkey bars begging to be played on. The luggage racks were intact, with curtains of different fabrics and colors hanging over them. It was an indoor playground on wheels—and we owned it!

My dad shifted the bus into gear as my mom sat down in the front passenger's seat. We began bounding down Ocean Avenue in our give-peace-a-chance bus, playing hide-and-seek in the amusement park on wheels. I ran down the middle of the bus on the rainbow wall-to-wall carpet, jumped on a green couch, and launched myself into the luggage racks, which turned out to be a tunnel of fun as we bumped along the road. The squeals coming from my sisters below made me smile inside and squeal a little back.

"Off to the General Community Gathering!" my dad yelled from the driver's seat. Dad was a district leader for an elitist fundamentalist group called the Disciples of Light. We had been a part of it for as long as I could remember. It operated under the Catholic Church, with men in positions of power and women who were subservient and referred to as "handmaids." The belief was that the group was "fighting the empire of evil," which was considered to be the world. There was no dating unless the marriage had already been arranged, strict obedience to the leaders, lots of speaking in tongues, and people falling to the ground "slain in the spirit."

It was our entire social network. If you weren't in the Disciples of Light, you were less than us and we were strictly forbidden to be with you. I was so grateful when Grace's family joined, although I worried my dad would kick them out because they didn't follow the rules. We had to go to these GCG prayer meetings every Sunday *after* we'd already gone to mass for an hour and a half; it was a whole lot of praying in one day.

"Maggie, God was calling me to buy this bus; it is for His glory to build up the Disciples of Light and carry souls to the General Community Gatherings. Imagine the number of people we could have praising God."

My dad was the district leader for the fifty or so families who lived down the shore. He, along with the other six district heads, set the rules and enforced them for the families inside of their territories through the head of each household, the man. He was throwing a lot of money around for clout, paying for the private school educations of the kids of the leader of the Disciples of Light community, Francis Tallic, and buying a house in London to expand the community's reach.

Mother stood up, one hand on the back of the front passenger's seat, and walked down the carpeted aisle and sat down on the sunflower cushioned chair with the Formica table in front of it. She took a small sheet of paper and a pen from her purse and continued her endless to-do list, writing, crossing out, writing again, and staring out the window with a small twitch happening in her eyes.

I caught myself staring at her and looking for her at the same time. I stuck my head out of the lime-green curtains and watched as she tried to straighten her smile. I wished I could have been my mom's friend, that day and many days into the future. I would have told her she mattered, that she was allowed to ask my dad to turn this amusement park around and bring it back to its rightful owner. I would have told her that she was lovable and she didn't have to follow my dad's every domineering dream. She needed such a friend.

I found a place in the middle of the bus. My body sank into the light-blue-and-pink upholstered chair that had been nailed to the floor but still had the ability to swivel. I stared out the window and watched the trees grow bigger as we went farther from my ocean. The farmland began to spring up around the bus, open spaces with lush green grass on all sides.

I purposely sat on that side of the bus because a barn where some of our horses were would be visible on that side. I liked to drive by the barn, but I never liked seeing my trainer, Jim, working with other riders. I had a fantasy that he worked only with me; I was his wonder rider, his protégé. I had two horses at Jim's barn, Julius and Irish. Julius was the one I trained on; we were leasing him, and it was as if he knew he was temporary. Irish was the real prize, a massively beautiful colt that my dad bought me for hunter/jumper competitions. I couldn't ride Irish yet because he was just a year old and wasn't saddle broken. I worked with him every day, though, and we were making huge strides. It was an amazing feeling to have an animal so powerful, and yet I knew I could tame him because we were building trust in each other; I could feel his energy so clearly, and he, mine. Once we had trust, he would never abuse his power. I was sure of it. It was the opposite of my father's power; his, I would never be able to tame.

I knew I would be in trouble if I ever said it out loud, but I found Jim to be very handsome. My mom felt sorry for him because he was in a wheelchair. "That poor man . . . ," she would say when she dropped me off at the barn. I didn't think Jim felt sorry for himself, so I wondered why my mom did. I asked him during my interview to be accepted to train with him what had happened to his legs, and I got into big trouble with my father for that. It was worth it, though, because in some way I knew that moment bonded us. I don't think people asked him what happened very often; they just looked at him, pretending not to see the wheelchair but staring at it at the same time.

I'd been training with him for three years now, and I loved the barn and being around the horses as much as I loved the ocean: the smell of fresh wood shavings, tack, and dust mingling together; the sound of the smooth leather saddle crackling as I rode; and the partnership I had with both Irish and Jim. We relied on each other, and I understood the rules. Jim said I reminded him of himself. He told me I had the talent and the drive to make it all the way to the World Cup, just as he had before his accident. We only disagreed on one thing: he didn't like me riding Lady at our family's barn, which was just a mile or so away. He said it would ruin my form, since I only rode her bareback. But I just couldn't give that up; beating my dad gave me the shred of worth I needed.

"Here we are, gang. Made record time," Dad said. He must have been starting some new record, because this was our longest trip by far; it had taken over two hours. He pulled our new bus right up to the front door of the high school where the Disciples of Light met every week. "Let's head in."

I wanted to ask my father if we could just stay in the car while he and Mom went in to pray.

Just then Mary asked if we could stay on the bus.

"No, we are all going in to pray."

I couldn't help wondering what would happen if I said those same words to my father. No one in my family ever got hit but me; I told myself it was because I was the strongest, but my smile wavered as I tried to believe that story.

"Are you going to leave it parked here, Richard?" Mom stood and smoothed both her hair and her to-the-floor floral printed skirt and made her way up to stand directly behind my dad by the front door of the bus. I didn't like how all the women were mostly silent and walked behind the men—except for Helen, Grace's mom. The male leaders were supposedly anointed by God, but Helen would always say to Grace and me when we were alone, "We are all anointed by God, men and women alike." That made more sense to me.

My dad paused as the Disciples of Light community surrounded the bus. He opened the front door with finesse, inviting everyone who could fit on board for a look.

Francis Tallic was the first in line, with his wife, Pricilla, close behind. Walt, their fourth son, followed behind with his right hand wrapped in an Ace bandage. He was not handsome, and his lack of smarts was kind of hard to believe, not to mention that he picked his nose in public. The last time he was at our house, he put his whole hand on the electric stove top, resulting in second-degree burns.

Francis Tallic was wearing a plaid button-down, khakis, and his signature shoes that gave him an extra two inches on the heel. His pants were always too long so he could hide the help with his height, and he stood assured without blinking, his brown eyes looking upward upon heaven, his posture too straight, and, as always, one hand in the air, praising God.

He looked down, only to nod to my dad and ascend the orange steps into the bus. His wiry frame looked unimpressive next to my dad's, but his voice commanded the attention of everyone boarding the bus, who fell silent when he opened his mouth.

"You did it, Richard. You rose to the calling of Jesus Christ and bought the bus, just like I told you," Francis said. "Margaret, you are a true handmaid for Christ. Your fiat will earn you a place in heaven. This will be of great service to our Disciples of Light community, bringing people to our General Community Gatherings and to the heart of Jesus."

There were still a hundred people filing out of the school to take a look at the mystery bus, and I spotted Grace and another friend, Erin, in the crowd. I opened the window in the middle of the bus, stuck my head out, and waved Grace and Erin to the back of the bus. I ran to the back and opened the emergency exit to let my friends on board.

"How did the red jeans go over with your mom?" Grace asked as she climbed aboard.

"Let's just say they're yours now."

"Sorry, Kath. You can wear them at my house; my mom won't tell."

Mr. Tallic held a glass bottle of holy water up in the air and announced, "This bus will be for God's glory. May all those who ride in this bus be ever closer to Jesus and His infinite mercy."

He walked down the aisle of the bus, dousing everyone from left to right, opening the luggage racks, spraying water without remorse, and making puddles of holiness on the floor. As he walked by, we were required to say "In the name of the Father, Son, and Holy Spirit," and make the sign of the cross on our bodies. All grown-ups and kids complied as he made his way through, and when the parade was over, he was at the back of the bus next to the door I had opened. He concluded, "This bus is freed from evil and is restored to the service of the Lord. Let us go inside and praise God."

We began to file into the high school gym for the charismatic Catholic prayer meeting. Erin and I walked Grace to her family's spot in the back of the gym and then continued on through the maze of chairs, which were placed in circles that got smaller and smaller as we headed to each of our family's ordained spots.

"My mom took my Gloria Vanderbilt jeans away last night," Erin said. "She said your dad told my dad that she had to do it."

Things were getting stricter. The last district head meeting had been at our house, so I hid in the alcove and listened. They talked about starting a "Camp Hope," where all the children would be required to go for two weeks of intense training in the ways of the community. Then they began talking about arranged marriages, and I had to put my hand over my mouth so I wouldn't scream when I heard one of the leaders say the marriage between Walt Tallic and me was approved. My two older sisters were also arranged to Tallic boys, Francis Jr. and John.

We got to Erin's family's seats, which were right behind ours. I greeted Mr. and Mrs. Dunn, winked at Erin, and continued to the center of the circle. My family was already seated, and I caught my dad's punishing eye as I sat down in the assigned empty seat between Mary and Rachel. As soon as I leaned back in the hard wooden chair, the music began and the whole community rose to their feet.

We turned in unison and watched as the Tallic family began their procession from the back of the gym. We watched Mr. Tallic, Mrs. Tallic, Francis Jr., Mark, John, Walt, Matthew, Jimmy, Gertrude, Faith, and Thomas sing with all their might, hands swaying in the air, parading down the aisle to take the eleven empty seats in the center circle with my family. The kids sat down in age order, like the rest of us.

Spontaneous prayer broke out in the crowd as an upbeat version of "Abba Father" started to blare from the speakers. The music ministry was decked out with tambourines, guitars, cymbals, and a piano synthesizer.

Hundreds of people were jumping for Jesus and shouting out their prayers with arms raised toward heaven. The ground was vibrating, and the bright lights seemed to be dancing in their sockets. A woman who must have been new to the community, since I didn't recognize her, was being prayed over by four men who were drenching her with holy water and yelling for Satan to "extinguish his hold on her." She dropped to the floor, slain in the spirit, and the people around her got louder in their praise.

The praying in tongues began and quickly turned into a swell of noise loud enough to lift the roof. In some ways I liked it, because it was the only time in my life when I was allowed to raise my voice; there were no real words, but it felt like I could get some sensation to run through my body. I did throw in one "Gloria Vanderbilt jeans are cool," when I was sure no one could hear me. It was important that our lips were in constant motion, as my parents checked to see if we were being given the gift by the Holy Spirit. Rachel held my hand and chanted "God's glory" mixed with some gibberish we had practiced to make her sound like she was learning to pray in tongues. I looked at Mary but couldn't hear what she was saying, and Maggie went full bore, jumping, swaying, hands in the air, eyes closed triumphantly, praying in tongues, and then switching to "God, You are my one and only Savior. You died on the cross for my sins. I don't deserve Your mercy. You are my rock and my salvation."

My father's arms were in the air, and he was jumping up and down with serious conviction. It was a competition between Mr. Tallic and my dad, which screams of praise God would hear first. My mother looked peaceful, her eyes closed, her hands clasped in the middle of her body, and her lips just barely moving.

"Gloria Vanderbilt jeans are cool. I love Gloria Vanderbilt jeans." I decided to throw two more in.

The music ministry began an upbeat, charismatic song that kept the crowd in a frenzy of movement, song, and praise. Then another song, and another. As the third song came to an end, people were still praying out loud, but quieter, and a sort of anticipation filled the room.

There were footsteps from behind as Luke Thomas made his way to the center of the circle. Mr. Thomas and his wife were in my dad's district. Earlier, I had heard my dad telling Mr. Tallic that he had high hopes for them. They were relatively new to the community, so time would tell.

Mr. Thomas stood emotionless and almost limp in his tall body. His fading curly hair was combed back, and he was wearing a white pressed shirt and blue dress pants with a brown belt that somehow seemed to be choking him. His arms were looking for something to hold on to for balance.

My father stood, raised his hand and his eyes to the sky once more, and walked to Mr. Thomas. Dad extended his arm to touch Mr. Thomas's shoulder. The community reciprocated and reached out their arms toward Mr. Thomas, watching as my dad prayed over him out loud. Mr. Thomas was over six feet tall, with a lanky frame and a long brown beard that he was trying to use to hide his fear, which was coursing through the room.

"Anoint my brother Luke with Your words, Jesus. He has come to praise You; use him as a vessel of Your love to fill this Disciples of Light community with Your message of mercy."

The whispers of prayer lifted the room. I could feel the energy rise; the building was being carried to outer space to meet the mother ship. People began shouting . . .

"AMEN, AMEN, LORD ON HIGH!"

"THANK YOU, JESUS!"

"GLORIFY YOU, LORD JESUS CHRIST!"

"YOUR NAME BE PRAISED!"

"WE ARE ALL SINNERS; WE DON'T DESERVE YOUR MERCY, LORD!"

"Stand tall, brother. You are filled with the Holy Spirit." Dad's voice grew louder and stronger as he continued to pray over Mr. Thomas.

Mr. Thomas straightened his body and looked out to the crowd of worshippers. His hands were glued to his hips so he wouldn't take off running. My dad took Mr. Thomas's right hand, placed the microphone in it, and slowly backed away. My dad's arm remained outstretched as he took his seat next to my mom, just a few feet away.

Mr. Thomas's eyes darted around the crowd, looking for a safe place to land. His feet were fastened to the floor, and he leaned forward again. He opened his mouth and snapped it shut again.

I looked at my father, whose eyes were wide and impatient, with his arm still outstretched to Mr. Thomas. Mr. Thomas began to lose tears; they streamed down his face and gathered on the gym floor.

My dad and Mr. Tallic shared a nod, and the music began to play. The picking of the acoustic guitar made me close my eyes. The melody was rhythmic and subtle; it reminded me of swaying in the wind, and I gave myself permission to keep my eyes closed, knowing my father was fully focused on Mr. Thomas. The singing began to take over.

I opened my eyes as the guitar began to be drowned out by voices. One by one, people stood and repeated the chorus until the entire community was on their feet, singing in unison, *"Rain down, rain down . . ."*

The energy gathered in my head, and the goose bumps were everywhere as my father and Mr. Tallic together walked the three steps to Mr. Thomas and placed their hands on him. I stood up and caught Grace's eyes; they looked afraid, as I imagined mine did.

The music stopped, and the gymnasium became a temple of silence.

Noises came out of Mr. Thomas's mouth. They were not words; they were throbbing sounds, unpunctuated concoctions of emotions hitting the air with force and conviction. His eyes were opening and closing with the rhythm of the noise, and his head was being cast back and forth on his neck as his body was held still by my dad and Mr. Tallic.

I could hear the prayers being raised around me, but I couldn't move my eyes from the scene unfolding in front of me as Mr. Thomas looked less and less like himself and the sounds kept manifesting out of his mouth.

"Should I take the children outside?" Mrs. Dunn whispered to her husband behind me, with no response. "Don, what is happening?"

I took Rachel's hand firmly in mine and looked for the nearest exit, just in case.

Mr. Thomas wilted and my dad caught him before he hit the floor. Mr. Tallic took the holy water out of his back pocket and began covering Mr. Thomas's body with the blessed liquid as he made the sign of the cross on his own body.

The community followed suit and began crossing themselves over and over again, and after two minutes my father helped Mr. Thomas to his feet. Mr. Thomas's face was gray, and his eyes were grasping at anything that would hold them.

My father walked with him to his seat. He reached for Mrs. Thomas's hand and placed Mr. Thomas's hand in hers while Mr. Tallic blessed that section of the community with the holy water. Then he headed back to the middle of the circle, where he stood waiting for my father to take his seat.

"Our brother has just received the gift of tongues, the language of the Holy Spirit. Our Savior, our Lord Jesus Christ, has just given me the direct translation for our community. Brothers and sisters in the Lord, this is what our brother has just been told, directly from the Holy Spirit to our hearts. Open your sinful hearts and hear what the Holy Spirit is telling you this day." Mr. Tallic stood tall. His voice was sure, and the room became devoid of sound as we waited for the anointed message straight from heaven.

He closed his eyes, stretched out one arm, tilted his head to the ceiling, and said: "'My faithful followers, you are in the right place, this is your calling, and you are doing the ordained will of God by being part of this community, the Disciples of Light. I call you deeper into this ministry and ask you where will you be of service, where can I manifest My love for you? I cannot love you more than to give you My only son, whom you crucified. I forgive you, My lost sheep, and now I ask for your service and your penance to be manifested in this community. Be on your knees, for the time is near when I will separate My flock from evildoers; I will bring legions of angels to carry you home. I ask you again to be of service to this community, to bring glory to Me through your service.'" Mr. Tallic's entire being shook. He opened his eyes and looked around the community as my father stood and led the crowd in an ovation that blew the roof off the high school gym.

Only the district heads, like my dad and Mr. Tallic, could "interpret" what people were saying in tongues, and it always had something to do with growing the number of people in the community, giving money, and being obedient to the district heads.

When the meeting ended an hour and a half later, I headed to the bathroom. As I was washing my hands, Mrs. Dunn and Mrs. Catalano came in. The bathroom was the only place where the women said what they really thought. They rarely cared if any of us kids heard.

"Did Tony get the call from Richard last night?" Mrs. Dunn whispered to Mrs. Catalano as they stood by the sink.

"Tony said he would talk to me about it tonight. What's going on?" Mrs. Catalano asked.

"Francis Tallic has decided we are no longer allowed to wear lipstick, starting with the next GCG meeting," Mrs. Dunn said. "Did you see Margaret? She doesn't have any on today, and you remember she and Pricilla Tallic were the first two to stop wearing eye makeup right before we got the order. Now the last of the color will be leaving our faces."

"I've already given up eye makeup, highlighting my hair, the clothes that I love—and now this?" I saw Mrs. Catalano in the mirror, touching her hair and making a face at her prairie skirt.

"I told Don I would think about it, but after today's display I'm realizing how insane this is becoming. Plus I am really beginning to feel awful from the inside out," Mrs. Dunn said.

"I know neither of us paid much attention when they said women weren't allowed to work outside the home anymore. I was knee-deep in diapers and knew I didn't want to go back to work until the kids were all in school, but I should have stood up then. This 'head of household' thing where the man makes all the decisions—but really Richard and Francis are making them—is not sitting right with me. Men are 'heads of households' and women, by design, are cooking, cleaning, doing laundry, and everything related to the kids?" She caught her breath and continued: "So now we're left with mousy-brown hair, a wardrobe straight out of *Little House on the Prairie*, and a whole lot of decision-less work. I feel as if I am watching the not-so-slow demise of women."

The bathroom door opened, and both women rushed to turn on the water and wash their hands. Grace's mom walked in with her high-lighted hair, perfectly placed makeup, and a skirt above her knees, and both women watched in silence as she walked to the stall and closed the door. Mrs. Smith never felt the need to follow the rules.

"Ugh," Mrs. Dunn said under her breath.

"I know. What are we doing, giving up the last of our beauty prod-ucts?" Mrs. Catalano whispered back. They walked out of the bathroom and the door shut behind them.

I began washing my hands again. Grace's mom walked to the sink, and I caught her eyes in the mirror.

"Hello, Mrs. Smith. How are you?" I asked.

"Hello, sweet girl. Grace was so looking forward to making the drive up here with you today. I'm sorry you couldn't ride with us. And please, call me Helen—all of that 'Mr. and Mrs.' stuff makes me feel like you're talking to my parents."

She bent down to my level and looked me straight in the eye. "Will you tell me if you ever need anything? I know sometimes kids need a place to just sort stuff out, and I know you and Grace have that kind of friendship, and you can trust me too."

The place where my father hit me on the wrist felt like it was break-ing out in hives as I listened to her. I quickly checked to make sure it was still covered with my long-sleeved shirt and pullover sweater.

"Um, I'm fine." *Keep eye contact; tell her with your eyes.* "Thank you. My mom won't let me call you that, but I will call you Helen when I come over. Maybe Grace can ride home with us. Will you ask my mom? She'll say no if I ask her."

"That is quite a ride your dad bought. I can imagine what your mom thought when he parked it on Ocean Avenue! What a saint your mom is. I'll see what I can do to have Grace ride with you. Come over soon; we love having you."

"I will, Helen. Thank you." I wasn't sure if I should hug her or run out of the room as fast as possible.

"We really care about you, Kathleen."

She hugged me, and we walked out of the bathroom. I wish she had stayed just one minute longer; maybe I would have gotten the courage to show her my wrist.

We were the very last family to leave the General Community Gathering. I rode home without Grace, in the bus that my mother hated, rummaging through my brain for happy thoughts.

CHAPTER 4

Early Winter, 1977
(Two and a half years earlier)

It wasn't a surprise when I learned that my mom was pregnant again. My dad told the Disciples of Light at every GCG that it was a direct request from God to build a large community of believers to serve the Lord.

She was simply huge; she had to sit down on her butt and go up the stairs one at a time. The doctors were worried about how big she was getting, so they had her do an ultrasound—and there they were: two big babies. There were no twins on either side of the family, so my dad was able to tell the community that this confirmed his prophecy of growing the Disciples of Light.

I was very excited to be having a day in New York City with my mom. I walked out of my room to the main staircase, just so I could walk past the twins' room again. Their room would be closest to mine, and it had just been remodeled. I counted twenty steps and turned right into the beautifully lit room. There were two hand-carved wooden cribs that had yet to be dusted with linens, two commissioned stained-glass lamps that hung from the twelve-foot ceiling above their cribs, and a beautiful Persian rug.

I was dressed in a white "Shirley shirt" (I gave that name to any shirt Shirley ironed), a blue-and-yellow cardigan, and velvet blue pants that were as soft as my baby blanket, which I still slept with as a pillow every night. I started walking down the main staircase, holding on to the railing and taking the steps two at a time. When I got to the landing, I saw the limousine waiting for us out in front of the house. I let out a squeal and ran to the kitchen to find Shirley.

"Shirl, Shirl . . . they're here. I'm so excited."

She was leaning over the counter in the center of the kitchen with a broom in one hand and a dustpan in the other.

"What's wrong with your leg, Shirl? You're holding it funny," I said.

"Oh, it's nothin'. Just a little fall last night coming off that there bus I take home. I bet you're excited, little Ox; you is gonna have a good ol' time with your mama today," she said.

As she walked to stir some concoction of sauce she had going on the stove, I noticed that she couldn't put much weight on her left leg. She walked back over to me, holding on to the counter.

"You're in pain, Shirl. Where's Mom? I'll get her to take you to the doctor," I said.

Shirley never let me tell my mom when she was in pain; she just worked harder. I wanted to take her suffering and stuff it into my dad's unbroken body.

I walked to her side of the counter to read my mom's list to her. Shirley wasn't a good reader. She had worked on a cotton plantation most of her life. Her mom had said there was no reason for her to read. She never knew her dad.

"It says 'Nothing sweet for the kids this weekend,'" I told her. "Can I help you?"

"Of course you can, little Ox. I didn't know your mama didn't want anything sweet this week, so it's a little too late. Lookie here . . . sweet padayda pie." She put a bowl in front of my nose that smelled like the gingerbread man's house. "Sweet potatoes are a vegetable. Help me finish this up; your mama will love it."

She took a scoop of the sugary treat with her finger and plopped it in my mouth.

"Yum!" It tasted like Halloween, Easter, and Christmas put together, and Shirley helped herself to a scoop.

The phone rang, and Shirley took her time to walk the short distance to the wall-mounted phone. "Flanagan house," she said into the avocado-colored receiver as she leaned on the wall to take the pressure off her left foot.

"He what?" Shirley stood straight up and threw a hand over her mouth. "Tammy . . . you betta not be lying to me, girl . . . ," she said in a hushed and serious tone as she faced the wall and put her back to the kitchen.

I ran through the kitchen, up the pitch-black servants' staircase, and down the long hall as fast as I could. I tore into my parents' room, grabbed the phone, and stretched the cord that was attached to the wall until it was taut. Only the twisty rubber part attached to the receiver would reach all the way into the bathroom for the privacy I needed. I carefully held the receiver, unscrewed the bottom circle, and took out the silver microphone piece so they couldn't hear me on the other end. I put the receiver down on the floor and closed the door and locked it—it was the only door that had a lock in our home—so I could listen to Shirley talk to her kids.

I had researched how phones work in the library so I could eavesdrop on my parents' phone conversations when my father was at work to see if I was in trouble for something I did or didn't do. It also came in handy when the district heads' meetings were on the phone so I knew what weird rules were coming down the pipe.

"Tammy, you give that phone to Winney so she can tell me what in the world is goin' on over there." Shirley was not pronouncing her words well, and her voice was wet with fear.

"Hi, Mama; don't worry, Mama," Winney said.

"Winney, tell me Chad didn't steal Mr. Swanson's car. The boy is thirteen!"

"Well, Mama, I didn't know where he was, so I went ta lookin' for him like you taught me to do, and I found him the first place I looked. He took the car to the basketball courts on Third Avenue to show Mikey," Winney said.

"Put that boy on this phone," Shirley said.

There was some fumbling, and then Chad came on. "Ma, I borrowed the car. Swanson always tellin' me that he's gonna teach me to drive. Well, I showed him. I don't need nobody to teach me; I learned it myself."

I closed my eyes, my ear pressed hard against the phone so I wouldn't miss a word. I pictured Shirley's kids as if in a movie. I had never seen them—Mom said that would be inappropriate—but I had listened to them countless times from this spot on my parents' bathroom floor. I wanted to be in a different family.

Winney was the oldest, and she sounded the most like Shirley, with her accent on the wrong syllable and me always trying to fill in a letter at the beginning or end of a word to make sense out of it. She was in charge of her five siblings and two cousins while Shirley was with us, and I imagined that she carried the responsibility of her family in the weight of her body. I pictured her as short and wide, with unruly hair that had never fully taken shape and a face older than her years.

Tammy was the tattletale, the one who called the most. I pictured Tammy with long, beautiful brown legs and a face you couldn't take your eyes off, like a TV star's. Tammy seemed to wisp in and out of conversations with her mama, always dancing with her words and braiding her hair—at least, that's how I always pictured her.

Chad might be young in years, but he was the oldest when it came to experiencing the world. He gathered trouble, lined it up, and knocked it down with swagger. I imagined him to be tall for his age, the size of a full-grown man, which didn't help the situation, since everyone always assumed he was older than he was. And I pictured him wearing a red baseball hat at every given moment—some nights even sleeping in it. Chad was never afraid; he was not afraid of the law, his mama, or telling the truth: whatever it was, he went at it at a full sprint. The other three kids were five, three, and one; they were Shirley's sister's kids. Her sister had died in a fire the year before, and Shirley had taken the kids. They never got on the phone.

Shirley tried to keep her voice quiet, but Chad's came through the phone with screams of denial and exhilaration, so she had to raise her voice to let him know she was still in charge. "Chad, you listen here, boy . . ."

"Ma, I borrowed his car—no biggie. It's back where I found it. He's too stupid to know I even took it."

"You are not showin' nobody nothin' by stealin' that car. You could have killed yourself and others. We are not done here, boy; you best be home when I get home tonight, and we will have ourselves a talkin'."

"Yeah, Ma," Chad said.

"Put Winney back on this phone . . . What is goin' on in that boy's head?" Shirley said.

"He's just Chad, Mama. Don't you worry about none of this; you have enough to worry about," Winney said.

"I will be home after eight if the ten bus is runnin' on time. Make sure the door is locked and the little ones are ready for bed," Shirley said.

"Love you, Mama," Winney said.

"Love you too, baby. I'll be home as fast as I can," Shirley said.

I could feel their love come through the phone as I sat on the cold, hard bathroom floor. I took my time putting the phone back together, thinking of Shirley's family, wishing I was in it. I walked out of my parents' room and made my way down the front staircase. I stopped at the landing in the middle of the stairs.

The view of the ocean out the large picture windows in the living room was majestic. I picked a spot in the ocean and swayed, pretending to be in the water across the street. I felt the tide take me right . . . left . . . back and forth, under the waves and over the whitecaps. I was floating on the waves, being carried and cared for by the powerful tide, the chill of the water keeping me awake. When I opened my eyes, I saw that the limousine that would take Mom and me to New York was still parked in front of our house. The man with the driver's hat was standing across the street on the boardwalk, smoking a cigarette, being paid for my mom's rudeness.

We were making a trip to the Upper East Side of Manhattan, where money grew on trees. We were going to a store where you had to make a reservation to get in the door, because they needed to know who was coming and how much sucking up would be needed. At least, that's what Grace's sister told me.

My dad let my mom wear whatever she wanted when she was pregnant. He said he wanted the community to notice her "for the glory of God." I helped her move the prairie skirts and long-sleeved turtlenecks to the back of the closet the day she found out she was pregnant. It seemed to make her happy—that and the fact that lipstick was included in the deal.

My mom sat in the limo, both palms facing down on her pressed suede skirt, looking out the window at the winter landscape, the gray sky crashing down on the Atlantic Ocean. She didn't make a single move toward her little flowered notebook, where she always wrote and rewrote her to-do list. That was a good sign. I squeezed my eyes closed so tight that I saw a burst of white in my eyelids as I made my wish for the day.

I spent most of the day waiting for my mom to remember that she had brought me with her, but I did get an embarrassing amount of new clothing I didn't need, including a fur jacket. I just kept putting things in the pile to purchase; she never checked the bill. My mom was going to have to change clothes a lot before those babies were born if she was planning on wearing everything she bought that day. But my wish didn't come true: my mom and I barely spoke. She was too busy shopping. I kept telling myself to care about the clothes I was getting instead, but it didn't really work.

In the limo on the way home, I tried again to make my wish come true.

"Did Grandmother want you to get married to Dad?" I asked, excited that we had an hour to talk.

"Of course she did; she loves your father. Of course; don't be silly." She said it all in one breath, without pause or punctuation.

My grandmother would get very nervous whenever my mom left the house, so my dad moving her from Syracuse to New Jersey after they got married left my grandmother in a constant state of panic.

"How come they never talk to each other?" I asked.

"Of course they do," Mom said.

I thought of our family pictures displayed so prominently above the piano. Last year's picture showed us strategically placed around the grand mantel in the living room, with a blazing fire in the fireplace. I thought we looked like a crowded family of strangers standing uncomfortably close to one another. I was in a white-red-and-black dress with a frog on the front, holding a candy cane. I did what I was told as the photographer moved furniture and mountains to get a genuine smile from us. The picture would be exhibited to the masses to ensure that we were seen as the perfect family.

I stared down at Mom's empty lap. My tongue throbbed with the questions that were stuck to it.

"Do you love me, Mom?" I said it quietly. She did not respond.

"Mom," I said. But it was too late; she was twirling her hair and humming her music to drown out the past.

I took her right arm, pulled it around me, and lay down on her lap for the rest of the drive home.

I noticed my dad's car running in the driveway when the limo pulled up. I told myself not to give up on my wish for the day.

"Boo! Did I scare you, Dad?" I settled into the plush leather seat of his car and closed the door.

"No, Kath, just lost in my thoughts," he said.

"What are you thinking about? Was work good today? Look at my new coat. Isn't it beautiful?" I was speaking too fast, but I couldn't slow myself down. "Did you see that huge fort Grace and I built in your library at your office? Where is your friend Ray that was here this morning with you?" All I could think of was how stupid I was for trying this.

I felt a sting in the air when I stopped to catch my breath. I turned to look at him from the side. His navy suit was disheveled. His hair looked bristly. His eyes weren't moving; they were fixed on the garage door straight in front of him, but his mind, it seemed, had been carried to a dark place.

I opened the door as unobtrusively as I could and slipped one foot onto the ground.

"Have you ever done something horrible to another person?" my father asked. He was still looking straight ahead. "Get back in and close the door."

I put my foot back on the floorboard of the front seat, but I wasn't willing to shut the door all the way. I tested my voice inside my head, making sure I sounded calm before I spoke.

"Mom is calling you, Dad." I pushed the words out quickly.

His hand grabbed my wrist and held it down hard on the leather console between us. He was silent, still facing forward. This plan wasn't working. I didn't know if he knew I was lying about my mom's calling to him.

I could feel hot redness moving up my chest and onto my face in the form of hives, and I continued to stare at him, willing him to snap out of whatever this was that was happening. I looked for the digital clock in the car to keep track of time: 5:34, 5:35, 5:36—my hand began to tingle under his grip—5:38.

"God's mercy forgives all transgressions," he said.

"Yes, Dad."

He let go of my wrist without glancing in my direction, opened the door to the Cadillac, swung both feet to the ground at once, and got out. He stood for a moment, looked behind him as if someone were there, and then put all ten fingers through his hair and walked up the driveway, smoothing his suit on the way.

I slumped down in the tan leather and rubbed my hand to bring it back to life. I got out of the car, put my new coat on, and walked across the street to the boardwalk. I leaned against the thick metal railing with my back to the ocean, watching my house and waiting for my dad to turn the light on in his bathroom. That would be my sign that it was OK to run in the back door and find Shirley.

When I saw the light and the shadowy figure, I ran across the street and into the kitchen. I had to shake this feeling my father had left in me. I found Shirley cooking up one of her amazing concoctions, which always started with butter and onions in the lime-green Le Creuset Dutch oven. My stomach growled. I loved her cooking.

"Miss Kathleen, what are you up to and where is your mama? She's gotta be downright exhausted." She turned to look at me and give me a hug. "Miss Kathleen, that there is softness like I never did feel . . . Whoooeee, girl, what's your mama gone and bought you?"

"I know, Shirl, isn't it great?" I pulled my matching muff out of my shopping bag and handed it to Shirley. "This is for you."

Shirley put her hand on the counter and took her time to get to eye level with me. I listened as her body protested and her knees crackled louder than the fire as they were made to rest on the hard floor.

"You know I love you, little Ox, and your fine thoughtfulness, but if your mama don't know about the present, I can't keep it; you know that just won't be right."

"But you're so cold all the time, Shirl, and it's so warm. Please. She doesn't even know I bought it. She didn't help me pick out one thing. She didn't even know I was there!"

"You are one sweet thing, Miss Kathleen, and I so appreciate you, but you know the right thing to do," she said, looking me straight in the eye with her forever bloodshot but beautiful brown eyes.

I used all my strength to lift her up to a standing position. She was younger than my mother in years but so much older in her body.

Dinner that night was in silence. It was one of those nights when my dad announced that no one under thirty was allowed to speak. Somehow, that meant my mom too.

"I have something to show you," Dad said to all of us at the end of dinner. After our encounter in the car I was not eager to see what he had to show us. Some of his veins in his neck looked like they were going to pop, and his eyes had a strange, glazed look. "Gather in the living room after you finish the dishes. It is amazing—a miracle, really." Then he stood and walked out of the kitchen, dismissing Shirley for the night on his way out.

We gathered in the living room on the light-blue velvet couches. I was wearing my very favorite orange shirt with the off-white embroidery around the edges. I stared at the embroidery and wondered if I could ever be as good a seamstress as Shirley. She had customized the shirt for me exactly the way we'd drawn it on the paper.

My dad came down the front staircase. He had changed into blue dress slacks and one of his white shirts, which he normally wore with a suit. His hair was combed, and the smell of aftershave still clung to him. He walked around to the front of the couch, settled his feet behind his imaginary pulpit, and began.

"You all know that there are certain people God picks to be His messengers, like Job and Abraham. I am one of the chosen ones, and what I am going to show you tonight is my ordination from God." He was looking past us and talking to the back of the room.

I looked at my mother, who sat uncomfortably on the edge of the newly upholstered chair. Her face was quivering as she tried to hold her smile in place, and her eyes darted between my father and the back of the room.

"God is merciful and forgiving even to the greatest of sinners. He has claimed you as His own, and He has a place for you in heaven."

I was silently praying that he wouldn't make me speak in tongues or get slain in the spirit, because sometimes he believed that it was real when I tried and sometimes he didn't.

"Follow me," my dad said.

He stood and walked through the living room and into the kitchen, with the five of us following like the quiet shadows that we were. He walked to the far side of the kitchen, almost to the mudroom, and stopped in front of the basement door. He turned his entire body around and looked Rachel in the eye. "Are you ready?"

"Yes," Rachel said, and then immediately looked at me.

He unlocked the dead bolt, opened the solid wood door, and headed down the rickety stairs with my mother close behind. I reached in front of Maggie and Mary, grabbed Rachel by the hand, and put her right in front of me without missing a step. Maggie and Mary, who were both still in their gray plaid polyester uniforms from school, descended the staircase after my dad and mom.

The basement was huge, fifteen large rooms in all. I clutched the railing, which was being held together with one nail, and noticed my mom holding on to my dad's shoulder instead of the railing that was about to fail us all. I stepped off the splintered wooden steps and onto the gray concrete. The floor sent icicles from my feet to my brain as we walked in single file through the first and largest room in the basement.

I watched the seasons pass by us as we walked: the large box with color-coded fake branches that we separated and put together each year for our Christmas tree; the Lenox Nativity set neatly sealed in its box; the plastic Easter eggs in all the pastel colors of spring; and, in the corner, the huge crucifix we walked the boardwalk with every year on Good Friday.

The cold, dimly lit rooms came one after another. I could only hear my rapid breathing and my mother humming "Bridge over Troubled Water" as we walked along. There were no windows, but I searched for them anyway. I needed to find an escape route for Rachel and me. I went through all fifteen rooms in my head, and each had its own degree of fear. He had to be taking us to the prayer room, but the energy felt like anything but a prayer. Ghosts were everywhere; I could feel them working through my body as I tried to calm myself long enough to create a plan. Rachel's tightening grip on my hand kept me in the moment.

I decided I could get us out of the basement through the bulkhead if needed. It would be harder for Dad to chase us to the abandoned sections because I had to crawl on my hands and knees on the stone-hard dirt floor to get to that part of the basement, and he was too big to make it through. He would have to go upstairs, around to the back of the house, and open the doors that were built flat into the ground—that is, if he even remembered those doors were there. I knew I was strong enough to push them open to get us outside and that we could get there and get out before he could make his way to the doors. The breath came back into my lungs.

"You're OK, Rachel; you're with me. Don't worry," I said.

"Are you sure? This feels really weird," she whispered.

"Let's think of this as an adventure, me and you. I promise, you're OK. Don't let go of my hand, OK?"

"I won't. Pinky promise." A tiny smile came back to her face, and her grip loosened. I wanted to play my somewhere-else game, but it was always next to impossible when Rachel was with me.

My dad stopped outside the prayer room door. He fiddled in his pocket for a key and gestured to my mother to move closer to him.

"This is a sacred place that houses the body and blood of Jesus Christ," my dad said as he opened the door and ushered my mother, Maggie, and Mary into the room. Rachel and I were supposed to walk in next.

I held Rachel with one hand on her shoulder and the other hand holding hers in the small of her back, not allowing her to take the next step. I could see my very pregnant mom, Maggie, and Mary standing inside the room. My mom was twirling her hair and shifting her weight from side to side. Maggie fell to her knees and began praying quietly in tongues, and Mary stood flat against the wall on the far side, not moving.

My brain was spinning. I couldn't let my dad get behind us or he would be blocking the door. I looked in his eyes. They had seemed to change to dark, dark black, and he was smiling at someone other than us.

"Go ahead, Dad," I said as casually as I could, and moved my hand from Rachel's shoulder to the door to prop it open.

I kept my eyes on his in hopes of guessing his next move. He looked at the door, then at me, and then walked behind us as I continued to hold the door. He was so big, and he stood so close behind me, that I couldn't move in any direction. I could smell the coffee on his breath as he forced us forward into the room. I turned to look at his eyes as he pulled the door shut, inserted the key, and turned it to the locked position from the inside. Rachel tightened her grip, and the moisture between our hands began to drip.

The room was painted blue in honor of Mary, the mother of Jesus. It was completely round, with a large concrete beam in the middle that was painted white for Christ. The blue walls were made of cinder blocks, and they were superbly uneven and chipped. The room was small; it would fit maybe ten grown-ups, and that would be tight.

There was a ledge at shoulder height around the room, also painted blue, and it was filled with candles. They were every color of the rainbow, and they surrounded the room in its entirety. New candles had replaced the old, and they all dripped their liquid down the wall and onto the gray concrete ground, beautiful strands of wax in different states of dryness and so many beautifully blended colors. The wall behind the wax had been changed to the color of the candle that had fed it. There was no natural light, and the place in the ceiling that used to have a lightbulb was empty, so the only light in the room was the flickering candlelight. It always struck me as odd that we were never allowed to play with matches for fear of fire, but there was at least one candle burning in this room at all times.

There was no furniture, only twenty or so pillows of different fabrics, sizes, and colors on the ground and up against some parts of the wall.

I had logged countless hours in this room, either hiding from the chaos above or sent here by one of my parents to repent for my "sins." I liked to put my hand on the center beam, close my eyes, and walk in a circle, extending my other arm out as far as it would go.

My dad moved slowly to what he deemed the front of the circular room.

"Look closely for the miracle; it awaits you in this room, at this moment." His voice was commanding. "Jesus lives here in the flesh and blood, and He has asked me to make it your residence. Each one of you."

Now that my eyes had adjusted to the light, I could see that there was something bulging from Dad's front right pocket, but I couldn't tell what it was. Maggie was still on her knees with her eyes shut, murmuring in tongues. Mary was standing on a red pillow with her palms stuck to the wall behind her; her eyes were protruding out of their sockets. And Mom was holding her belly in a protective stance, a question waiting on her lips.

My dad turned and reached behind him and took the *capsula* from the ledge. It held the Eucharist that he had stolen from St. Catharine's the week before. It wasn't "legal" in the church to have a Eucharist in your home, but we almost always had the Eucharist in our prayer room. He held it above his head. The wafer-like Eucharist was glorified in a twenty-four-carat gold *capsula* that wrapped around it with opulence. It looked especially transcendent with the candlelight hitting the gold, then the glass that held the wafer in place, and then the gold again. It was sending lightning bolts of color around the tiny room.

"Margaret, do you believe this is the actual body and blood of our Lord and Savior, Jesus Christ?" he asked.

"I do," Mom said. She was moving a lot from one leg to the other, still holding on to her pregnant belly with both hands.

"Maggie, stop that gibberish and get over here. Do you believe this is the body and blood of Jesus Christ?"

"Of course, Dad," she said as she moved to stand against the wall with Mary, who had not moved in the slightest since we arrived.

"Mary, tell me you believe."

"Yes, Dad."

"Kathleen, what is your belief?"

"You are holding the true body and blood of Jesus, Dad." I put charismatic holiness into my words while I contemplated rushing my dad and grabbing the key that he had put in his left pocket or the weapon I was now sure he had in his right.

"Rachel, do you believe this is the body and blood of Jesus?"

"Dad?" she said.

I squeezed her hand too tight in mine to make her say the words she needed to say to buy us more time.

"Yes, Dad; yes, Dad," she said.

"God Himself has given me a prophecy that must be carried out today. I am, above all, *His* faithful servant. Part of that prophecy has been carried out today with the life of my friend Ray, and now it is your turn. You have all been chosen for a very special reason. First you must see the miracle . . . where this message came from this morning." He turned completely around and set the *capsula* on the shelf next to the plethora of flaming candles, and then he put his finger on the wall next to a black area where a candle used to be.

There was dark soot on the wall, and I stared at it, holding my breath as my dad translated what he clearly thought we should be seeing.

"Look at the confirmation I received in my prayer time this morning. It is He. He is holding His staff in His right hand, here"—he pointed to the place on the wall covered in soot from one of the burning candles—"and calling to me to follow Him. He has asked me to be like Abraham." He looked strange: his skin was aglow; his smile took up too much of his face; and his eyes were dancing with a darkness I had never seen before, not even in him.

"Look at the pained expression on His holy face, His disgust at sinners like you, and His unwavering mercy to forgive. The crown of thorns on His head, reminding us that each of you crucified Him and He died to forgive you. See, here"—my dad pointed again to the ashes on the wall where he saw Jesus—"is His robe draped by the angels across His tired body, a rope braided around His midsection that has been tied and retied throughout His thirty-three years on this earth. And His feet—He has sandals that are worn through to the bottoms. This Jesus appeared on the wall this morning as confirmation of what God is asking me to do."

This was not like the Eucharist question; telling him I believed that a talking Jesus was smoked onto our wall in our basement was not going to get us out of this. I needed to throw him off his calculated plan, and

the only element I had on my side of the ring was surprise. If he didn't
see me coming, and if I hit him with all my force, I might be able to
knock him into the wall hard enough to hit his head. I breathed in a
very scared breath and looked around the room. Tears came as I touched
Rachel's hair and tucked a strand behind her innocent ear. I hated that
I might not be able to protect her. Maggie's eyes were closed, and tears
were streaming down both cheeks onto her uniform. Mary looked like a
statue frozen in fear and solitude, her eyes wide-open, staring at my dad.

"We will meet in heaven and . . ."

"DAD . . . Mom!" Maggie's voice sounded like she was out of her
mind.

I looked at my mom and heard the whimper come out of her
mouth that sent all eyes to her belly. Her hand reached out for support
on the center beam. Her head fell to the side and her legs wobbled. My
dad snapped out of his hypnotic state and ran the three feet to her side
and stabilized her.

"Something is happening, Richard," she said, with palpable fear in
her voice. Her face was red, and her body looked frail even though she
was so big in her belly.

"It's OK, Margaret, I've got ya," my dad said. "It's a miracle—you
have saved us all." Their eyes met, and they searched for each other in a
wave of emotion. I watched them meet; I saw their connection.

"I'll get some water," I said.

He balanced my mom on his body, reached into his pocket, and
threw me the key. I caught it while still holding on to Rachel's hand and
unlocked the door. I opened it wide, checked to see that my dad was not
looking, and put the key in my shoe. Rachel and I began to run, and I
could hear Mary close behind us. I pushed the door at the top of the stairs
open so hard that it smashed into the counter and made us all jump.

"What the hell was *that*?" Mary said.

"I don't know, but one of us has to bring Mom some water," I said.
"Rachel, no matter what—and I mean it: no matter what—you are to

stay upstairs. If I'm not back in ten minutes, run to the McDougals' house. Promise?" I crouched down on one knee and stared right into her big brown eyes.

"OK. Will you be OK?" she asked.

"Of course. I'll be back soon," I said. "Promise me you will go to the McDougals'."

"Pinky," she said, with tears running down both cheeks.

I filled a glass with cold water, wet a tea towel to put on my mom's forehead, and reluctantly ran back to the basement door, where I froze. The lock made it look secure, but I knew what was behind it. I opened the door and, without holding onto the railing, walked down the splintered wooden steps. I walked through the rooms, looking at them differently than I had a half hour ago. They were still dimly lit, but they were not terrifying. The seasons still had their boxes, and there was no joy in them. I felt older, more on guard than ever, and desperate to be invisible. The prayer room door was still open; I could see the flickering candlelight as I made my way to the room. It was impossible to be invisible and breathe as loudly as I needed to in order to get the air into my lungs. It felt like I had to swallow to breathe.

Mom was lying with her head propped up on the one giant gold pillow, the rest of her body supported by other pillows tucked in around her. Maggie was at her feet praying silently, and my dad was on his knees beside her, talking quietly to her.

The energy in the room had shifted from unexplained darkness to something that felt like love, and I sat and watched as my dad gathered my mom in his arms and began to assuage her fear. He cradled her and reminded her how to breathe. He told her to love her breath, to make it loud and let it take over.

"It will only be a few more seconds . . . You can do it . . . I've seen you do it before, and we will do it together again. I love you," my dad said.

Who was this man? He was undemanding and tender. He fit in his body, yet I didn't recognize his body or his voice. I had never seen his muscles that relaxed, and his hands looked gentle as he pulled a strand of blond hair off my mom's forehead, the way Shirley did to me and I did with Rachel.

I felt as if I were opening a gift as I watched my parents display raw, unmasked emotion. I had never heard such kindness from my father. He was telling her over and over that he loved her, that her body knew how to do this, and that they were about to meet two new souls that were the unique and amazing genetic combination of the two of them.

"Margaret, God has spared us," Dad said.

My dad was quick to move as soon as my mom's contraction stopped. I could hear his heart beating. His eyes were the lightest hazel I had ever seen them, and his mouth had a less tainted smile than usual.

My dad lifted my mom back up to a standing position, and I was amazed that she was able to walk after all I had seen in the last few minutes. She walked through the basement with me in the lead, up the stairs, and through the kitchen—and we'd almost made it to the side door in the living room when another contraction started. My dad walked her through the pain again. Maggie followed.

I noticed Mary and Rachel watching from a distance on the landing of the steps. The contraction lasted only about a minute, and the four of us watched in silence as this man none of us knew helped our mother with his words and his body.

When it was over, he opened the door and led her down the steps to the car. The door closed behind them, and without words the four of us ran to the arched windows in the front of the house and watched my dad place my mom in the front seat, run around to the driver's side of the car, slam the door, and pull the car out onto Ocean Avenue.

I sat on the radiator and pulled Rachel onto my lap. We sat in silence. It was dark, and I stared at the ocean through the eyes of the moon as it lit the places it liked the best. I tried to promise myself a future where I would be safe.

CHAPTER 5

Summer, 1978

The next time I saw my mom, she was coming home from the hospital with two big, beautiful baby boys. I was in love in an instant. We all were. Plus my dad's prayer for two boys had been answered, so he was able to boast to anyone who would listen that God had heard his prayer. Michael had an adorable round face and blue eyes, and Richard Jr.—or Ricky, as we would call him—was a little bit smaller, with features like a porcelain doll. They were perfect babies, in my estimation.

School was out for the summer, and life had a routine and rhythm to it. One of my dad's New York City clients was taking up all his waking hours, and Shirley had basically moved in with us to help my mom with the twins. As a result, I had more safety than usual at home. I would wake up not remembering what day it was and not needing to know, which was one of my favorite things about summer. There was nowhere to be but at the beach with my friends or at home with Shirley and my six-month-old baby brothers.

I climbed out of my bed onto the cold hardwood floor and headed to my bathroom, picking up my clothes from the night before and putting them on along the way. As I began to put toothpaste on my orange toothbrush, I was startled by my mother's scream.

"Help! He's not breathing! HELP!"

The volume of it rattled the mirror above my sink, and I threw my toothbrush on the floor and ran. She was still screaming as I turned into Ricky and Michael's bedroom. She was hunched over Michael's crib with her ear to his mouth.

"Mom, what's—"

I didn't get my sentence out before she yelled, "Call nine-one-one! Call nine-one-one!"

I ran down the long hall to the large brown door of my parents' bedroom and kicked it open, wishing the phone would materialize in my hand. I followed the cord to the base of the phone and pushed the plastic hang-up levers. I chased the receiver end to the opening of the balcony and saw Mary sitting outside with the phone in her hand wondering what just happened. I flung the door open with force. She looked at me with her usual disgust, but before she could let loose on me, she saw my face and stopped. "What the hell is wrong with you?"

I ignored her, grabbed the receiver out of her hand, and quickly dialed 911. She saw the numbers I was dialing and the stress in my body, and she just listened as the 911 operator picked up on the other end of the phone.

"We need an ambulance!" I felt like a grown-up, with the weight of the world pushing me into the earth.

"What's wrong?" she asked. She sounded so calm that it made me more nervous. She wasn't seeing the urgency of the problem, and I needed to transfer my urgency through the phone and onto her lap.

"My brother isn't breathing! My mom is with him, and we need an ambulance. PLEASE GET AN AMBULANCE HERE!" I became a robot, dictating our address, phone number, and last name to this woman I had never met but who was now somehow responsible for my brother's life.

Mary and I ran to the twins' room. My mom was holding Michael in a green blanket, trying to wake him up. He was loose in her arms, like she was afraid to touch him, and I stared at his dangling feet. Maggie was in the corner on her knees reciting, "Jesus, Mary, Jesus, Mary . . ." And Shirley was behind my mother, positioned to catch her if she fell.

My mom shrieked again, "Call your father!" Mary ran down the hall to the phone.

The ambulance arrived and two paramedics raced up the stairs to my mother, who was in hysterics holding Michael and screaming her familiar chant of "Jesus, Jesus, Jesus, Jesus . . ." She also added "Mary, Mother of God; Mary, Mother of God" into the mix.

Shirley and I watched as the paramedics took Michael out of my mother's arms and laid him on the Persian rug next to the rocking chair by the window. Through the window, I saw people walking down the boardwalk, unaware of the mounting fear on this side of the glass.

Michael was turning an unrecognizable shade of blue, and my mother was screaming at the ceiling for answers.

The men seemed to be in their own world, speaking a different language as they filled the floor around my brother with tubes and contraptions.

Shirley walked to my mom and held her tightly to keep her mind together. I couldn't move my eyes from Michael's face. His blue eyes were partially open but not moving, and his little body was listless.

"Jesus, Jesus, Jesus . . ."

"Ms. Flanagan, it's OK; Michael will be just OK. You watch—you OK, lady." Shirley was holding my mom up by the waist, and my mother's eyes were wild with fear.

Ricky began to cry. No one moved to pick Ricky up, not even me; we just listened to him cry from his crib in the hope that he could transfer some of that breath into his twin brother's lungs.

One of the paramedics was breathing into Michael's mouth while plugging his nose, and after about a minute the right color began to move back into Michael's face. We all began to breathe again as my dad blasted into the bedroom with a look of terror on his face.

"Mary called me. What the hell is going on? Oh my God . . . ," he said. His knees hit the ground with a loud bang, and he shifted his stare blankly from the paramedic's face to Michael's.

Michael looked tiny as they picked his body up off the floor and strapped him to a huge rolling gurney. The paramedics were taking turns next to the gurney to breathe much-needed oxygen into his lungs as we all helped roll it quickly down the hallway. My dad and the paramedics carried the gurney down the massive staircase. Shirley placed Michael's cashmere blanket over Michael when they reached the bottom, covering his still-lifeless body, and rushed out the front door that we never used. I looked at the waiting ambulance with the circling red-and-white lights, the back double doors open.

We walked down the white porch staircase, onto the cement walkway, and toward the ambulance and Mrs. McDougal, who was standing next to it, holding Maggie and Rachel tight. My parents were right next to Michael, my mom holding on to his left foot, which was sticking out of the blanket. My dad was on the other side holding Michael's hand.

My mom looked at Mrs. McDougal, and when their eyes met, something was exchanged between them. It felt as concrete as words, but I couldn't understand it. They both knew a truth that I had not been told yet.

Maggie broke into my thoughts as I heard her ask, "Can I kiss him, Dad, please?" Michael was being wheeled into the back of the ambulance, and my dad took that moment, picked Maggie up, and let her kiss his exposed foot as they continued to wheel the bed into the ambulance. Mary was standing inside at the front windows, watching us. She hadn't moved since making the call to my dad. I wished I had thought to ask to kiss Michael; I wanted him to know I loved him. I also kept thinking about how I wanted to be the one to have kissed Michael last, to touch his sweet, innocent skin as they wheeled him away. I made up for it by telling myself that I would be the first to touch him when he got home. I would insist on holding him for hours to make up for always having gravitated toward Ricky. I had always favored Ricky, so I figured somehow this must all be my fault. I had always reached for Ricky more, held him more, and pampered him more—and the sudden realization of his being my favorite threw me into a state of intense guilt. Somehow, Michael's being sick was God's way of punishing me for loving Ricky more.

My mom insisted on being in the back of the ambulance with Michael. My dad got in the front seat without arguing.

Shirley, Maggie, Rachel, Mrs. McDougal, and I held hands and watched as the ambulance made a U-turn on Ocean Avenue toward Fitkin Hospital, where my brothers had been born just six months earlier.

I watched the ocean across the street, and again I was taken by how little had changed in the outside world. I watched the waves crash, and I tried to eavesdrop on the conversations the couples were having as they walked our still-beautiful boardwalk. I saw three kids about my age playing tag on the beach, running in and out of the salty water, and I wished it were me playing, without a care in the world.

I broke free from the stronghold of hands, remembering that Ricky was upstairs in his crib, probably still crying and scared to his core, knowing something was wrong. I ran from the street, across the grass, up the front steps, through the grand wooden doors, across the sunporch, through the living room, and up the staircase. I was annoyed at the large size of our house as the intensity of needing to know that Ricky was OK grew inside me. I ran down the long hallway toward him, and my heart began to settle as I heard beautiful oxygen escape from his lungs in the form of a cry.

I picked him up and wrapped him in his favorite blue blanket, the one with the tiny brown monkeys on it. I cradled him, but he would not stop crying. We sat in the rocking chair together, but I knew he felt alone. Ricky's brother wasn't there, and that was the farthest he and Michael had ever been from each other.

"Michael will be OK, and he'll be back home soon. You're OK; you're with me," I said.

The day felt like ten days wrapped into one. Every time I looked at the clock after not checking it for what felt like hours, only fifteen minutes had passed. I did not let Ricky out of my sight, and I wouldn't until I heard that Michael was healthy. I wanted to be the one to tell him.

Ricky was smiling again in his high chair as I fed him too many teething biscuits and watched as he put them everywhere but his mouth. There had not been an update from my parents since the ambulance pulled away.

I went to the front windows with Ricky to see if life had changed outside the house. It was as if no one knew the news yet, and that was why all those people outside our house were moving and breathing normally.

I saw the South End Pavilion to my right, down the beach a little way. I had spent countless hours with my friends in that spot, swimming and going up the cement steps to the top of the pavilion to drop candy on our unsuspecting friends sitting on beach towels below. We ran the beach and the lifeguard stands. We charged candy to our parents' tabs and ran in and out of the salt water as we had been encouraged to do in our childhoods. We always climbed the lifeguard stands as it got dark and made our plans for the next day. It was beginning to get dark right now.

I looked left and saw North End Pavilion down the beach a distance. The same rituals were happening there right now. Different friends, different cement steps, but the same lightness of life.

I was in the middle of those two worlds, unable to make plans for the next day until I knew this day's outcome.

❖

It was as if my mom appeared out of nowhere late the next morning. She took Ricky out of my arms and walked silently to the impeccably upholstered wing chair in the living room and sat down. I wanted to follow her, but I just stood up from the chair in the alcove and stared at her. This was a different woman from the mom I'd had last night. Her eyes were so swollen, I was not sure she could see. Her face did not have any questions on it, only pain, and she was holding Michael's blanket in her hand so tightly that her knuckles were white. I became afraid to be in the same room with this stranger.

My dad walked in the side door and made his way to the wing chair, bent down, and put his ear next to Ricky's nose to check his breathing.

"Kath, please gather your sisters."

It was barely audible. With questions surrounding my every step, I walked into the little den off the kitchen and found all three of my sisters watching TV.

"Dad wants to talk to us." I spoke as if it were programmed inside me. I heard myself say the words, turned right around, and walked back to the living room. I thought somehow maybe this would help the outcome.

"God took your brother to heaven today," my dad said, with the voice of a preacher. He was standing straight, but I could sense the slumped soul inside his body. He got the words out, and the tears followed right behind them. I had never seen my dad cry. He had seen my tears and so often caused them, so they meant nothing to him. But his tears meant something to me. I wanted to bottle them and give them back to him the next time I needed to explain how much he had hurt me.

I did not fully understand what my dad was telling us.

"God took your brother to heaven today." I said it out loud in a muffled voice so I could better understand its meaning.

Michael was dead? When it hit me, I rejected it. My dad walked away, toward the fireplace and his album collection, and my legs followed him.

"Can I ask you something, Dad?" I was trembling.

My dad was down on his knees and looked me in the eye. I felt our pain fuse; it was a feeling of knowing him that I had never felt. This pain was exposing him for what he was: a human, a father who had just said good-bye to his son and his wife as he'd known her. I saw him for the first time in my life as a man with questions and no answers. I heard his silent screams at God. I felt his eyes searching mine to find Michael.

"Dad, can we pray that the doctors made a mistake?"

"Once," he whispered. "We can pray *once* that he is still alive," he said.

I said the spontaneous prayer without blinking. "God, can our little Michael still be alive? Can the doctors have made a mistake, and can he come home to us? Please. I promise to take good care of him."

My dad's tears hit the red rug one after the other, and I couldn't stop staring at them as they betrayed our prayer. He got to his feet, and I jumped to attention. He walked through the living room, past the family that was still gathered on the blue couches, and out the front door. I sat down on the floor and felt the wetness of his tears in the rug. I rubbed the tears deep into the carpet.

Then I went and sat on the floor next to my mom. Shirley was behind her with tears running down both cheeks. Shirley looked at me and held my eyes firm with hers; they were warm and strong, and I leaned into them in my need and confusion.

My mom stared at Michael's blanket, which she was still clutching. Her face was hollow.

I could feel that she would not return to us. She would be a different mother now, and we would be different children. A different family. She had lost her mother to mental illness, had buried her father at a young age, and would now bury her child. She had gone to her somewhere-else place; I could tell from the new color of her eyes and the way she held her breath and her body so still that she would stay there. It was as if she were the one who had been taken.

I wanted to touch her to remind her that I was still breathing, that I still needed her.

"God's will." My mother spoke the words with her eyes glued to the blanket. "The rosary; we need to pray the rosary. Is it five thirty? Where is my rosary?"

I was still watching my mom an hour later when members from the Disciples of Light began pouring into our home. I felt lost in the crowds of tears, prayers, and prophecies that were happening around me. I needed to go check on Rachel and explain what was happening, but I had no words for her; I needed more time. I saw the side door open again, and I let escape from my lips the first sound I had made since my prayer with my father: "Grace."

Grace walked in with her mom and dad, and she made a beeline for me. I watched her run toward me and thought that, whatever it was, it must be serious. She put her arms around me and I heard her say, "It's OK, Kath."

I couldn't feel her arms. She took me to the alcove, sat me down on the couch, and put a blanket around me. My body hurt from not having moved, and it tingled as it came out of numbness. I was grateful for the pain; I wanted more of it.

"Grace, I need to hold Ricky," I said as I clung to the soft blanket that covered me.

"Got it," she said. Grace got up and walked straight to her mom and whispered in her ear. Her mom looked at me, stood up from the piano bench where she was talking with some other women, and walked straight over to my mom, who was sitting on the couch with Mrs. Thomas and holding Ricky in her arms.

My mom held him as if he were a shattered glass bottle. With a sweet smile on her lips, Helen took Ricky from her, tucked his special blanket around his feet, and made her way to me. My mom never looked up.

"You tell me if you need anything else, little one," she said as she very lovingly laid him in my lap and turned and left the alcove, tousling my hair on the way out. It loosened my body to be treated without sadness.

I was overwhelmed at the feel of Ricky's warm skin and the smell of his breath on my arm. I decided that I would be his twin, the person closest to him, and I would not let him go. The tears were allowed to come then. I felt them breaking down the dam in my body, making their journey up to my eyes, and spilling out onto Ricky's blanket.

I stared into his eyes and watched him breathe for a long time, and when I had cried myself out, I stood to take him to their room for a nap. I realized all my words must change: it was not "their" room anymore. He was the only boy in our family now.

I took Ricky around to the sunporch, through the baking kitchen and den, and up the back stairway to avoid the traffic of sadness swirling around the downstairs rooms. I rounded the corner to his room and saw Shirley sitting in the rocking chair, crying.

"Oh, Miss Kathleen, I'm so sorry . . . I just wanted to feel close to him." She was choking on her words and trying to make them proper.

"No 'sorry,' Shirley; please stay with us."

I laid Ricky in the crib and climbed in after him. I positioned his head at a slight angle so I could feel his breath on my face. As I listened to Shirley's tears, I pulled him close to my body, trying to fill the void that Michael had left. I stared at his deep-hazel eyes and whispered, "You are not alone," into his little ears.

CHAPTER 6

Summer, 1981

It was the middle of June. I had just gotten home from working with my horse Irish. We were doing so well together: we had a rhythm, and I felt powerful, being able to tame him little by little every day. I knew he was beginning to trust me, and it meant everything.

I was sitting in the alcove, reading about Egypt from our new *Encyclopædia Britannica*, which smelled of fake leather. I watched, only half-shocked, as my dad pulled up in front of our house in a thirty-eight-foot Pace Arrow motor home. It was massive. I ran out the side door and down the driveway just in time to hear him tell my mom and my sisters that he had decided to take the next eight weeks off—and we were leaving in the morning. He looked like a kid, with his hair pointing in all directions, his polo shirt untucked, and brown sandals on his feet.

"Richard, can we go inside and talk?" my mom asked.

"Come on, girls, I'll show you the new rig," he said, ignoring my mother and waving us inside. "Where's Ricky?"

"Napping. I should go check on him." The frustration in my mom's eyes turned to anxiety. Sometimes, even just hearing my brother's name made my mom panic even though it had been almost three years since

Ricky's twin had died. She stood in the grass and watched us file in behind my dad to get a look at the mobile home.

I tried not to jump up and down so I wouldn't hurt my mom's feelings, but it wasn't working; there was a definite skip in my step. All my sisters had it too.

We followed my dad up the steps and into our new compact version of home. It smelled like new leather and Pine-Sol, and all the built-in furniture still had plastic wrap on it.

"Come here, girls," my dad said. He was hunched over the kitchen table, unfolding a map. "We are going to circle the great U-S of A. We will see it all: the Mojave Desert, the Grand Canyon . . . hell, I might even take you to the cattle ranch in Montana where I lived for a summer when I ran away."

"You ran away, Dad? When?" Rachel asked.

"I was fourteen, and I hitchhiked from Nutley, New Jersey, to Bozeman, Montana." He smiled at Rachel. "I wanted to be a cowboy."

"You never told us that, Dad. Was it awesome?" I asked.

"It was, until my parents showed up three months later," he said.

"How did they know where you were?" Maggie asked.

"Well, the day they showed up is the day I learned that every letter gets a postmark showing where it originated. After I'd been gone awhile, I sent them a letter to tell them they would never see me again. They got in their car, drove across the country, and carted me back to New Jersey. Bye-bye, cowboy."

"Tell us another story, Dad," Rachel said.

"I have a better idea," he said. "Let's leave tonight! You girls run in and pack whatever you want for our trip."

We scrambled out of the motor home and ran into the house to pack. Rachel was behind me laughing as we ran though the side door. I was concentrating on what books I wanted to bring. I stopped in the kitchen to grab garbage bags. There was no time for the organized type of packing: this was going to be a free-for-all.

Up in our bedroom, Rachel and I bumped into each other as we ran from the closet to the trash bags, throwing clothes, toothbrushes, and stuffed animals into the bags.

"Don't forget PJs, Rachel," I said. "What books do you want me to bring for you?"

"*The Velveteen Rabbit, Doctor Dolittle*, and that one you've been reading to me about the boy on the beach with the horse. I love that one," she said.

"Got it. Let's hurry so we can claim our space in the motor home before Mary gets there," I said, rummaging through our bookcase under the window. We threw a few more essentials into the bags, and I made two trips, carrying the bags to our new mobile home like Santa on Christmas.

I put the trash bag with our clothes in it in the storage compartment that my dad had left open on the outside of the motor home. Then I joined Rachel, who was unpacking the other bag in the top bunk in the back of the motor home. If we could get unpacked, my parents wouldn't make us move. The space was cramped for two people, but it had a tiny storage area on one side and a window that ran the length of the bed on the other. There was a bookcase above the pillow at the head of the bed, and it had its own set of lights for late-night reading.

My mom and Ricky were the last to enter the motor home. Ricky was dressed in his checkered pajamas, and my mom looked like she was going to a gathering for the Disciples of Light. She was dressed in a long skirt with blue and pink flowers and a long-sleeved white shirt that buttoned up past her collarbone. She made her way to the passenger's seat, put Ricky on her lap, and stared straight ahead into the dark night.

The next three weeks were a blur. I loved us being in the motor home together. We were a family on wheels, wandering from one highway to the next with no need to get anywhere. My dad was always the one driving, and I stayed out of reach of his arm, so life was good.

We had a large detailed map of the United States in the motor home, and every time we stopped for gas, we continued the line we were drawing in thick black ink to trace our journey from the last town to the current one. The line started in New Jersey and then ran south to Florida and then west to Arizona.

It was that time in the afternoon when the Monopoly games were over and the excitement of looking out the window at new scenery had faded, and my sisters and I had gone to our favorite corners of the motor home to be alone. I was sitting behind my dad on the sleeper sofa, reading my favorite book, *A Tree Grows in Brooklyn*. I looked out the window and wondered what it would be like to be Francie Nolan. She was so brave.

I could hear my parents talking behind me. I turned my head to the left slightly and stole a look at my mom, who was sitting in the front passenger's seat. She moved between fixing her hair in the pull-down mirror to making a grocery list, all the while balancing Ricky on one knee.

I remembered how carefree she used to look sometimes when we drove in the car together. Now her hands were shaking and she was touching Ricky's shoulder every few seconds, making sure he was still there.

"But Ricky can't swim," my mom said. "He will sink to the bottom."

"Don't be so dramatic, Margaret. He'll be fine. We'll get him a life jacket and keep an eye on him," my dad said.

"I have to put my foot down on this."

"Yeah, OK, Maggie," he said. "We're going to be there shortly, so you finish that list of yours."

"Please, God, not a boat," she whispered, staring at her grocery list.

The map was on the table across from me. I got up, found Lake Powell just north of us on the map, and drew a solid line to it.

We were supposed to stop at the Grand Canyon for a few days, but instead my dad had come out of the KOA campground office six hours ago and announced that he had just rented us a fifty-three-foot Adventurer houseboat. We were headed to Lake Powell. He threw me a guidebook and said, "Do a little research for us, will ya?"

I devoured the book, reading it to Rachel in our bunk bed. Lake Powell was in two states, Utah and Arizona, but from the map it looked like it was mostly in Utah. It was the second-largest man-made lake in the United States after Lake Mead. It was huge: almost two hundred miles long and twenty-five miles wide and over 130 feet deep on average.

Rachel came up from behind me and asked, "What does a houseboat look like, Kath?"

"We are about to find out. Look," I said.

My dad pulled the motor home up in front of a dock that had a row of houseboats attached to it. They were bobbing up and down on the small waves rolling in on the beach surrounding the dock. There was a big sign made of driftwood that said "General Store."

We ran to the door of the motor home. I bounced up and down, waiting for the sign from my father that we were allowed to open the door and get out. Rachel was in front of me, wearing her polka-dot bathing suit and matching cover-up, and Maggie and Mary were already in the stairwell. Through the windshield I could see a huge body of water directly ahead of us. It was calm, unlike the ocean, but I had read that the waves could get as high as six feet during a storm.

My dad stuck his thumb in the air, and Maggie opened the door. My sisters and I tumbled out of the motor home into the blue Utah landscape, which looked like it had been freshly painted. My mom came down the steps of the motor home clutching Ricky's hand. She stood on the final step, stuck her head out, and looked left to right.

"Margaret, you are being ridiculous," my dad said from behind her. "Get out here and give the kids the list. Let's go."

"Come on, Ricky, you'll be fine," she said to my brother as she carefully stepped out of the motor home and handed Maggie the list to divvy up between us.

❖

I walked into the general store in my bare feet. I looked at my portion of the list, then at Rachel's. We had the nonperishable section: healthy cereal, crackers, pasta, red sauce, beans, and rice. Rachel and I gathered everything on our list, pretending to be in a race to the finish line.

"Mom, can we get these?" I asked, holding up the Suzy Q's, Cap'n Crunch, and Pringles.

"Yes, hon," she said without looking at me. I watched her in the life jacket section as she moved from rack to rack.

"You sure are buying a lot of groceries," the man behind the counter said as he added them up on his manual calculator. "How many of you are there, little girl?"

"Seven, but my mom will buy a lot more than we need," I said as I stuffed a package of Twizzlers into the bag. "She'll pay once she picks out a life jacket for my brother. Can I take these bags now?"

"Sure, kid."

Rachel and I ran out of the store, bags in hand, to claim our spot on the boat. My dad was standing on the roof of the boat, paying no attention to the man who was trying to give him the required walk-through.

We ran through the houseboat excitedly, looking for the perfect space to declare as ours. We agreed on one of the bedrooms down below and hid our sugary goodies under the bed. Then we went upstairs to explore the floating house. Maggie and Mary came aboard with their own bags of sugary treats and settled into the bedroom next to ours.

My dad yelled from the deck on the roof, "One of you girls, go back into the store to see what the holdup with your mother is."

"OK," I said. I left Rachel by the blue slide on the back of the boat and skipped back to the general store. My mom was in the same place she'd been when I left thirty minutes before. She was holding Ricky's hand and circling the racks of life jackets.

My body tensed. I could see my mother's fear as I walked to the end of the small aisle. Her breath was shallow, and her skin looked yellow, almost jaundiced. I could see her straining to swallow, and I felt her panic.

My mom looked up, stretched to her tippy-toes, and said, "Sir, excuse me. Which of these looks safer to you?"

The man behind the counter looked at her but didn't answer.

Her body started moving in circles again. She was like an uncontrollable child as she threw one life vest after another on the floor behind her. Now Ricky was staring at her with questions shining bright in his big, beautiful eyes.

I leaned against the row of swimsuits and watched my mom. I sensed her screaming on the inside. She needed the life jacket to come with a guarantee that Ricky would make it to be one hundred years old.

"All aboard!" my dad screamed from the houseboat.

"Jesus, Jesus, Jesus . . . ," my mom chanted as she walked to the checkout counter.

"Add these, please." She placed four life jackets and two large bundles of rope on the conveyor belt.

"Sure. That will be eight hundred twenty dollars and four cents," the man replied, eyeing my mom suspiciously.

My mom put on the smile she used for pictures and counted out nine one-hundred-dollar bills from her skirt pocket.

"Here, Mom, I'll take Ricky," I said, and tried to take him out of her arms so she could juggle the last bag of groceries and the collection of life jackets that were now hanging from her arm.

"NO, Kathleen, don't you . . . Here." She handed me the bag of groceries, squeezed Ricky tighter at her hip, and left the money on the counter.

"Ma'am, ma'am, I need to give you your change," said the man, calling to my mom as she tried to fasten Ricky into one of the life jackets while heading out the door. "Excuse me, lady, you have eighty bucks coming your way."

"OK, have a nice day," she said over her shoulder.

I shrugged at the man and went to catch up with my mom, who was heading to the boat.

My dad was standing on the dock. When we reached him, he took Ricky from my mother and stepped onto the back of the boat. My mother had no choice: if she wanted to get Ricky back, she had to get on the boat. She looked like Grandmother as she straightened her posture, forced her right foot forward, and stepped onto the boat, never taking her eyes off Ricky. Once on the boat, she took Ricky from my dad, clutching him with one hand while grasping the steel pillar holding up the covered deck with the other. She was completely still.

The covered back deck was large, with a seating area with cushions on one side and a built-in table and chairs for dining. It led to sliding glass doors into a living room and a nicely appointed kitchen at the helm of the boat. The fake leather smelled new, and some of the cushions were still wrapped in plastic. My dad told us there were three staterooms.

"Untie that rope," he hollered to Maggie.

"Got it, Dad," she shouted from the back of the boat.

We were off.

My dad let each of us take a turn driving the boat, and after only half an hour he stopped and dropped anchor. There was not another boat in sight. Red clay rocks jutted up all around us, looking majestic and peaceful, with sandy beaches resting at their bottoms. The water was four shades of blue, with green thrown in for good measure. The scenery deserved to be on a postcard.

My mom had disappeared into her stateroom and closed the door. Ricky was with her, and I wondered if she would come out.

"Well, if ya want to eat, ya better get fishing . . . ," my dad said as he pulled out the fishing gear.

I took two rods, baited them for Rachel and myself, and cast them off the back of the boat. I looked around—me in my daring multi-colored two-piece that I couldn't believe I was allowed to wear, and Rachel smiling as she played with the worms that were our bait. I tried to capture this scene in my brain so I could report it back to Shirley in a letter—every detail.

There was a tug on my line, and I heard my dad yell, "Reel it in!" His voice was steady, helpful. "I got ya. Now reel it in," he said as he steadied my shoulder. It was a strange feeling to have him so close and not be afraid as he helped me reel in the line. His calm and his desire to help me made me feel so special, as if we were building the world together, not just catching a fish. I didn't want it to end.

"What kind do you think it is?" I asked.

"Bring it up here and let's get a look."

I reeled in the line with all my might. My dad was going to be proud of me. I just knew it. The fish came out of the water with a fight and began flailing around on the boat deck.

"Pick it up; get ahold of it," my dad said.

"Got it—I got it," I said.

"That's a striper. You caught yourself a striper, kiddo."

I held it up for Maggie to take a picture.

"Dad, will you get in the picture with me?" I asked.

My dad put his arm around me, and together we held the line that held the fish.

"Do you know how to fillet a fish?" he asked.

"No."

"Go get a bucket from the storage downstairs, fill it with water, and put your fish in it. I'll teach you to fillet it when we're done fishing," my dad said.

"All right . . . who's next?" I heard him ask my sisters as I ran down the stairs for the bucket.

I woke up early the next morning with the excitement of the previous day running around in my brain. We had anchored in a shallow cove for the night, and from our window I could see the sun just beginning to hit the red rocks above us.

I slid out of bed, careful not to wake Rachel, and made my way to the galley kitchen. I loved how everything was latched shut in all the rooms, especially the kitchen. It felt safe. I opened the latch on the refrigerator and pulled out our leftover fish. I mixed it with a can of corn, toasted an English muffin, and made my way to the back deck to eat my well-earned breakfast and write to Shirley.

Mom and Ricky woke next and joined me, Ricky teetering back and forth with his life jacket on.

"This is a perfect spot. I told your father we should stay right here for the rest of the trip. Don't you agree?" Mom said.

"Sure, Mom. It's beautiful. Can Ricky sit on my lap to eat?" I asked.

"No, sweetie. Ricky . . . he'll sit here, with me." She pulled him up on her lap. One end of a rope was tied to the back of Ricky's life jacket and the other to my mom's wrist; it kept him from moving more than about two feet away from her. The life jacket had become officially part of him while we were on the boat. He had not taken it off once, not even to sleep in the bed with Mom and Dad—and even still, my mom had not taken a deep breath since she'd come aboard.

Since Michael died, Mom had kept Ricky next to her no matter what she was doing: cooking, sleeping, going to the bathroom, lying on the beach . . . He was her little shadow.

"I told your father we all love it here and there is no need to move us around on the lake so much. We won't be moving today," she said as she fed Ricky a bite of English muffin.

I knew she loved this spot mostly because the water was only three feet deep. There was sand on both sides of the cove, and the previous night when we had dropped anchor, Rachel and I discovered that we could make real clay pottery out of it. It was thick and sticky, like Play-Doh in the form of sand, and I was excited to make presents for Shirley and Grace today.

It was almost an assembly line. Mary and I gathered the sand in our cleaned-out fish buckets and sent it down to Maggie and Rachel, who picked out the rocks and got it ready for shaping. Then we all stopped to shape the clay and bake our pieces in the sun. We were on round three, and I was going to make a ring tree for Grace to put her jewelry on.

"Include your brother," Mom said from ten feet down the beach.

Ricky was walking toward us with a priceless grin.

"Ricky, run!" Mary yelled to him.

"Come on, Ricky!" I said.

"Yay, Ricky can play?" Rachel said, looking at my mom questioningly.

Mom was sunbathing in the foldout chair, a glass of white wine in her hand. The rope that had connected her with Ricky was still attached to her wrist, the other end dangling off the side of the chair.

Maggie blessed herself with the sign of the cross, looked up to heaven, and said, "Thank you."

We all sat in the sand and made a circle with our feet touching. Ricky was in the middle, jumping and acting rambunctious, like a dog off leash. We took turns burying each other in the sand and spoiling Ricky as much as possible until Mom called us for dinner. The day had flown by. I could feel the heat on my back where I had gotten too much sun. It made me smile.

My dad had decided we would cook over an open fire on the beach for our second night. Everything tasted better cooked out there. After dinner, we put out the fire and climbed back onto the boat to clean up. Rachel and I were allowed to sleep on the first floor, where there was a makeshift bed crafted from the top of the kitchen table with a mattress fitted on top.

Our bedroom for the night had a view out the back of the boat. Rachel was already asleep next to me, and I wiggled my way to the other side of her so I could see my parents, who were sitting on the back deck. Ricky was already asleep, tethered to my mom on the couch. I could feel the boat moving. Apparently my dad had pulled up the anchor.

"Hon, please," my mom said as she moved farther away from my dad. "Let's go back to the cove and drop anchor there; it's safer."

"I'm trying here, Maggie. I've spent two days in this one cove when we have hundreds of miles to explore. Let's see where we land in the morning if we drift for a while."

"No—the man at the store told us that we MUST anchor every night. He said that. You heard him say that. Please drive us back to the cove and drop anchor—please."

My sunburn started to itch, and I began to feel myself slipping into sleep.

The next sounds I heard were my mother's screams: "KATHLEEN! RACHEL! KATHLEEN! JESUS, JESUS, JESUS . . ." I heard my mom's voice in my sleep. "KATHLEEN! WAKE UP!"

I sat straight up in bed and instinctively pulled Rachel onto my lap. The houseboat tilted violently to one side and then upright again so much so that we were both tossed into the air. A strong wind ripped through the boat. And shadows moved across the interior walls at a fast and frantic pace. I rubbed my eyes with one hand and hung on to Rachel with the other.

"What are they?" Rachel's voice was two octaves higher than normal.

Bats. Hundreds of them, flying in the houseboat, trapped and agitated.

I tucked her small body into mine. We were tossed hard into the windows as their movement combined with the storm now raging outside rocked the boat. Even though I tried not to, I screamed.

Rachel's grip loosened as we were tossed against the windows again. "Don't let go of me!" I said. "Hold on tighter!" Her brown hair whipped around her face from the force of the wind tearing through the open windows and doors.

"Get on the floor!" Mom yelled as she began to tie a thick braided rope to Rachel's foot. I grabbed Rachel off the bed and held her between my legs on the floor. Ricky was silent and bewildered, already tied to the braided rope next to my mom. I took the thin blanket off our bed and wrapped it around Rachel and myself.

"Margaret, don't tie them together—you'll all drown," I heard my father scream above the sound of the wind and the chittering of the bats. I could hear his voice, but I couldn't see him in the blackness swirling around us.

My dad came back up the stairs with Maggie and Mary close behind him, all three ducking as the bats darted around the kitchen. Maggie and Mary joined us on the ground, and my mom began tying us together.

The bats were everywhere, and I put Rachel's head under the blanket so they wouldn't hit her as they darted around in circles, desperately searching for an exit.

"Richard, we have to jump! I just need to tie two more! Jesus, Jesus, Jesus!" my mom screamed. The floor felt like a Slip 'N Slide. There was rain pouring in, and the only thing I could do was hold on to Rachel.

My dad started to drive the boat through the storm, and my mom went to work tying Maggie and Mary into our labyrinth of rope. I felt sure our boat was taking on water; we were sliding from side to side and I felt several inches of wetness following us. The wind got stronger and seemed to scream as my dad drove into the darkness of the lake.

I decided we could not go overboard all tied together—that it was a crazy notion and my dad was right: we would all die. I could feel the rope loosening a smidgen as I worked with both my hands in between waves to untie Rachel's ankle. Once I had freed Rachel, I just needed to do the same for myself.

My dad began steering the boat into the waves, so instead of being thrown from side to side, we were now being thrown in the air every time we went into a trough. My dad gunned the engine, and we moved faster and faster over the waves, which at least helped force the bats to clear out through the back opening of the cabin.

"If this storm gets any worse, here's what we're going to do!" my dad screamed from his spot at the wheel. I was so happy someone other than my mom had a plan, because I was pretty sure hers was going to kill us all.

My dad told us to brace ourselves, because he was going to drive as fast as possible until he beached the houseboat. Then we were supposed to jump to safety.

My mom was holding Ricky tight with both hands. She continued her rhythmic chant of "Jesus, Jesus, Jesus, Jesus" loud enough for all of us to hear. Maggie joined in, praying in tongues.

"Richard, let's jump! Jesus, Jesus, Jesus! Get up, kids—we're going to jump overboard!" She was trying to manage getting to her feet with Ricky in her arms. I went into high gear trying to untie the knot on my foot. There was no land in sight; it could have been miles away.

"Got it. I got it. Oh my God. OK," I said. Now I needed something to tie Rachel and me together, but I couldn't see anything, and we were flying into the air with force about every twenty seconds. I protected

Rachel's head with my arms every time we were jolted upward, and I tried to soften the blow as we came back down. I was more grateful for the latches on the cabinets than I had been that morning.

My mom began shouting at Rachel to get her to stand.

"I've got her, Mom," I said.

"Get up—get up—Jesus, Jesus, Jesus!" my mom screamed from her crouched position on the floor. She held tight to Ricky as we were all thrown into the air again. We landed hard on the ground, and I moved Rachel under the kitchen table, which created a border on three sides. I hung on to the leg of the table with one hand and Rachel with the other. We weren't getting thrown around as much here, and I was able to look around the space.

"Come over here—it's safer!" I yelled to Mom, Maggie, and Mary, but the wind and the chaos were carrying my voice away before they could hear it.

"COME HERE!" I screamed.

Mary looked in our direction, and I let go of the leg of the table to gesture for her to come. She and Maggie began to move toward us, which forced my mom and Ricky to join them. We were able to meld our bodies together under the table, where we formed a solid mass that made us more stable, and the violent tossing around subsided.

My dad was yelling into the storm with a wrath that brought new creases to his face. He was being thrown from left to right as he held tightly to the steering wheel and taunted the storm. The next wave threw him to the opposite side of the cabin, and the boat began to do a circle around the wave; with no one at the helm, it began to turn on its side.

My dad pulled himself up and, crouching forward, made it back to the steering wheel. The boat did a dramatic turn and faced the next wave.

"Good try, you bastard," he said, laughing.

The next wave hit with intensity, and this time my dad was ready. He white-knuckled the steering wheel and braced himself for the impact as we hit the wave head-on.

The boat began to stay level longer, and I didn't have to hold on to the leg of the table quite so tightly. Rachel cried softly into my shoulder as she continued to grip my skin with her nails. Ricky was wrapped tight inside a blanket, so I couldn't see his face. My mom's eyes were closed, and she continued to lean left and then right even without the help of the waves, all the while continuing her chant. Maggie and Mary were behind me, and I could hear Maggie still praying.

The next wave was less intense, and I could feel the circulation coming back into my fingers.

"Bastard," my dad said, keeping his hands on the wheel.

I stood to look out the open window while still holding on to Rachel. We were soaked to our skins, and I was shaking from the cold and the adrenaline. Mary got up and turned the lights on. I looked around to survey the damage. There were still inches of water inside the boat, and everything that hadn't been latched down was floating in it.

"Thank you, Jesus," Maggie said.

Mom stood up, one hand on Ricky. "God's mercy."

"Why the hell wasn't the anchor thrown down last night? Who did I tell to throw anchor last night?" my dad demanded.

"Richard, we . . . ," my mom began.

"I wasn't asking you, Maggie." He walked to the back of the boat to throw the anchor over the side. His steps were loud and angry.

CHAPTER 7

I woke up with a gasp and was relieved to see the sunshine out the tiny window of our stateroom. Last night, after my dad had dropped the anchor, we had listened from our beds as he paced upstairs in the main cabin. I had fallen asleep with the sound of his heavy footsteps and the lingering flapping of bats' wings in my ears. I listened for movement upstairs.

It was quiet now, and I was hungry, so I thought it was likely safe to make my way to the kitchen. My clothes had been strewn around the stateroom from the storm, so I grabbed the first shirt and pair of pants I could find, since I wasn't allowed to wear my bathing suit for meals. There was a pretty piece of orange yarn in my pants pocket, so I tied my hair up with it. I came up the stairs and saw my dad sitting in a chair at the back of the boat. I tried to turn around and head back down the steps, but it was too late.

"Come out here."

I made a conscious effort to sound as lighthearted as I could when I got to the back of the boat. "Good morning."

"Sit down."

I was hoping that was just a suggestion, so instead I leaned against the side of the boat to keep my distance. Even when he was sitting down, he was intimidating.

His hands were clenching and unclenching. "What do ya think about last night?"

My voice came out as a whisper: "Crazy."

His body stiffened. "Did you just call me crazy?" He began to forcefully push himself out of the chair. I straightened up to run, but his hand smashed into the left side of my face before I could get very far. The next thing I knew, my body was in the air, and the sound of the water as I hit it filled my ears.

I was fully clothed; my ears were ringing, and my arms and legs were moving in all directions, trying to get away from the pain in my face. *Somewhere-else place, somewhere-else place,* I just kept saying in my mind, in the hope that I could conjure up one.

I started screaming apologies while I struggled to keep my head above the cold water. The orange yarn I had tied in my hair was floating past me. I spotted a beach not too far away, but there were no other boats. I was trembling in the water, making circles with my hands to keep myself afloat.

I have to get back on the boat.

I can't get back on the boat.

I looked at the houseboat, and my dad had disappeared from the back deck. I wondered if he was going to leave me here. I closed my eyes to try to steady my breathing so I could think of a plan. The darkness behind my eyes startled me, and I opened them wider and involuntarily threw my head backward, into the water. I had a metallic taste in my mouth, and I realized the inside of my mouth was bleeding.

I saw my clothes through the blue water. My green Izod shirt was ballooning out around me, and my pink Dockers pants felt heavy with my body stuck inside them. I was taken with the image for a moment, trying to find my somewhere-else place. My canvas tennis shoes were weighing me down, and the distance between me and the boat increased as I lay on my back and swam in the opposite direction of the boat, never taking my eyes off it.

I heard the engine start up in the water, and my body began to shake uncontrollably. There was enough blood in my mouth that I had to spit it out. I watched the red liquid disperse, forming patterns in the blue water.

As the boat turned toward me, I could see my dad behind the plexiglass window, driving it forward, chasing me. I needed a plan. A wave caught my face; I coughed more blood into the water. The boat was headed right for me.

I turned away from the boat and swam as fast as I could toward the beach.

The boat narrowed the distance, still pointed right at me. *Is he going to run over me? Swim, just swim. Get to the beach.*

I could hear the engine getting louder behind me, and I became scared that I would be sucked under the hull. I stole a glance behind me and saw the boat turn abruptly and then pass me. A few seconds later, my dad beached the boat on the sand.

I could stand in the water now, and I walked quickly, perusing the beach for a place to run and hide. The terrain was flat, with red rocks protruding up at a dramatic angle all around us.

I stopped when the water was up to my knees and saw my dad standing on the front of the boat. He had something in his hand. It was the size of a small thick stick. My wrists began to tingle with the memory.

Dad stood fiddling with the thing without looking up.

I kept walking, but toward the boat now. I couldn't hear my mother's voice reciting Jesus's name the way she did when bad things were happening. I concentrated on my feet as I struggled to lift my shoes out of the mucky sand and clay on the floor of the lake. I was just a few steps from the boat when I looked up to meet my dad's shadowy eyes. I heard my mother's words come out of my own mouth: "Jesus, Jesus, Jesus."

He was loading a gun.

I couldn't move. He put a tan-colored backpack on and then reached for the holster that was sitting on the railing. He wrapped it around his waist and gently and carefully placed the .45-caliber pistol into it. I couldn't take my eyes off the gun. I screamed so loud in my head that I thought I heard small bursts of brain cells exploding. I put both hands on my knees to steady myself, letting my head fall toward the ground, and I spit the blood that had gathered inside my mouth into the sand.

He jumped from the boat onto the beach next to me. He was too close.

I looked up at him and then back down and watched the drops of blood falling from my mouth mix with the grains of sand and turn them shades of red. I counted how many clear drops of water fell from my body in between the red drops of blood. Two, three, four. Red drop of blood. Start over: one, two, three . . .

"I am going to kill you. We are going for a walk, and I am going to kill you. Don't say one word, not one. Do you understand?"

I nodded my head.

My mom walked out to the front of the boat with Ricky in tow. She was watching me but never made eye contact. She wasn't crying, she didn't seem upset, she wasn't humming or twirling her hair or chanting "Jesus." My brother asked her a question, and she leaned down to answer him.

"Stop with the drama. Now," my dad said, "follow me." He turned around and began to walk toward the rocks in front of us.

I began to follow him. I decided not to pray.

He was left-handed, and the gun sat solidly in the holster on the left side of his body. There was a leather strip with a snap on the end locking the gun in place. If I were able to push him down, I might be able to unlock the gun and get it from him. But tears started to flow down my cheeks, stalling my faint attempt at bravery. My dad was at least twice my size; there would be no way to get possession of the gun.

I thought of Shirley. I missed her. I needed some of her grit right now.

The sun was relentless as we walked up the beach and onto the red rocks. My clothes had dried quickly, and they felt like sores on my body because of the heat trapped inside them, burning my skin. I still tasted blood inside my mouth, but I could tell the bleeding had slowed. I spit the blood out as it gathered in my mouth. I could feel the dried blood on my forehead where his wedding ring had left a cut above my eye.

My dad stopped abruptly just as we were climbing up the second red rock. He put his hand on his holster and looked at me. I looked him straight in the eye and tried to keep my lips from quivering. *Don't let him see you scared.* He took the backpack off his back, took out a large canteen, and drank from it. The water stayed on his lips as he smirked at me, put the canteen back into the backpack, pulled out a large rimmed fishing hat, put it on his head, and started moving again. *Don't let him see your thirst.* He picked up the pace.

The dried red mud on my shoes made them feel like clay pots baking my feet. My brain felt foggy, and it was difficult to put energy into anything other than just putting one foot in front of the other. I looked around for opportunities to run, but even if I found one, there would be no way to outrun a bullet. Time was all I had now.

We made it over the first set of red rocks and began walking on another beach that looked identical to the one where we had started out. My dad stopped to drink more water from his canteen. Almost involuntarily, I stuck my tongue out, looking for moisture.

It was about twenty minutes later when my dad stopped again. He rearranged his hat on his head and glanced in my direction. He took his canteen from his backpack and unscrewed the top. He put space between the opening of the canteen and his mouth so I could see the clear, wet liquid hit his tongue. It was his second canteen and his fifty-fourth sip of water since we had left the boat.

My eyes were drooping from exhaustion and sunburn, but I still stared him square in the eye. It was the only power I had.

The beach ended again and we were faced with more red rocks coming out from the earth. I could see the top; maybe that would be the spot. I looked at my dad in front of me to see if I could read his mind. His left hand rested on the butt of the gun inside the holster.

I was surprised my body was still moving forward, since I knew my fate. We were almost to the top. I could feel the pureness of the terror on my skin; I felt it mixing with the blood and the sweat and the exhaustion, and it was becoming harder to focus on the next physical step ahead of me. I was dizzy; the red rocks before me looked like a bonfire that we would need to cross. I willed myself to take the next step.

My dad stopped ten feet ahead of me. Sweat dripped from his face, and he was breathing hard through his mouth. He turned toward me, removed the lid from the canteen he had been holding, and took another long sip. I watched him swallow and tried to feel the fluid running down my own throat. He avoided my eyes and placed the canteen back in his backpack. By this time I had lost count of the number of sips he'd taken since we left the boat. I looked at him. *You can't break me. I hate you. You can kill me, but I won't let you break me.*

He swiveled from his right foot to his left, looking for solid footing at the top of the rock. He looked so tall standing above me, with the blue sky as a backdrop. He took his time and carefully rolled up his left sleeve. He took the gun from his holster and held it in his left hand.

Run. You have a chance. Don't let him break you. I miss Shirley.

I was wobbly and hunched over my functionless legs. He opened the cylinder, spun the metal chamber filled with bullets, and closed it again.

I stood up straight, wiped the sweat off my forehead, and stared at the gun. My fear and exhaustion gave way to an unexpected courage. *Look at him. Be brave when you die.* I tried to swallow, but the air stuck in my mouth.

I was floating. I felt so light, I couldn't keep my body on the ground. I took a deep breath, and it felt clean going into my lungs. I smelled water; I had never noticed the smell of water before. It was alive; I could feel the particles, the absolute wetness. I looked at my dad, and I could see the gun reflected in his eyes.

He lifted the gun, looked through the sight, and aimed it at me. My eyes were wide-open. I thought of Shirley and her kids. I thought of Rachel and wondered who would protect her. And I thought of my dead brother, Michael.

He turned the safety off, slowly pulled back the hammer, and looked at me, steadying his aim at my head.

"OK, kiddo, you ready?" The blue, cloudless sky behind him made his body look fuzzy. I stayed focused on his eyes. They were a dark shade of hazel. They moved continuously—calculated, powerful, and paranoid at the same time. He was looking at me as if he didn't know me.

"What do you want to say to me?" he asked, looking past me. He shifted his body again and balanced his weight on his right side. Once he was settled, he repositioned the gun.

"What do you want to say to God?" he asked.

"Will you tell Shirley and Rachel I love them?" I said. I tried so hard not to cry, but as the words came, the floodgate broke and the tears were a continuous flow down my cheeks. The salt tasted foreign in my mouth, and my body shook violently.

He moved his finger onto the trigger in slow motion, and I could feel the pressure he was putting on it. I kept my eyes on his. Then my head shrank back and to the right as I cringed and fought to stay on my feet.

He fired two shots, one after the other, both flying past the left side of my head. The sound ricocheted off the rocks. I could hear the echo along with the buzzing in my ears. I lost my balance and fell to the ground, landing in the fetal position, the hard rocks holding me. I covered my ears. I was sobbing out loud.

"Get up." I think he was laughing. "Stop the drama and get up."
His foot was on my thigh, shaking me back and forth.

I stood and kept my face to the ground. *Look at him; I have to look
at him.*

But I couldn't look at him.

"You look like a fucking wreck. Here," he said. He opened his canteen, poured some of the water on his handkerchief, and threw it at me.

"Clean yourself up, for God's sake," he said.

I sucked on the towel for the moisture and then placed it on my
face and wiped from my forehead to my chin. I looked at the handkerchief. The dark reddish-brown color turned my stomach.

He threw me his canteen, and I wanted to throw it back to him,
but instead I quickly opened it and drank the water as fast as I could.

"Let's get back to the boat," he said as he motioned for me to give
him the canteen.

I started walking down the red rocks behind my dad, stopping
twice to vomit.

I had no sense of direction, and my body felt as if it weighed twice
as much as it should. I followed my dad to the bottom of the huge red
rocks and back onto the beach, watching every step of the way the gun
that was back at his hip, locked in the holster.

We walked the beach until I saw our houseboat. Rachel, Mary, and
Maggie were splashing in the water next to the boat. I could see my
mom and Ricky in the chair several feet away from them. I started to
cry softly.

When we got close, Rachel ran to me. "Where have you been?
Why are you so dirty? You were gone all day . . ." Her questions made
me cry harder.

I got down on both knees, looked at her beautifully innocent eyes,
and said, "I love you, Rachel." I couldn't force myself to tell her I was
OK. I stood up slowly and headed for the boat.

"Hi, sweetie, get cleaned up for dinner," my mom said as I passed her.

CHAPTER 8

Spring, 1985

It was almost summer again. I was a sophomore at St. Rose High School. I was sure Mary, who was a senior, hated the fact that Robert, one of the most popular guys in her class, was trying to date me. Mary and I passed each other in the hall without acknowledgment; we went to the same parties on the weekends, wishing the other wasn't there; and we were cruel to each other every place in between.

We left the Disciples of Light that year because my dad and Francis Tallic had a tug-of-war over power. My dad was starting a new community, and he was doing his best to recruit families. My dad's rule was that I wasn't allowed to date anyone but Robert. He said Robert reminded him of himself at that age. Robert's group of friends was the same as mine, so I went along with dating him so I could go out on the weekends.

When Grace and I found out that our friends Karen and Marie O'Neil were going to Ireland for summer vacation with their family, we decided their house would be a great place to hang out for the week they were gone. They had a big house just off Ocean Avenue, several blocks from mine, and we knew Karen and Marie would be more than happy to secretly leave us a key.

We decided to throw the party on Saturday, three days before the O'Neils would be coming home. Robert was out of town, and my parents thought I was staying overnight at Grace's house. We planned for something simple: a few people and some beer. We would make everyone smoke outside.

"What do you mean you lost the key?" Grace said as she punched me with her middle knuckle. "Idiot."

I tried to laugh as I covered my upper right arm protectively, trying not to let her know that her punch had landed squarely on the large bruise that Robert thought I deserved for having a cigarette last weekend—even though I had told him we were *not* dating and it was none of his business.

"It's gotta be in here somewhere—hold on," I said as I rummaged through my brown leather purse with tassels coming off the bottom. "Shit. Well, I'll just climb in the window."

"What window?" Grace said.

"The one I left unlocked. Ha! Who's the smart one now?" I said, turning and heading for the kitchen window. We had been in and out of the house all week, using it as a private getaway. I climbed in the window, landing on their wooden farmhouse table, and ran around to the side door to let Grace in.

"Let's get this stuff inside before someone sees us," Grace said.

"No one's going to see us. If they do, we have our story. Don't freak out."

"Whatever—just help me with the cooler," Grace said. When we walked into the O'Neils' sitting room, with the mahogany wood chairs and stuffed down pillows in all different patterns of black and white, I immediately felt at ease. The house was more like a beach house, a place of comfort with an eccentric flair: it was filled with trinkets, paintings, and furniture from their travels abroad that somehow worked so well together. The old grandfather clock next to the wicker furniture by the window begged you to sit, chat, and pay no attention to time. The thick off-white carpet massaged your feet as you walked across it, tempting you to lie down and snooze in its comfort. Where my house was grand, with everything in its exact place, theirs felt lived-in.

Walking through the sitting room and up the three steps back into the kitchen, I noticed the family pictures on the walls. The O'Neils had four adopted girls, and in each photo the smiles on their faces were intense. I wondered what happened in their family when they weren't in front of the camera.

I made my way around the large farmhouse table, unpacked our twelve-pack of Budweiser, and put it into the fridge, minus the two that I was about to open.

"I'm so grateful your sister was cool enough to buy us beer. I always have to drink wine coolers when Robert is at the party, and they are sugary-nasty."

"He is such an asshole," Grace replied.

"Try telling my dad that. Yuck."

I gave one of the now-open bottles of Bud to Grace, we clinked them together in a toast, and I took one long sip from mine as I made my way out of the kitchen. I liked the numbness alcohol created in my brain. I walked down the steps and into the sunken living room, with its corduroy conversation pit surrounding the television.

"OK, tell me how many people you really invited over tonight," I said as I walked up to the back of the conversation pit, stepped into it and onto the green cushy fabric, and took another long draw from my beer. "I invited maybe ten? OK, maybe more like fifteen. Everyone is coming around seven." I put my beer bottle on the table and grabbed the remote to switch the TV on.

"We said we would invite two people each," Grace said as she moved around the couch and sat on the opposite side of the pit. "OK, I invited about the same, maybe a few more."

"Oops," we said in unison, and laughed. We both moved closer to the middle of the couch and started watching *Happy Days* as we waited for seven o'clock to roll around.

I touched the bruise on my right arm and flashed back to last week's party. Robert's strong words as he slammed my arms into the dirt echoed in my memory. "I said NO SMOKING. Did you think you could sneak off and I wouldn't find out?"

I had panicked and tried to casually walk away from the group that was smoking behind the brown car across the street when I saw him coming. I waited until I was far enough away from the streetlamp that lit the road before breaking into a run. I was desperate for him not to see me.

The blackness made me feel safer as I ran deeper into the forest by his house. But as I slowed down to try to see through the trees in the dark, I heard his voice behind me.

"Kathleen. Stop right now. KATHLEEN!" His voice was raspy and winded, and my body broke out in goose bumps.

I crouched down behind a large tree and tried to slow my heartbeat, which was pounding behind my eyes. The rhythm of the beat sounded like a heavy-metal song that wouldn't let up on the drums. I pulled my knees into my chest as tightly as I could and dropped my head in between my legs to make myself invisible. I didn't know where I was exactly, but I remembered that the forest went on for a way before ending at the neighbors' property. I decided to make a run for the neighbors' house.

"Where are you, goddammit?" His voice was getting closer. I needed to run; I couldn't just sit there and wait for him to find me. The moon poked through the trees, and I could see my white shirt as if it were lit by a flashlight. I stood up and started to run as fast as I could toward the distant light of the neighbors' house, not sure what I was going to do once I got there.

I heard his six-foot-two body cutting through the forest and closing what I imagined was a short distance between us. Sweat mixed with tears and made its way down my face as I turned my head to get a glimpse of him through the moonlight, my feet driving forward.

By the time I turned back around, it was too late: my body slammed into a chain-link fence. I felt the impact as the fence gave only a fraction, and then I was flung backward onto the hard ground. I sprang up even before I could put together what had just happened. I saw Robert. He was walking now, a victory walk, his eyes focused and taunting as he covered the short distance to my stunned body.

He grabbed both of my arms so hard that my body collapsed and hit the earth again. He pushed me down flat and rested his body on my hips, his knees pinning my arms to the ground between my shoulders and my elbows. I could feel his knees digging into my flesh, where the bruises would form. His breath was forced from the running and the anger, and it smelled like stale beer.

I wanted to close my eyes, but I forced them open wider and held my breath. The pressure he was putting on my arms cut off my circulation, and my fingers began to tingle as he screamed, inches from my face.

Grace's voice brought me back to the O'Neils' living room: "I'm getting another beer; want one?"

I watched her walk up the steps to the kitchen. I worked to slow my breath. "No, I'm good. I'm going out to have a cigarette," I said as I covered the bruises on my arms and made my way to the backyard.

Our small party quickly turned into more than fifty people, all drinking, dancing, and smoking in every room of the downstairs and the game room in the basement. At ten fifteen, Grace came to tell me that Maggie and Mary had arrived to pick me up for the night: she said something about my dad changing his mind. I sprinted up the stairs and out the front door. There were so many cars parked outside, it looked like a parking lot at a Bruce Springsteen concert.

"You are dead when Mom and Dad find out," Mary said with a glint in her eye. Since we hit high school, Mary wanted me in trouble, and she was jealous. It was a bad combination.

"Wouldn't you love that," I said, glaring at her.

In a soft voice, Maggie said, "I'm worried about you. Come home with us. Dad wants you home. It's curfew."

"I'm staying at Grace's tonight; Dad said it was OK. I have to start telling people they need to leave."

Maggie touched my shoulder, made the sign of the cross, and then turned and started the ten-block walk to our house.

I tripped up the front steps and then made my way back down to the basement. My head felt lighter, and I liked the feeling of the beer in my brain.

From a distance we heard, "The cops are here! The cops are here!" It sounded like Kappy's voice, and I wondered if he was playing one of his pranks. Grace and I ran up the basement steps together, following the voice. At the top of the stairs, we saw the red and blue swirling lights breaking into the darkened living room. The lights were circling, and people were scrambling in every direction to get out of the house. We sprinted to the back door and saw two policemen with flashlights grabbing the kids who were leaving the house and attempting to sprint across the back lawn.

Bonnie, a good friend from school, caught up to us. "Upstairs— let's hide," she said.

Grace, Bonnie, and I ran up the stairs, sending one of the framed family pictures smashing to the ground behind us. The sound of the shattering glass made Bonnie scream.

"Shut up," I said. "Master bedroom—get under the bed!"

We ran down the short hallway and began jockeying for space under the bed. And then we got very still.

The light from a policeman's flashlight shone through the bed skirt as the officer started down the hallway from the staircase. "We know there are people up here. Come out and don't make us come find you," he called in a stern voice. I decided to take my chances and wait it out. No one moved a muscle, and the sound of our breath slowed with his footsteps.

I could see the policeman's feet walking from room to room, the light from the flashlight guiding his steps. He walked into the bathroom off the hall, and I heard another friend, Ellen, scream. Another policeman joined them in the hall, and I lifted the bed skirt just a bit to get a better look.

The policeman reached around the right side of his belt and produced handcuffs. Ellen screamed again, this time loud enough to shake the house. Her body was so tight, it looked as if she would snap if he touched her. He took one of her arms and put one handcuff on and then took the other cuff and attached it to the wooden banister at the top of the stairs.

Ellen's tan had vanished, and she looked like an apparition standing there, crying, one hand over her mouth.

Now there were three police officers on the second floor. I carefully let the bed skirt drop back to the ground and watched the shadows of their legs getting closer. Grace slid her arm under mine, and we held on to each other, letting only small breaths escape our lungs.

I had been the last one to climb under the bed, and two pairs of officers' feet were now eerily close to my body. One of them stepped back, and I thought I heard him draw his gun from its holster. He dropped to his knees and pulled the bed skirt up.

"It's more kids," he said to the other policemen as he stood up. "Get the fuck out of there," he said to us.

I was closest to him and dragged myself out from under the bed. He took my right hand, then my left, and put them behind my back and handcuffed me. He told me to stand next to Ellen and her tears.

They handcuffed Grace and Bonnie and marched us in single file down the wooden staircase and over the broken glass. I looked around the house, trying not to fall down the stairs with my arms behind me. The lights were on now. The damage was everywhere. Some of the windows were open, some were shut, and one side window had been shattered; there was glass all over the rug. The chairs in the sitting room were on their sides, and I could see crystal glasses with cigarette butts in them on the coffee table. The place looked like a cyclone had just hit.

We walked out of the O'Neils' house, and I saw my sisters in the small crowd that had formed outside. Maggie looked panicked, and Mary was laughing. She waved at me as the officer released my hands, put his hand on my head, and pushed me into the back of the police car.

The four of us were squished into the back of the patrol car, sitting straight as boards in utter silence, desperately trying to think up our defense. We pulled up to the station in less than three minutes; I knew because I had been watching the clock on the dashboard, hoping to turn back time.

They put us in the cell with seven other kids they had snagged from the party. I knew them all, and there was a thread of fear that was running from one set of eyes to the next. The cell was so clean, it looked new; but the lightbulb above us was broken, as if to remind us that we were in jail. Otherwise, it was spotless. Even the toilet in the left corner looked unused.

One of the policemen walked over and asked for our names, addresses, and the name and phone number of the person we wanted to call to pick us up.

"Who are you going to call?" I asked Grace.

"I guess I'm calling whoever answers at my house. You should come home with me," she said matter-of-factly.

"You. Who are you?" The officer looked at me.

"Kathleen Flanagan. Nine-oh-nine Ocean Avenue, but I'm supposed to sleep at her house tonight." I looked at Grace.

"Are your parents home?"

"No, my cousin is taking care of me this weekend," I lied.

"Then we'll call your cousin. Is she eighteen? What's the number?"

"Yes." I squeezed Grace's hand harder as the number to my cousin's house came out of my mouth. I held the black receiver with both hands and listened to the ring that would ultimately lead to my being given away to whoever was on the other end. I stared at the policeman, who was standing next to me with a smirk. I think the police were being highly entertained by the stupid kids who had tried to have a party.

Patty answered. "Hello?"

"Hey, Patty," I said, with all the collectedness I could muster.

"What's up, Kath?" she said, hearing the panic in my voice.

"Patty, I had a party at the O'Neils' tonight, and the police came, and now I'm at the police station. Will you come get me?" Patty knew the O'Neils, and she was friends with the oldest sister, so she knew they were out of town. I had to do very little explaining.

"Ask them if I can come get you on my bike," said Patty. "I'm grounded, but I could sneak out on the bike. My dad will hear if I try to take the car."

My options were limited: either ask if she could bring me home on her bike or call my dad. I turned to the officer.

"My parents took the car on their trip. Can she come get me on her bike?"

"I don't care if she rides a unicycle; she has to be eighteen and willing to take responsibility for you," the policeman said, staring at me.

"That's fine, Patty. Come quick."

Four people had been picked up so far. All the parents seemed to be joking with the police.

"Takes me back," Mr. Kappy said.

"Boys will be boys," Mr. Flaherty said.

The police knew everyone who walked in the door, and their demeanor was opposite to what they had shown us. I relaxed a little more, realizing their job was to teach us a lesson—and they had done that. They had sufficiently scared the shit out of each and every one of us.

I heard the laughter from the police stop abruptly, and I looked to the door to see who would be the next one sprung from our cage.

I gasped as my father walked into the station. I looked at Grace and saw her hand fly to her mouth.

"No," she whispered.

"Oh my God," I said. "What do I do?"

"Can you refuse to go with him?"

"Where is Kathleen Flanagan?" my dad asked the policeman behind the front desk. My dad's hair was wet and slicked back just right. His jeans had been altered to hit directly on the front of his shoes, just so, and he had on a black-and-white striped golf shirt. His eyes hadn't found mine yet, so I studied them as they roamed the room to find me. The whites of his eyes were more of a gray, and the hazel color looked electric.

"Yessir. I'll go and get her." The policeman almost saluted as he turned and walked toward our cell.

"Kathleen?"

I stood up, and my dad's eyes found me. He made it across the room in three steps and was standing next to the policeman before the policeman could get the key in the door to open it.

"I'll get her," he said to the policeman as he walked into the cell.

My head was pulsing with my heartbeat, and I looked at Grace. "I'll see you later." I smiled at her and walked toward my dad. I'd only taken half a step before he grabbed my arm and cut his fingernails into my bruises, pulling me forward. He signed the paperwork without letting go of my arm, and we headed outside.

He pushed me when he let go of me outside, and I started to walk around the side of the car.

"Get in the back," he said.

I rocked back and forth in the back seat. I couldn't make any words come out of my mouth. Nothing could fix this. My tears tasted like sweat. I stared at the back of my dad's head, waiting for any movement; but he was completely still, which scared me even more.

When we pulled into the driveway, he said, "Get out and wait for me on the side porch." I got out of the back seat quickly and walked up the driveway, checking behind me every three seconds to make sure he didn't surprise me. I sat on the fourth step, as close to the side as possible, where the moon wasn't lighting the path up the steps. I was twirling my hair with one hand and biting my cuticles with the other, and my feet were tapping on the wood below them.

I noticed that the porch steps were a dark green and that the fence around the pool was extra tall. I needed to remind myself of normal things, colors and crystal-clear pools. Then my eye caught the woodpile that was down the stairs and to the right against the house, and I simply could not pretend to be OK. My body started to shake.

I heard the car door open and then close, and I started to count out loud: "One, two, three . . ."

He rounded the corner, grabbed me by my right arm, and pulled me up the steps with only one of my legs touching the ground. He was silent as he continued to hold my arm in the same position and look up and down my body. I was trembling and unsteady in my legs, and my eyes were trying to focus on his, but I could not see them through the dark.

"You are a disgrace to this family and you are no longer part of it," he said.

His body was towering over me, and the muscles in his arms were bulging. I unconsciously raised my left arm to cover my face. At that moment, he dropped my right arm. I was unprepared to hold my weight on my own, and my body slumped to the floor of the porch.

"Get up and take your shirt off," he demanded.

"Dad—what? I'm sorry, Dad." I stayed on the ground with my knees pulled into my chest as tightly as I could get them and my head between my knees to protect my face.

"GET UP."

I lifted my face to see him, but it was so dark, I could only see his silhouette, and it made me wince. I straightened at the knees and made my way to a standing position. I could tell he was fidgeting with something, and as my eyes adjusted, I saw him taking the belt off from around his jeans.

"Don't make me take your shirt off," he threatened.

I lifted my white shirt quickly, in case he tried to hit me in the stomach as I raised it, but he didn't. He just stood and watched. Then he stepped into the porch light. His eyes were wide; the whites of his eyes were moving like liquid in a jar. He was smiling, and he looked almost patient.

I pulled my shirt over my head.

"Cover your face," he said, his voice tempered and quiet, and I did what he said.

Both of my arms were glued to my bra, elbows touching my torso and my palms on my chin holding my shirt over my face. I stood like a statue, trying not to let a single cell inside of me move. I could see through the white shirt enough to know that he was staring at me and moving his hand up and down the belt.

He moved three steps forward and said, "Turn around now. And bend over."

I felt a drip of sweat run down the inside of my arm as I turned around. With my back to him, I bent over and waited. My left leg was visibly twitching.

He slammed the belt on my back. My body shot straight up in the air, and I screamed with pain. The heat on my back was so intense, it felt as if it were melting from the inside. My head wobbled from left to right as I staggered toward the hammock as I struggled to regain my footing. I turned to make sure he wasn't winding up for another blow.

"You will be sleeping in the garage. Make yourself comfortable," he said, and he walked into the house through the front door. I heard the door lock, and then the dead bolt, and I fell to the ground.

CHAPTER 9

Three weeks later, my dad made an announcement at dinner. "God has ordained that Kathleen come back into the home for His glory," he said.

"Oh, Kathleen, how wonderful," my mom said, looking at her plate of chicken Parmesan. I didn't mind sleeping in the garage because I didn't actually ever spend a night there; it was way too dark and creepy, and it smelled like worms and dirt. From the first night, I stole into our pool cabana, which was attached to the garage. It was a really comfy room, with a white down couch peppered with orange and white pillows with circles of different colors on them. The two opposing chairs were covered with the fabric from the pillows, and the ottoman was a dusty pink color. There was a bar in the corner with a fridge, a little sink, and three bar stools. It was small and cozy, and, truthfully, I would have liked to live there until I left home for good.

I was stunned that my dad still believed I was sleeping in the garage when he knew it shared a wall with the cabana. Every night I waited to be caught sleeping there, but no one ever checked on me.

Shirley knew where I was sleeping. Every morning there was a different treat from her waiting for me just inside the cabana door when I woke up. One day it was warm banana bread, another it was clean clothes and a toothbrush. I was only allowed in the house during the day when my dad was at work or when we had dinner as a family, so I spent the days with Shirley, listening to her stories about her kids and learning the correct way to iron a shirt.

I would lie on the white couch in the cabana and watch until all the lights in the house—at least the ones I could see—were turned off. I could see people milling around before bed; I could even see Rachel climb into bed, and I wondered if she missed us going to sleep together. We always talked before sleep took us, and I found myself hoping she noticed my absence.

I learned that my dad had a ritual of walking the house before bedtime every night. He made his way around the house, turning the lights off and locking the doors as he went—first in the sunroom and then the living room, the dining room, the two kitchens, the den, and the mudroom. He must have gone up the back steps to bed, because that was the last light I could see being turned off.

Now that my banishment was over, I was getting ready to go to a party with Grace. I decided to wear my favorite Levi's, the ones that had only about ten wears left in them before the holes were in the wrong places. I had spent hours washing and drying them to give them the worn-out look, and now, just a year later, I wasn't washing them at all in hopes of getting a few more dates with them. The white button-down was a good choice, with the suede vest over it. My makeup was minimal, mostly because if either of my parents noticed I had it on, I'd be sent upstairs immediately to wash it off. As I walked down the hallway to go down the front staircase, I heard Mary getting ready in her room: she was going to the party too. I decided to stop in.

"Hey, Mary," I said as I started toward the bed, and then I stopped. It was completely covered with jeans, skirts, shirts, sweaters, and everything else that had calmly waited in her closet to be ripped from the hanger, held in front of the full-length mirror, and hated.

"You should wear your new jeans and the orange shirt from Florida; they look great on you." I also offered to let her borrow my funky gold earrings as a momentary truce between us.

"Thanks," she said. She sounded defeated, and the wounds in her voice brought out my better self. I really wanted her to love not only what she was wearing but who she was.

A strange thought crept in: I realized we were both dealing with our family in the best way we knew how. We were different players, but the unbelievable loneliness and feelings of not being good enough for the world were the same for both of us. I saw in a moment of clarity not only that my dad kept us all apart emotionally but that he actually pitted his children against one another on purpose. He never wanted us to love each other, and when we tried, he played referee to put us back in the ring. Last week, when I complimented Mary on her outfit, my dad commented, "That's certainly not what she said about your outfit when you left the room." Mary denied that she said anything bad, but the words were out there, and so, for me, they were true.

I knew that Mary had been born with an extra drop of essence; she was a beautiful spirit that loved to learn, and when she chose to be kind, she was very kind.

Unfortunately, she was also born with a spirit that could be easily molded by flattery and attention. She had decided that she was not lovable, and she was not willing to try to claw her way out of it. Being part of the Disciples of Light, we had been taught that women should be completely subordinate, men make all the decisions, and religion is at the core of everything we do. She endured this family and the world around us, keeping her mouth shut and her gratitude meter high while she slowly died inside.

The confusion of being part of this family had taken its toll on her, and I had just this second realized we were in it together, that we didn't need to be enemies. We could take this mercurial family experience and make it bearable, not so lonely, a sanctuary with just the two of us.

We could look back at the shattered pieces as adults, together, and try to put the puzzle pieces in some kind of order. Two sets of eyes could make more sense of the insanity.

In a flash, I understood my life as all the pieces came together for a split second, and I sat completely still and tearful, surrounded by discarded clothes. I heard a scared and partially crippled little girl inside me say, *I deserve to be loved.*

Mary settled on my recommendation after trying on every other shred of clothing, and as we headed down the imposing staircase, she topped off her outfit by putting my earrings in her ears.

I heard muffled voices coming from the den, and Mary and I followed the sounds. As I got closer, I realized that one of the voices was Robert's—and I stopped dead. I could hear my dad explaining why his gun collection was so amazing and Robert commenting that his own father had a similar collection.

I started twirling my hair and told Mary, "I don't want to go out with him."

"Why?"

"He'll hurt me."

"Don't be silly. Come on. I don't want to keep Dave waiting."

Mary walked into the den, and I reluctantly followed her.

My voice sounded far away as I asked, "Is Grace here?"

"That's no way to greet our guests. You're going with Robert tonight," my father replied. I stood there still confused as to whether or not Grace had arrived.

"You can go out with Robert tonight, or you can stay home," my father said, breaking the short silence. I will never understand why I didn't stay home.

"Have them home by eleven thirty, boys, no later," my father called as we walked to the door. My eyes widened; my curfew had never been later than ten p.m.

"Yes, Mr. Flanagan," Robert replied.

As we began to walk down the side steps to the waiting cars, I thought of asking Mary if we could drive together. I was reminded that my moment of clarity upstairs only had room for one of us. "See ya," she said dismissively as she and Dave walked to his blue Honda.

The drive to Todd's party was short, and Robert gave me his usual warning to drink only two wine coolers—and absolutely no smoking, or else. I tried to stay calm as we walked into the party, but I needed to find Grace.

"Has anyone seen Grace?" I asked the first group of girls I saw.

"She had to stay home tonight."

Shit.

Robert kept me within arm's length the next two hours, and I tried to act as normal as I could. I saw my friend Colleen at the party, and I had a desire to try to talk to her, but she looked away when our eyes met. I was trying to pay attention to the story Mary was telling about her boyfriend, when Robert stood up from the couch and announced that we were leaving.

"No. I don't have to be home for another hour and a half, remember?" I said as I checked the clock hanging over the bathroom.

"Leaving." He grabbed his extra beer and my one wine cooler and headed for the door as I hugged my friends, trying to pretend it was my idea to leave early.

We were halfway to my house, and my heart was starting to settle. Suddenly, Robert took a turn and started heading in the wrong direction.

"Where are you going?"

"I just had an idea." He stepped on the gas pedal.

I noticed the beat-up yellow "Dead End" sign as he turned onto the rocky, abandoned street. There were trees on three sides of us—thick,

312.22.2.2222222.

dense trees. Robert drove all the way to the end of the street and parked in the overgrown foliage.

"Ah, there."

"Where?" I asked, looking at the darkness all around us.

He leaned over the leather seat and kissed me on the lips. His mouth was wide and his tongue invaded the back of my throat. I hardened my face and kept my lips tight, my body recoiling into the seat. I turned my head slightly toward the window and said, "We need to get going."

He reached over and locked my door and the back door behind me.

"Wait. Stop!" I said, pulling my face as far as I could from his.

The space inside the car was shrinking, and I was having a hard time catching my breath. A tiny glow came from the dashboard, and I tried to focus my eyes, but there wasn't enough light to see.

Robert reached across my body and grabbed the lever on the side of my seat to push it backward. I felt it hit the leather of the back seat, and my eyes tried to find a place to land on the ceiling of the car. I was holding my clenched fists tight against my thighs and listening to him fidget in the driver's seat. I sat up and tried to find his eyes in the darkness. I heard him glide his seat as far back as it could go, untie his shoes, unzip his jeans, and pull them off his body. My eyes caught the white of his underwear, which were stuffed inside his jeans, as he threw them in the back seat.

"Robert, what are you . . . ," I heard my voice say. It was weak, barely audible. I looked at the window, and there was a foul air of sweat fogging it.

Robert pushed my body back flat onto the seat and climbed on top of me. It was hard to breathe. He moved his hands to my headrest to stabilize his weight. His shirt covered part of his body, but I saw a flash of his white legs. I looked up to find his eyes, but it was too dark and I could see nothing.

I wasn't cold—I was frozen. The word "fight" was stuck in my throat, and I lay there in silence. Robert unzipped my faded Levi's; I heard a tear as he pulled them down to my knees and then put one foot between my legs and pushed my jeans down to the floorboard with his foot. I was unaware of my arms or my hands, but my eyes were wide-open, darting from the window to the dark face inches from mine.

He tore my underwear. His right hand moved down to maneuver himself to align with my body while his left hand kept him from crushing my body. He pushed himself inside me. It felt like shards of glass being forced into me: dry, cutting, unforgiving. His head was tilted toward the roof, and I could feel the pounding of my flesh against the leather seat. I heard a scream and registered it as my own. The pain ricocheted through my body, up to my head and down to my toes. My legs trembled, and the smell of his sweat washed over me.

He forced himself inside me again, then again and again. His moaning kept me in the moment. It sounded as if he were mocking me, laughing at me, while he was tearing me apart. His face began to quiver, and I felt his fluid mix with my blood as he screamed out my name in the airless pit.

When he was finished, Robert turned the radio on and re-dressed himself. He reached into the back seat and threw a pair of sweatpants at me before he got out of the car. My whole body was shaking, and both my feet were asleep from lack of circulation. I worked at a frantic pace. I took off my shoes and jeans, used the jeans to clean up the liquid I could feel on the seat and on my body, stuffed the jeans away under the seat, and put on the extra-large sweats. I was panicked that Robert would open the door and see me half-naked.

Robert was leaning against the car, drinking a beer. Dire Straits was playing on the radio: *"Money for nothin' and your chicks for free."* My eyes had finally adjusted. I memorized the scene outside the glass window. The green trees swaying in the breeze, the cracked and unkempt concrete road, the sturdy silver pole with the "Dead End" sign fixed on top of it. My mind stopped on the word "Dead," and I stared at the bold, black, all-consuming letters until I couldn't see them anymore.

On the drive home, I was terrified to look to my left, to have to see him. He pulled into my driveway, and I was completely still. Robert came around to the side of the car and pulled the door open. He gently took my hand from my lap, where it was sitting paralyzed, and lifted me out of the car. My legs took the subtle hint, and as I began to walk the short distance to the steps, I was painfully reminded of the attack. It felt as if a thousand sharpened pins had been stuck between my legs, and the pain of walking was almost too much to bear.

My mother was standing at the door, watching me cringe as I walked up each step. I felt as if my body were going to tear up the middle, and all that would be left would be two empty halves. Robert was all smiles as he greeted my mom, walking me to the door, trying to hide how much he was propping me up as we approached. I pictured the inside of his body, saw a black, unrepentant soul, and damned him to hell for the smile on his face.

"Kathleen, what is wrong with you? Are you drunk?" My mom spit the words at me with an accusatory tone. Robert released me once we were on the porch, and I stumbled a bit before gathering my balance.

Robert almost leaped down the steps to his getaway car, and I began to feel sick to my stomach. "I think I'm going to throw up," I said, and launched myself to the side of the railing, where I vomited into the shrubs below while my mom watched.

My mom was silent as she followed me up the stairs and down the long straight hall, past my brother's room, and to my bedroom, where I saw the light was on. It was taking a very long time. I felt pain with every step. Physical pain, but also a pain so deep inside, I didn't know it existed until now.

"Kathleen, what's wrong with you?" my mom said.

I let the sweatpants slide to the floor. I could feel the swelling between my legs.

My mother's eyes displayed shock, but the only word that came from her mouth was "Oh!" as she took a step backward. I lost the fight not to cry. I was crying so hard I couldn't imagine I would ever be able to stop. I felt the vibrations inside my body, fighting their way to the surface in a panic. There were so many of them, I was drowning inside. I needed to find a faster way for them to get out or soon I wouldn't be able to breathe.

I looked down to see if I recognized my new body. The skin between my legs was swollen and red, and it was hanging inches below where it belonged. There was dried blood on the delicate skin, smeared on both my thighs.

"I will run a bath." My mom was methodical, robotic.

She walked me into the bathroom off my room, and began to run warm water into the tub. "Get in. I'll get you a Sprite to settle your stomach." She had to have seen the look of terror on my face when she told me she was going to leave.

"I don't want Sprite, Mom. Please don't leave me alone; I'm really scared. I didn't . . ."

"I'll be right back," she called from my bedroom as she made her way down the back stairs. I began counting seconds until she was back in sight. One, one thousand, two, one thousand, three, one thousand . . .

She entered the bathroom again. "Here you go," she said.

She started out of the room again and this time I didn't say anything; I just followed her with my disbelieving eyes. I knew what she was doing.

"Good night, sweetie."

I did not know that emptiness could have a sound. I wanted my tears to fill that porcelain tub so I could sink deep into the abyss. Every cell in my body was cold and exposed, and there was not a blanket in the world large enough or thick enough to make me warm. I stared at the old stark-white porcelain tiles on the wall at the side of the bathtub. They were like a canvas, immense and blank.

I sank beneath the water with my eyes open and my soul closed. I waited for my lungs to give up and allow the tears and the water to take my breath and my life away.

❖

After the rape, I ended up having to tell my mom that something was wrong: I was in constant physical pain. I couldn't imagine how to find the words to escape from the prison I felt I was in. I finally just blurted them out.

"Mom, something is wrong down there," I said, and pointed between my thighs, not having the confidence to say it more specifically. She was sitting in the family room alone, surrounded by her paperwork as if it were a friend. She looked up for a split second, and her eyes held blankness.

"OK, sweetie, I can take you to see Dr. Erickson. I'll make an appointment."

Dr. Erickson walked into the small sterile room. I had a badly patterned blue hospital gown on with a blue sheet covering my legs. He had been my doctor since I was little—I think he may even have delivered me—but I was yearning for anonymity.

I was simply horrified as he casually asked me to put my feet in the stirrups, which he pointed to at the end of the table. The way they were on the table meant that my legs would be spread open for him to see between them. My body collapsed in on itself, and I began to cry as I laid my head back on the crinkly paper on the table. There was a high-pitched ringing in my ears.

"Margaret, do you want to stay?" he asked. Oh my God, this was much worse than I had anticipated. I would rather live with this pain for the rest of my life than put my feet in those silver foot handcuffs, and now my mother was staying in the room.

I didn't move fast enough, and before I knew it, Dr. Erickson was placing my feet into the stirrups, all the while asking my mom about our house and whether the traffic of the summer bothered the family. My body was a hard shell, and I held my breath and waited, clenching the sides of the table.

Dr. Erickson suddenly changed his line of questioning, and as if it were coming from another universe, I heard him say, "Margaret, this looks like a forced sexual encounter, the way the skin has been torn." I drew in a deep breath to hold. For the first time since Robert raped me, someone else knew, and soon my mom wouldn't be able to pretend it hadn't happened. It felt like hope: maybe my body wasn't so dirty.

I repeated his words in my head, *"forced sexual encounter,"* and my body loosened just a touch. My lips parted, and I took a deep breath. Maybe it wasn't my fault.

My mom tucked her upper lip as her right eye started to twitch, and she said, "That can't be, John; Kathleen has never been sexually active."

"Margaret, her hymen has been broken. The tender skin in this area has actually been torn in more than one place, and whoever did this to her also gave her genital warts. She is in discomfort not only because of the tearing of the skin but also from the irritation of the warts on her body. She is in a lot of pain, and I would imagine it is not just physical." Dr. Erickson stood and walked to the sink and began washing his hands. He must have thought I was dirty too.

I wanted to scream, "He raped me! It was disgusting, awful . . . Please put him in prison, and please don't make me look at him at school tomorrow." The adrenaline was moving rapidly through my body. My legs, which I had thought were frozen in place, were now trembling on the table.

I was silent, and it was as if no one knew I was in the room. I pushed my legs together and sat up, trying to cover every inch of my body with the blue sheet, which seemed to have shrunk in the last five minutes.

"We'll need to freeze the warts off, and in the meantime I can give her some cream for the pain. Margaret, you, Richard, and I need to talk," he said.

My mother and I walked to the car without speaking a word. As I got into the station wagon, I wondered in earnest about what would happen next. Would I be the laughingstock of school? Would my father beat me when he found out? Would Robert be arrested? It wasn't a secret anymore, and I straightened my back in the seat and closed the door.

"Do you want to go get ice cream?" my mom asked as I settled into my seat with more self-respect than I'd had since it happened.

"What, Mom?" I couldn't formulate any other words. Ice cream was Mom's typical stop after doctor or dentist appointments, but the offer felt inappropriate after having just been told with certainty that your daughter had been raped and given a sexually transmitted disease.

I watched my mom's cold unfazed face the entire drive home as my mint chocolate chip ice cream melted in the bowl.

If only we had pressed charges, I would have been able to hold my head high, walk with dignity, and believe that men were not allowed to do whatever they wanted without paying the consequence. I can imagine looking at Robert behind his lawyer's table and telling the truth of that night: ". . . nothing but the truth, so help me God." But I never got that chance. My mother and I never spoke of the rape again.

CHAPTER 10

Spring, 1986

It was about noon. I was walking home from the beach at a slow pace, my wet towel around my shoulders. The salt from the ocean was tacky on my skin, and I shook out my hair so it would dry faster. The hot wooden planks under my bare feet were a nice contrast to the coolness I felt on my skin from my swim in the ocean. I gazed across the street to our house and did a double take when I saw the silver Cadillac in the driveway.

"Damn—I thought they weren't getting home till tonight," I said out loud.

My parents had been in London for almost a week. They had bought a flat there in hopes of growing the Disciples of Light or a similar community across the pond. It had been a wonderful week for us stateside: Shirley had stayed with us and we had cooked together, enjoying the peace and freedom. I had spent a lot of time at the beach, and when I wasn't enjoying the sand, I was riding and training with Jim at the Equestrian Center or working with Irish at our barn. Irish was progressing at a quick pace because of the hours we spent together. I was set to compete on Julius in the hunter/jumper competition come July. Julius was fantastic in the competitions, well versed with the courses, and had taken home several blue ribbons last year. I was grateful that Jim was letting me lease him for the season. It was a real vote of confidence. I wished I could ride Irish in the competition. Eventually he would be my show horse, but that was still a long way off; I hadn't even placed a saddle on him yet. I needed to get to the barn today to check on things, since Mary was threatening to have a party there last night.

It had rained the last two days, but Jim and I trained anyway. It was marvelous to ride in the rain. There was a wildness to it, a sort of surrender to the elements that made me light in my body and more connected to the sport of hunter/jumper. About once an hour, Jim's electric wheelchair would get stuck in the mud, and I would dismount and use my full force to pull him out, both of us cackling at the sight we knew we must have been. He was an industrial-strength man, stocky and well-built from the inside out. He stuck it out in the rain with me and refined me in my stances and horsemanship. I knew every inch of that muddy arena, and I was feeling confident in my growing skills.

As I walked in the side door and put my wet towel on the stairs, I could hear my dad's voice coming from the kitchen.

"Who had the party?" His voice was edgy and thunderous. "Who had the party at the barn?"

I looked at Mary, waiting for her to speak up.

"It must have been you." My father was looking at me.

"It wasn't me," I said as I marched into the kitchen. "I didn't have a party at the barn!"

My dad's breath was heavy. "Don't you dare lie to me."

Mary was sneering at me; my dad's protruding eyes and flaring nostrils were coming toward me. He walked up to me and bent down to face level, two inches away, and practically screamed, "Put some clothes on and meet me in the car."

My father was waiting for me in the car when I got into the passenger's seat. We began driving and I stayed quiet as he started steering the car toward the barn.

My father turned left onto the dirt road, the tires kicking up dust behind us, and I could see the barn from a distance through the fruit orchard. I loved the smell of a barn: the hay, the grain, even the manure. It got inside my nose and made me feel like part of the earth. Up until this visit, I had always had a sense of calm heading to the barn; I knew the silence there, the sense of aloneness. The undemanding brown-eyed animals always offered me a place to belong.

"I didn't have a party, I just didn't . . ."

"Stop." The back of his neck was flushed, and I could hear fear pounding in my ears.

But along with the fear there was something else: I was curious. Curious how my dad would hurt me. Curious how I would hide the markings of his abuse tomorrow. Curious as to whether my mom would be waiting for us when we got home or if she would be hiding upstairs, pretending not to hear the door open and close. Curious if Mary would feel guilty or at all accountable.

"Follow me." We got out of the car and walked the fifty feet to the barn door in silence. My dad opened the huge sliding door to unveil the trappings of the party. The barn was in shambles. There were dozens of empty beer bottles on the floor and hay bales broken and thrown about, and all the saddles, bridles, blankets, and leads were on the floor, looking desperate for a place to hang.

I forgot about my punishment, I was so angry. How *dare* Mary allow her friends to do this? This was *my* barn! I had spent countless hours cleaning this barn and feeding and brushing these amazing creatures. I had hung every last one of these saddle racks and cleaned every last bit of this tack with Lexol soap and conditioner. This was my sanctuary, my place to be with the animals I loved. I ran to open the stall doors to check on my horses. All of the stalls were empty. When I'd left the barn at seven last night, they were all tucked away in their stalls with fresh hay and grain. I didn't care about Beau, my dad's bad-tempered horse, but I was panicked and needed to set eyes on Lady and Irish.

I took off past my dad to the pasture. They must have been left out all night because of the party. They had to be feeling out of sorts, especially Irish.

"You are going to clean every goddamn inch of this barn . . . ," I could hear my dad yell at me as I ran to the pasture.

Lady noticed me first; I swear that horse could smell me. She began to trot toward me and I ran to her. She was a mare of loyalty, not a mare of perfection. Jim called her a "regular" horse; it was the only thing we disagreed on. She would never show with me, never have a ribbon around her neck like Irish would, but she was the only weapon I had against my dad. She would win against him every time, and for *that* she would always have a special place in my heart. I yanked on her beautiful black mane and jumped up onto her back, and we ran the short distance back to the barn.

I put Lady in her stall after moving the sleeping bags out of the way. I felt a wash of gratitude flow over me that the partygoers hadn't burned my barn to the ground, given how much Mary smoked and the fact that hay and cigarettes don't mix well. I headed back to the pasture with a feed scoop full of grain to get Irish. All I had to do was shake the scooper and he came running. On the far side of the pasture, my dad was trying to corral Beau into the corner of the fence so he could get a lead rope on him, but Beau wasn't having it; he would make a break for it every time my dad got too close.

Atta boy, Beau, give him hell!

Irish was not a "regular" horse. He was a Thoroughbred, and he pranced like one. The gliding movements of his body were impeccable. I watched his red, immaculately groomed mane blowing in the wind and the muscles in his body pulsing with his movements. He was over seventeen hands tall and amazing to watch as he cantered toward me. Jim had told my dad to buy Irish based on his stature and grace, and he'd been right. We had worked together since he was a colt, almost every day for five years, and our trust was undeniable. Once I could get

Wholly Unraveled

a saddle on him, we would move him back to the Equestrian Center and I would train exclusively on him. We would learn from each other and become one for those blessed moments over the jumps. But for now, it was about putting a halter on him and leading him around the pasture a bit to further grow our trust. It was such a thrill to be in charge of this animal.

After working with Irish for a bit, I led him into his stall, laid fresh hay on the floor and in the corner hayracks, filled the individual troughs with fresh water, and gave him and Lady healthy scoops of grain in their buckets, which were attached to the stall guards. I pieced together remnants from my grooming box, which were strewn all over the barn, and brushed the two horses, cleaned under their feet, and looked into their warm brown eyes.

My dad finished settling Beau into his stall, and I unconsciously took two steps backward when I heard his footsteps coming closer to the tack room. I had organized the mess, put all the tack back in its place, remounted the two saddle racks that had been pulled from the wall, and placed the saddles in their spots. The only thing I couldn't fix was the folding saddle stand; someone had broken it in two, so I threw it away.

My dad's voice broke the silence: "Come out here."

I walked out of the tack room to find Irish out of his stall, my dad standing next to him. Irish was tied to both walls of the barn with lead ropes, and he had very little slack on either side. My dad had a grin on his face, as if keeping a secret, and his arms were relaxed behind his back.

"I think it's time we ride Irish—what do you say?" My dad was standing next to Irish, loose in his posture. Irish was past agitated. His right hoof was trying to dig into the concrete floor in a scuffing motion. He was in Beau's halter, which was making his nostrils flare; it didn't have his own smell on it or the endless hours of training we had built into it. I couldn't imagine for the life of me how my dad had gotten it around his neck.

131

Ride Irish? We were more than six months away from that step. The most I'd done was put a saddle blanket on him. I hadn't even had a saddle on his back yet—and my dad wanted to get on him? Jim had fostered my ability to intuit the horse, work with him until he was entirely comfortable with every step, and only then add another. My dad was a gun-slinging cowboy at heart; he just might be crazy enough to try this, and I could promise him it would not go well—for either of them. I couldn't imagine my dad trying to get on him: Irish didn't even want my dad next to him. If my dad went through with this, it could scar Irish and remove all the trust we had built.

"Jim says he isn't ready." Fear was crawling up my legs. I looked in my dad's eyes and something clicked. I could hear Irish's powerful breath.

"I wasn't asking your permission."

"I can't. Really, I can't. He needs so much more time, please." I heard my pleading and was embarrassed.

"Get on him," he commanded. I knew that tone, but I didn't know which I was more afraid of: my dad or getting on Irish.

I walked the ten feet between us and felt the vomit rising up the back of my throat. I looked at Irish, and the whites of his eyes were so large, our fears were melding together.

My dad brought a stool over to the left side of Irish and then held on to both sides of the halter. Irish was pulling at the ropes, turning his head from side to side, and his ears were pinned to his head. I stood entirely still on the stool and brushed the favorite spot on his neck. I could feel the pulsating adrenaline running between us.

"It's OK, boy. I'm going to sit on your back for just a minute, OK? We will do this together. I know, you're OK. It's just me."

"Enough of that crap—get on the horse!"

I heard Jim's voice in my head: *If you're scared, so is Irish. You're in charge here; you lead him, tell him what you want him to do.* I held his mane and kept talking in a melodic voice, although I could hear myself stammering.

"I can't do it. Please, Dad."

"Get on the damn horse." He let go of Irish's halter and took a few steps backward.

I brushed Irish's neck several times. His hair was rigid and coarse, standing at attention. I swung my right leg over his back and tried to land gently. Irish began to strike his front right foot in front of him, aiming for my dad. My dad jumped to the side to avoid the impact and slammed into the stall door.

Irish thrashed his head from side to side to free himself from the lead ropes. One ripped from the wall, and Irish reared up on his two back legs and freed the other rope. I felt a sharp sting in my thighs, and I could feel his mane abrading my fingers as he took off in a full gallop. I ducked in time to dodge the black wrought-iron saddle hook that was dangling from the ceiling as we tore out of the barn.

I opened my eyes and saw blurry silhouettes in a room. There was a throbbing inside my brain. The pain was so intense, I involuntarily closed my eyes again. My body was heavy and taut. It smelled like bleach.

I heard one of the silhouettes say something, and I opened my eyes again with excruciating pain. I could feel my body shaking, as if there had been a sudden drop in temperature.

"Kathleen, you have been asleep for a long time. Do you know where you are?" I recognized the voice but couldn't place it.

I wanted to say no, but the words were stuck in my head. My mouth was so dry, and I tried to focus on saying "water," but nothing came out.

The voice began again. "Move your right hand if you know where you are." I was frozen. "OK, it's OK, just relax. You're OK. You have a head injury and you're in the hospital."

I tried to make out the word "Jim," but it came out sounding like "Iiiim."

"Yes, yes, it's me, Jim. I'm right here. Your brain took a beating. Just relax and breathe. Can you squeeze my finger?" He slipped one finger under my right hand, and I squeezed it.

Everything felt damp. My body was tense, as if I were bracing for a fall. The smell was burning my nose, but my vision was coming into focus. I could see Jim next to my bed in his wheelchair. An IV was coming out of my arm, and I was wrapped in white blankets. I took a full deep breath; Jim smiled at me and I tried to smile back.

My eyes darted to the door, which was opening.

"It's about time you woke up." My dad walked in with a McDonald's bag in one hand and a cup of coffee in the other. "Your mom said you would want a cheeseburger and fries. I even got ya a Coke, even though the doctor said not to give you caffeine." His eyes never touched mine; they went right to the window on the far side of the room.

Jim wheeled himself to the door. "See you tomorrow, kiddo." I watched the door slowly shut behind him.

"That's the last you'll see of him—and Irish, for that matter. He's fired and I shot that damn horse," Dad said.

"Deeeaaad?"

"Dead as a doornail. Never saw it coming either." My dad had his back to me, eating the McDonald's fries.

A part of me believed that I deserved all the beatings. I closed my eyes and saw the gun pointed at my head at Lake Powell, and I wondered if he had used the same one to shoot Irish. Something deep inside me finally broke.

PART TWO

broken (adjective):

(of a person) having given up all hope; despairing

CHAPTER 11

Spring, 1992

There was the usual chill as I walked down the narrow, sticky steps to what we affectionately called the Dirty Dungeon in the Old Market district of Omaha. Of course, I was late for work, so I needed to do my best not to be noticed. I opened the door to the crawl space that served as a pub and smelled the familiar combination of liquor and cleaning products. There was really no way to abolish the smell; it just seemed to get thicker with time.

"Maaaaryyyyyyy," said Pascal as he came from around the thick wood bar to get my hug. He was a wiry Armenian man with a loose smile and a hurried gait, who always wore a pressed white shirt. "Good night last night, Mary. Good night. Made some real money," he purred. This place was a front for his cocaine dealing and not so much about the booze I was pouring.

"Good to hear, Pascal. I'm just here to serve!" I didn't remember past about eleven last night, but I was pleasantly surprised with the $187 I had in my pocket when I woke up this afternoon.

I had moments when I wanted to tell him my real name wasn't Mary, but I knew better. Kathleen had run up too much debt. I had twenty-two credit cards that were maxed out and all the debt collectors looking for me, and I couldn't rent an apartment in my name because I'd been kicked out of a few; plus I owed the utilities. Turns out they won't turn on your gas or electric at a new place until you settle your bill from your old place.

Being someone else was pretty easy, really. I had stolen my sister's birth certificate years ago and gone to the DMV to get a license in her name. Now I was "Mary" to credit card companies, utilities, apartment complexes, and employers.

I had left my home in Spring Lake to go to college and slowly over those four years broke the ties to my family. My two older sisters went to a ridiculously strict Catholic college, but somehow I talked my dad into a slightly less Catholic university in Omaha.

Other than the pungent smell, the bar was clean and orderly. The smattering of booths covered in faux red leather and the sturdy wooden tables were all aligned, each chair knowing its place, ready for another night of disorderly conduct. I was grateful to Pascal for that: cleaning was not my thing. I hadn't even cleaned when my landlord had put the eviction for "pigsty" conditions on my door a year ago. I'd just moved.

"A new guy will be dropping 'stuff' off in about an hour, so I'm going to have you run to the bank for me before he gets here."

"I don't do bank runs, Pascal," I said as I pretended to diligently check the bottles behind the bar for stocking. I knew doing bank runs was part of the job; I just didn't need him taking it for granted.

"You do if I give you your paycheck."

"Ah, now, that sounds like a threat, Pascal, and I hate those. Ask nicely and tell me it's the last time, and I'll go for you."

"Your wish is my command, princess," he said, then walked into his office on the far side of the bar and closed the door.

It helped Pascal's drug-dealing business that the French Café, the most expensive restaurant in town, was located directly above us. It was easy to tell the difference between the people who came to buy and the people who came to drink.

Clearly, Pascal must have put me on his account, but I'd never asked. I liked walking around with $20,000: it meant I could pretty much buy my way out of anything. The drug money gave me an adrenaline rush. It reminded me of walking home with a bag full of candy in my childhood and not getting caught. I craved that feeling. It made me defiant—and defiance was what I needed to mask my fear of the world.

I tried to think of what day it was so I could settle into the shift. Wednesday? Nope. Thursday. So that meant early rush and nonstop until close. Alio, one of the other bartenders and my friend, would be in for work soon. I poured myself a shot of Jägermeister, downed it, then left for the bank.

The night took on its normal tenor, and Alio and I got into our rhythm working the bar, slinging drinks, and flirting just enough for the tip.

"Will you pour me another shot of Jäger?" I asked.

"Yeah, but, here, first give this to the cutie at table eleven." She slid a whiskey with ice back across the bar.

"Got it. Is he not a tipper, or are you playing hard to get?"

"We'll see. Hey, isn't Logan coming this weekend to see you?"

"Fuck. What time is it?" I spun around to check the clock behind the bar. It was 9:16 p.m.

"Really? You forgot?"

"No—I mean yes, I forgot. I betcha a hundred bucks he's sitting at my place right now. Shit. Can you cover for me with Pascal? I have to go."

"Go. And make sure you eat something if he takes you out!" I heard Alio say as I gathered my things and bolted for the door, checking my pockets for my keys and just starting to get my buzz from the shots.

I checked how many fingers could fit between my size-two jeans and my skin. Two fingers fit between, which meant I was safe. I told myself that I could have a few pretzels tomorrow.

I parked my beat-up red Nissan Pulsar in front of the duplex while scanning for Logan's car. He saw me before I saw him. He was sitting on my front steps with a beaming grin on his face. He had just driven eight hours, but, goddammit, he was still smiling.

"Oh, babe, I'm so sorry. There was a snafu at work and I had to go in for a few hours. How long have you been waiting?" I said as I ran to him. He set the beer bottle he was holding on the stoop and stood up. Six foot two, steel body, with a short blond haircut that made his green eyes somehow greener.

I jumped into his arms and kissed his neck, pulling down the red T-shirt so I could smell him.

"Were you waiting long?"

"What time did I tell you I would be here?"

"Seven."

"Well, then, that's when I got here. I did help myself to a couple of beers. What's going on inside your house? It's a mess." He hugged me tightly as he spoke. "Hold on, let me look at you . . ." He put me down on the concrete steps above him and said, "I could lift you with a finger."

"That's because you're so strong," I said, and kissed him on the mouth to clamp down on that subject. His lips turned to velvet. "Let's go in."

"Nope, I have a surprise I've been dying to show you all day." He took my hand and cupped it in his.

"All day? What are you up to, Logan?"

He carried me to his Bronco, opened the door, and set me down in the passenger's seat. He got behind the wheel and took a right out of my neighborhood, followed the slight curve around the strip mall, drove another mile or so through the darkened park with the vacant swings, and stopped in front of an old Victorian building standing three stories high. I loved it when people had a sense of direction—maybe because I wasn't born with one. The building had a charming front porch with a swing, a tea table with two chairs, and potted geraniums welcoming us as we walked up the steps.

When we reached the top floor, he took a key out of his pocket and opened the wooden door in front of us. It was the only door on this floor. I could feel my heart racing, hoping this wasn't what I thought it was.

"Logan, what . . . ?"

"Shh, wait for it. Look."

I could see three small rooms unified with the same beautiful hardwood floors and white wainscoting on the walls. There was a queen-size bed on the floor in the living room in front of the fireplace, which already had wood stacked inside, ready for a match. The bed was tidy, with sheets, pillows, and a dark blue duvet cover. The tiny kitchen had an old table with two chairs and was set with place mats, dishes, and mismatched wineglasses. It looked like something out of an old novel.

"Logan, what's going on?" He was almost dragging me through the place. My feet were heavy and I felt a bead of sweat roll down my back. He began to show me around, pointing out all the details of the apartment.

"There's a bathroom right through there with a cast-iron soaking tub. Wait until you see it. It's ours, baby. I rented it yesterday and spent all day cleaning and setting it up for us. I signed a year lease. Plus it is only a few blocks from where I want to open my fitness club."

"Wow, this is just amazing! Um . . ."

"I've made us the most delicious dinner." He grinned, and I could tell he wanted me to go to him and shower him with kisses.

I certainly didn't know what love was, but I had told Logan that I loved him. I was trying to do what normal twenty-somethings do. But

I was not a normal twenty-something. My life was a contradiction. I wanted the love he poured on me, but I didn't want to let him in.

I wore the engagement ring he had bought me last year when I promised to marry him. There was nothing not to love about this man—even his mom was amazing—but I simply could not have him move here; I needed distance between us to cover who I really was inside: a broken, unlovable person.

I was twirling my hair and looking for a window to open so I could breathe again. I walked past the bed and opened the window overlooking the street.

He was so devoted, so genuine, so unselfish, and so categorically trustworthy. But when we were together too much, he had this way of making me want to break my cardinal rule: no one gets close.

Logan touched me from behind, a gentle touch that startled me.

"It's OK, little one, we can stay on slow mode. You're OK. I love you."

I turned toward him. I ran my hand up his forearm and all the way to his face. He was just staring at me.

"Talk to me," he said as he kissed my lower lip.

"Nothing to say, baby."

I wanted him to stop talking. This was exactly what I was afraid of: he was starting to seep into my heart. It felt warm but too open for my comfort.

When I met Logan two years ago, I was immediately drawn to him. I could feel his intense goodness. I was so attracted to his body, but anything other than kissing was terrifying to me. It had been that way since I was raped. The only advice about sex I ever got from my mom was "You are going to have to make love to your husband when you don't want to." I decided after the rape that I would never make love with anyone. Making love and rape seemed to involve the same actions. I decided that I wasn't interested in either.

I kissed him full on his mouth, trying desperately to feel something in my body besides frigidness and fear. When thoughts of the rape came to mind, I would pretend it had happened to someone else, but it never worked. Instead, I was trapped in Robert's car on a dead-end street and reliving the brutality every time I was physical with Logan.

I went through the steps one by one in my mind and tried to make my body follow them. I wanted to be physical with him the way other woman allowed themselves to be with men, but my body froze. I was unable to respond to his tender touch on my hollow and now naked body. I moved mechanically on top of him until I felt him get hard. I kissed him, keeping my eyes closed, and touched him gracelessly with just two fingers, reminding myself to stay right here—not in the past—to move more, to kiss his ear. He was lightly touching my face, but all I could do was hope that his orgasm would be fast. *Please let it be over. Please let it be over.* I could feel the hard part of his body enter me, and my legs went straight and tense. I made breathy noises to cover my rigidness.

"I love you," I said, my eyes shut. "Kiss me." He kissed me, spilled inside me, and collapsed on top of me. We were silent.

"Baby, I love you," I said, placing my hand over his eyes and sliding it down to his mouth.

I pretended to sleep until I could hear his faint snore. I touched his face before I slid out of the bed, grabbed my clothes, and went to the bathroom. I wet some toilet paper with cold water and placed it between my legs to ease the burning.

I winced.

I sat on the toilet and replaced the now warm piece of toilet paper with a new cold one. I was angry at myself for crying as I waited for the pain to subside.

What if he found out I didn't respond to pleasure—that after we had sex I always cried; that it hurt so much. I didn't want him to know how damaged I was.

It had been easier to hide with the physical distance between us, but what now? This place was only a mile away from my apartment.

"Where's my little one?" I heard him call from the living room.

Shit.

"I'm in here—be right out." I squeezed the excess cold water out of the toilet paper and fastened it like a pad in my panties, threw my jeans and tank top back on, and thought of my mom as I put on my fake smile and walked to the bed.

"Hello, sleepyhead," I said.

"Come down here—I want more of you."

"I wish. I told Alio I'd go back and help her at the bar. I'm so sorry . . . ," I lied.

"Wait, we didn't even have dinner yet."

"Don't get up—it's late. Go back to sleep. I'll come back after work. You're OK if I take your car, right? Love you."

I grabbed his keys and flew out the door before he could answer.

I spent the next six weeks doubling up on night shifts, drinking until I passed out, and avoiding sex with Logan.

CHAPTER 12

Summer, 1992

I met Brock, Pascal's new dealer, the same night he had cleaned the bar out of gin. He looked like a well-educated surfer, with unruly curly blond hair and the attitude to go with it. He wasn't tall, but he wasn't short either—maybe five foot nine or so. I gave him Tanqueray even though he hadn't asked for it. I planned on bumming my smokes from him as long as he was at the bar; it was a bit of a game for me with handsome men.

"Don't be so selfish: light me one," I said from across the bar. He smoked my brand, Marlboro Lights.

"Get your own," he said.

I didn't miss a beat. I walked up to him, the wood bar between us, looked in his eyes, smiled with an attitude, and said, "Wait, let me guess. Family money and lots of it. Am I right?" Cocky men needed to be put in their place.

"Oh, a feisty one who thinks she has men all figured out because she uses her looks to deflect." He took a long draw from his drink and said, "Another, please."

"Get it yourself." I took off walking the length of the bar to Pascal's office, pretending I had reason to be there. "Asshole."

I yanked open the top drawer of Pascal's desk and pulled out a Marlboro Red—gross, but necessary. I grabbed the lighter from the plastic cup that held the pens, lit the cigarette, and walked back behind the bar. There were at least three new people waiting for drinks, so I went to work puffing on my cigarette in between pouring drinks and ignoring Brock.

Alio came around the corner and behind the bar to mix drinks for the private event she was serving in the other room. Brock caught Alio's ear: "Can you get me a gin and tonic, three limes? I believe I got a free upgrade to Tanqueray with the last pour from your pretty little friend, who won't serve me again." He had moved his seat from the end of the bar to the middle, just to infuriate me. He winked at the dirty look I shot him.

Alio looked at me: we always had each other's back; you had to in this bar. I nodded and she poured him his drink. Brock gave her a twenty and, loud enough for me to hear, said, "Keep the change."

I rolled my eyes and smirked a little as I shook my head; I could feel that he saw me. "I'm going to take that look to mean you like me." He cocked his head to the side and ran his fingers through his hair.

"You would," I said with my back toward him, walking to the far side of the bar and getting back to work.

Pascal made his entrance several hours later, a little after eleven. The place was mayhem, and I was already very drunk.

"Another round, and count yourself in again!" The shout came from the end of the bar—four good-looking guys dressed in business suits with loose ties and looser wallets. I pulled six shot glasses out of the washer and poured the tequila. I handed one to Pascal as he came around the bar and delivered the others.

"Do you mind?" I asked one of the men as I set the drinks down and picked up the pack of Marlboro Lights on the bar in front of the guys.

"Help yourself," one of them slurred as we all took our shots and washed them back with the limes from the plate next to the smokes. I took the forty-five dollars and four smokes and teetered back to the middle of the bar, reminding myself to fake the next shot as I slid my hand across the bar for balance.

"Mary—come, come." Pascal was standing behind the bar across from Brock. "This is Brock. Brock, this is Mary."

Brock had a nefarious grin plastered across his face.

"Nice to meet you, Mary. May I please have a Tanqueray and tonic, three limes? I'm a big tipper."

"We're acquainted, Pascal." I moved down the bar and took the next order.

"The Tanqueray-tonic, three-lime guy?" Alio asked.

"Yeah, what the hell, right?"

"OK, last call at midnight, outta here by twelve thirty. Pascal can pick up the slack in the morning. Party at your house. Unless Logan is there. Tell people." She was already taking another drink order.

I thought of Logan and the person I was when I was with him. I was softer, as if I had some kind of hope for the future—that maybe there was a white picket fence somewhere in the world and it wasn't such a scary place. In my drunken stupor, I knew that who I was in this bar was more likely the real me. Dirty, chasing a buzz to numb me out, and looking unconsciously for a way to end my life.

I hadn't eaten in two days, and I put two fingers between my cutoffs and my skin, then lit up a cigarette.

Last call went without a hitch; everyone was too drunk to argue. I settled the bar and put the cash in the safe, noticing the money I had picked up from the bank that afternoon was no longer inside.

"You ladies aren't going anywhere," Pascal said, leaning against the bar next to Brock.

"You're wrong there, Pascal, we're out of here; tonight's money is in the safe. See you tomorrow. I'll drive," I said to Alio.

147

"You sure?"

"No, but you can't," I said as I fiddled with my keys.

We stopped at the 7-Eleven for smokes. I bought three packs of Marlboro Lights and a small bag of pretzels.

"Dinner?" Alio asked.

"That's it," I said to the clerk, ignoring Alio. I hated how she watched me not eat.

"Who did you tell to come over tonight?" I asked Alio, changing the subject.

"Only the cute boys and the usual."

"How much money do you think you made?" she asked as we drove the short distance to my place.

"Dunno. I like to count it in the morning. You?" I asked.

"One hundred and thirty-two. Pretty good, but I thought that big party in the back would tip more." She checked her lipstick in the visor mirror. "Shit. Look at all those people outside your house," she murmured as she flipped the visor up.

"Dammit." I left the pretzels in the car and went to open the door to the building. I already had four eviction warnings at this place, and my neighbors would surely rat me out again with the size of this crowd. Oh, well. I was bored with the place anyway. I just needed a story Logan would believe for why I still wasn't moving in with him.

It was two in the morning, the music was loud, the bottles were accumulating, and my neighbors had been over twice to ask me to take it down a notch. I was sitting on the forest-green sofa in my living room, facing the fireplace.

"I need another empty bottle," I called to anyone. Someone from behind me handed me an empty Amstel Light bottle, and I threw it against the fireplace at the same time as the blurry person sitting next to me did the same. We high-fived and restocked our hands with empty bottles to cast them against the stone.

"One, two, three . . ."

Crash! The sound was fantastic.

I turned to reload and saw Pascal walk into my house. Brock was with him. Brock walked straight over to me.

"Nice place. I usually only destroy my place this bad when I know the maid is coming in the morning."

"Good to know."

"Want to join?" He held out a capsule that looked half full of white powder.

"What is it?" I took it from his hands.

"I have a feeling you don't care." He handed me a full beer, and I washed down the pill.

People were leaving, saying good-bye. I was talking—laughing, even. Brock touched my back as he walked by me to the kitchen, and it felt like a trillion feathers tickling my whole body. I followed him with my eyes. He came back very quickly with two very cold beers.

"What have you done?" I asked with a flirty voice. I never used this voice unless I was at work and there was a wooden bar between us—and I was going for tips.

"Taken you to heaven. Taste this."

It might have been the best sip of beer in my life. No, it actually *was* the best sip of beer in my life.

I tried to focus on the picture behind Brock to get my bearings straight. It wasn't actually moving, but instead of it being the very small picture it was, by a painter from Italy that I loved, it had traces of itself all over the large wall. Dazzling, really.

Alio had left with the cutie from table eleven before the baptism of the fireplace, and I was really wishing she were here.

"Who's with us on this ride?" I asked. Then I said, "Jesus," after a moment of lucidity.

"Anyone you want to be on it with you," Brock said.

For the next three hours or more, I was free. I felt kind. I felt vulnerable. I felt like a real person. I wasn't scared. I wasn't going to be hurt.

I wanted more.

After several more delicious hours, I found myself standing with Brock as he talked with some guy I had never seen before. I was fascinated by how staggeringly tall this stranger was, and the jittery nature of his body made me want to move my own. My toes felt amazing inside my shoes as I moved them around in the sweat that had accumulated between them. I twirled in a circle to get to the kitchen and made a mental note to do that more often.

I could hear the voices behind me, and they were so clear, every word echoing against the last with precision. And I was happy.

"Well, well, look who's smiling," Brock said as he came into the kitchen.

"Oh my God, you have to feel this." I closed the refrigerator door, positioned Brock with just enough room for it to open in front of him, and said, "Ready? This is amazing." I pulled open the door, and the cool breeze from the refrigerator entranced him for a moment, just as it had done to me. He closed his eyes as I watched. He left the door open, turned toward me, and ran his hand from my face very slowly down to my belly. I stepped away, but the touch lingered.

"Can I have more?" I asked.

"Does anyone say no to you?"

"Not yet. Don't be the first."

He smiled and shook his head.

"That's OK. I'll get it from Pascal tomorrow."

"I don't give any of this to Pascal; this is my personal stash." He reached out to touch me again.

CHAPTER 13

I had managed to avoid Brock's advances, and without much fanfare had put myself to bed shortly after he had refused to give me more of the magic pills. I had the same dream that night as the night before.

There was a stretch of grass two feet high and wild. At the end was a broad flowing ravine and a split-rail fence beyond it. Lady was there. She was lightning fast when I rode her bareback. Her withers pumped adrenaline through my clenched hands. My body moved with hers as she let me take control. Her black mane changed from coarse hair to a malleable and silent channel between us as I tugged ever so slightly to the right to clear the ravine.

The wind cut at the base of my cheekbones. I could see through the grass forest; I knew the trees, the wildflowers, and the ravines we would cross. I had recorded every turn during the hundreds of times we had trusted each other to make this ride. The sun highlighted the sweat on Lady's neck, and I leaned farther onto her withers, letting her know I was ready for her when it was time to jump. Her ears moved back a fraction of an inch, and I noticed the water was much higher than yesterday.

"We've got this," I said, squeezing her mane to urge her forward over the expanded water. I felt her shoulders launch as I squeezed my legs tightly around her girth, and together we hovered over the water for one brilliant second. The landing energized both of us for the next jump.

I heard Beau at a strong gallop behind us. My father was on top of the massive horse; I could hear him kicking his spurs into Beau's skin. I could picture him on top of his expensive Western saddle adorned with the filigree lace leather top and silver-embossed rope edge. He was gaining speed for the first jump as Lady and I prepared to leap for the second.

I began losing my connection with Lady. I could feel liquid where my hands met her mane. It was sticky and coarse. I looked down and I was sitting in a vat of blood; her whole body was a pungent liquid, and my legs were immovable in it. *I can't make the jump; Lady is dying,* I thought. What had been the fence was now a cave with my father's shadow at its hollow end, laughing at me. His left hand was holding the pistol in the air, pointed at my head. I screamed, but there was no sound, just silence and blood.

I gasped and opened my eyes, only to see the pale cream color of my bedroom ceiling. I jumped out of my bed onto a pile of dirty clothes on the floor, trying to catch my breath. I looked down at my legs to make sure they weren't covered in blood as I moved quickly to the bathroom. On the nightstand by my bed, the clock was flashing 12:00 a.m., and the ashtray was full of cigarettes.

My breath was rapid, and I looked behind me just in case before I closed and locked the bathroom door. I picked up the half-drunk beer bottle by the sink and took a long sip.

I pulled the scale out from the corner of the bathroom, yanked off my bra and thong underwear, and stood on top of it. I thought about putting one hand on the wall, but the cheating was too obvious. One hundred eight. Dammit. Too close to the danger zone. *Did I eat last night? God, I hope not. No, I didn't.* I stepped off the scale and got back on again and watched as the red digital numbers went to one hundred nine, fluttered, and went back down to one hundred eight.

No pretzels today.

"You here?"

Shit. It was Logan. I looked in the bathroom mirror and tried to locate a comb but decided it was more important to brush my teeth. I wet the toothbrush and shoved it in my mouth while trying to yell out to him.

"In here."

I pulled on my cutoff Levi's, which had been lying in the bathtub, and, in between spitting toothpaste into the sink, threw on a tank top without a bra. I rinsed out my mouth, splashed some water on my face, and took one deep breath before walking out of the bathroom.

Logan had on a blue button-down that was so neatly ironed, it reminded me of Shirley. His hair was tight on top of his head, and he was clearly ready for the day.

"What the hell happened? There's glass everywhere. Are you OK?" He hugged me tight, and I imagined I smelled like a cross between a brewery and a tobacco factory. "I thought you were coming over last night. I kept calling but you never picked up."

"No, I'm good. It was a super-late night at the bar, and Pascal and some of his friends came over afterward. No biggie." Disregarding his feelings was easier than feeling that I was in trouble. He stood there confused by my response to his concern.

"Uh, I need to get to work. I'll come over after? I'm working the day shift, so I can be there by six." I kissed him and walked down the hallway toward the kitchen.

"Good morning."

"Uh, hello?" asked Logan, who rounded the corner to see Brock propped up on his elbow on the couch, dressed in red checkered boxer shorts, no shirt, his hair smeared across his head.

"Oh my God!" I jumped backward as Logan positioned himself between me and Brock. It was silent for a moment as we all took in the scene.

"Er, Logan, this is Brock. He's a friend of Pascal and he needed a place to crash . . ." Logan didn't budge from his protective stance. *I've got to get out of here.* "It was nice to meet you, Brock. I gotta run. Logan, I love you, and I'll see you at six."

I looked around for my smokes. Logan was right: there was broken glass everywhere. I'd forgotten about throwing the bottles against the fireplace.

I tried to steady my hand as I picked up the pack of Marlboro Lights that was on the counter, grabbed my keys, and headed for the door without as much as a glimpse behind me.

I didn't actually have to work today. I was hoping both guys would leave my duplex soon so I could return and sleep the day away in peace.

Brock will be my sworn enemy if he says a word about the drugs. I started the car engine and drove toward nothing.

There were only two cigarettes in the pack I'd grabbed from the counter. I hadn't brought any money with me, so after I finished smoking the two, I headed home to see if Logan's car was still there.

I pulled around the corner and saw that the place where Logan had left his car was now occupied by a police cruiser. *Now what?* I parked my car three houses away and walked up to my open door.

"Can I help you, Officers?" There were two cops in uniform, complete with guns, standing in my living room.

"Are you Mary Flanagan?"

"Yes." I looked around. It looked a lot worse than I remembered.

"You have one hour to vacate the premises."

I didn't mean to, but I laughed out loud.

"Is this funny, miss?"

"I'll be out in ten."

I walked to my bedroom, turned, locked the door, and looked around. The walls were ugly and sad. There weren't any pictures hanging on the three naked nails. I was relieved to get the hell out of here. I went into the bathroom, grabbed the scale, and threw it on the bed along with my toothbrush and a black bag full of cosmetics I never used.

I pulled a suitcase out from under the bed and put the scale in first and then the toiletries. Then I stuffed the suitcase with the clothes from my open drawers, remembering to add a couple of aprons for work. The rest of this shit could stay.

I stopped to check the fridge for beer on the way. *Yes—a cold six-pack!* I headed for the still-open front door.

"Thank you, gentlemen. You have done me a huge favor. I didn't want to clean."

I walked to my car, threw the suitcase in the back, and drove in the direction of Logan's apartment.

There was no need for me to tell Logan I'd been evicted. He only mentioned once that I should go get the rest of my stuff and give up "that ratty place." After three weeks, we had established a routine. It was sweet: no drama and no friction. It was almost boring.

I caught myself staring at him from across the tiny kitchen. Was life really this simple? He left for work in the morning, going to a job he adored while I slept in. He had a ritual of tucking me in and kissing me on the forehead every day before he left. During the day, I ran errands for both of us, hung out with Alio at work, and went to the market to buy things for dinner—and to smell all the yummy food I wouldn't eat.

I was listening to him talk to his mom on the phone as he cooked. He was so relaxed in his bare feet, khaki shorts, and perfectly fitted blue T-shirt.

"Yes, of course, of course, Mom. It would be so great to see you. I know Kathleen would love to see you too." He looked at me and winked. I nodded and smiled back. *Oh, Jesus, not parents—I can't do parents.*

Their playfulness and real love made me feel the hollow, wounded space in my chest as I listened to their easy banter. It struck me as I listened further that Logan had a foundation of safety and love, which was why he could be so tender with me. I was jealous of their relationship.

"I love you, Mom . . ."

I was a third wheel in this kitchen. Their laughter slapped me in the face and reminded me of where I had come from, what I was running from. I walked to the bathroom. I looked in the mirror and watched myself cry, just for a second. Then I washed my face.

I came out of the bathroom to a huge hug and a tender kiss.

"My mom is going to come visit us; isn't that great?"

"Yeah, that's great." I forced a smile. "I can stay at my place when she's here."

"Don't be silly. It'll only be a couple of nights. I'm going to get a blowup mattress." He released me and walked back toward his dinner prep.

"OK, well, I'm headed to work."

"It's ridiculous that you even still have that place, Kathleen," he mumbled as he returned to chopping and stirring. I walked close to him. He put down the knife and turned toward me. My feet were on top of his and our bodies were pressed together.

"I love you, Logan," I said. It was easier to show my feelings when I was leaving.

"I love you too, baby. Forever." He wrapped his muscular arms around my body and rocked me for a very long time—until I pulled away.

Then I grabbed my things and left for work. I spent the drive concocting a plan to be away while his mom was in town. I wasn't going to give her the opportunity to sniff me out.

CHAPTER 14

I couldn't stop thinking about Logan and his mother, and it was messing with my night and, consequently, my tips. I didn't want to turn on the charm to customers; I wanted to run home to Logan and snuggle in bed next to him. I wanted to believe his arms and his words and his actions.

I grabbed the Smirnoff bottle and started making the drinks on the ticket Alio handed me.

"Gin, not vodka. What is wrong with you tonight?" Alio said. She came around the bar and started making the order herself. I leaned back on the wet bar and threw the freshly poured Smirnoff down my own throat to ensure it didn't go to waste.

"Nothing."

"Here, I'll mix; you deliver these to table four. They're cute—not that you care!"

"Pour us both a double of that," I said, pointing to the tequila she was already pouring.

"Cheers," we said at the same time, clicking the shot glasses together and downing the contents. Hopefully, the tequila would kick in soon.

"Just for the record, I'm worried about you," Alio said, looking right at me. "You're withering away."

"Don't, Alio." I picked up the tray of drinks and quickened my pace to table four.

As I set the drinks on the table, I heard Brock's voice. Raspy, as if he smoked too much, but confident.

"She lives. Now, where have you been? I haven't seen you since our rendezvous at your place," he said. Like a moth to the flame, I was drawn to his apathetic personality, which only made me crave his attention and approval more.

He was holding court with four guys who looked too dressed up for this bar, so I assumed they were just here to buy drugs and snort somewhere else.

"How was the couch? I never got to ask," I said, and shot him a poisonous look.

"This is why we're here, gentlemen: her charm and charisma." He smiled, unfazed.

"That's right. Served with a smile. Total is forty bucks, which includes the shot you're buying me. Want to run a tab?"

"Yup; put it on Pascal's tab. I have a present for you, if you're nice to me." He took his shot and cocked his head to the side.

"You wouldn't like me if I were nice," I said. I took my time walking back to the bar, not bothering to take any drink orders on my way.

I was standing in front of the liquor bottles with a list of drinks to make, and the bottles all looked the same. I looked down at the list for the fourth time.

"Come on, I need those drinks." Alio was standing on the other side of the bar with an empty tray.

I just couldn't get Logan off my mind. His love was seeping in.

I snapped out of it. "What?"

"No offense, but I might as well be working by myself tonight," Alio said.

"Works for me." I tugged on my purse, which was caught on the faucet, flung it over my shoulder, and shot Alio a nasty look.

Brock watched me walk to him without taking his eyes off me. He was smiling.

"Are you ready to get out of here?" I said, staring right at him with a tight but confident smile. I could see the stunned looks on the faces of the other men, and I chuckled inside.

"You bet I am." He stood up and followed me out of the bar.

We walked to a bar that had opened six months ago. It was lit by bare bulbs hung in bunches over each table. The décor was urban chic, with perfect touches from the past. There were old wooden tables mixed with modern but comfortable chairs. I chose the table in the corner. We both ordered drinks and shots and settled in.

"When are you going to give me my present?" I asked after the second round of drinks.

"Are you using me?"

"Yes." I leaned in a little closer. "Did you not know that?"

"That's why I put it in your drink already. To punish you," he said, laughing.

"If you did that, you're more of an asshole than I thought," I said, my voice clear, the sound ricocheting in my ears. "Are you serious?"

"Calm down. You won't be mad for long." He sat back in his chair and sipped his gin and tonic.

I got up and walked to the bartender, whom I knew, and asked to use the telephone in the office.

"Hi, baby, sorry to wake you up, but I knew you'd worry if I didn't," I said into Logan's ear softly.

"Hey, babe, what's up? What time is it?" Logan's voice was melodic and dreamy; the effect on me was intense. *Maybe I should cab it and curl up with him, ride the wave that's about to crash with him.*

"Go back to sleep. I'm great. I just wanted to let you know Alio needs me tonight. She's sad about her breakup, and she wants some company. OK? Sleep. I love you." I listened to his breath and wished what I said were true.

"OK, babe. I'll miss you. Be safe."

"I will." I hung up the phone and stared through the door. Brock knew I was coming back, that asshole. He had already ordered me another round of drinks.

"I'm leaving," I said as I picked up his smokes and lit one.

"No, you're not," he said. "If you were leaving, you wouldn't have walked back here."

I sat down and did the shot in front of me. I started to feel that welcome wonderful feeling of sweat between my toes, and I wanted to move my body.

"Let's dance," I said, and popped up out of my chair. The lightbulbs above the tables were throwing off a vibrant glow, as if they were all moving together.

"I have a better idea," Brock said as he grabbed my hand. He threw a hundred-dollar bill on the table, snatched up my purse, and walked me out of the bar.

His house was on the west side of town. It was modern and sparsely decorated, with expensive artwork lit to perfection. It was clean, with white walls except for the slate-colored one behind the fireplace, which was glowing.

"Turn the lights off; they're fucking with my eyes," I said from the deck off the kitchen. My God, I was even higher than last time.

The music was loud, and I was moving with it. My dress was blowing in the wind, as if choreographed to the music, and my bare feet felt like they were floating two inches off the earth. Brock turned down the lights with the dimmer switch and leaned against the double glass doors, watching me. He was sipping a beer, barefoot, with his light-green short-sleeved shirt unbuttoned. When I could focus, his face looked so inviting, still and staring at me. I walked over to him and kissed him, softly at first. My body was light and pliable, moving on its own. My tongue was moving in his mouth from one side to the other, chasing his. I was in charge, but it was a different part of me from usual. My mind wasn't looking around the corner; it was just here. No past, no future.

"Whoa, hold on . . . ," I said. I was breathless and light-headed.

"It's OK." He steadied me. "Have a sip of this," he said as he handed me his beer, and the liquid stimulated my insides. I poured a little down the front of my V-neck dress. The drops pulsed down in slow motion, and I could feel the bubbles between my breasts. I closed my eyes and twirled in a circle, pouring more of the magic down the front of me. The techno music had been written just for this night, and I danced to the cadence. The smell of lilacs was strong when I closed my eyes, but it went away when I opened them, which made me giggle out loud on several occasions.

"What are you up to?" Brock was standing close now, watching.

"Living. I'm living . . . ," I said, brushing my hand against his bare chest as I danced by him.

"Yes, you are. It looks good on you."

Hours later, my feet had run dry, but I was still light-headed and happy, my body still on hiatus from me. It was four thirty in the morning.

"I want to go to bed," I said, puffing on my cigarette. "I want to sleep with this feeling. OK?"

"Twist my arm." Brock took my hand, and it felt warm and sweaty.

"I won't sleep with you, but you can kiss me again."

"Let's not forget, *you* kissed *me*. I'm going to Mexico tomorrow. I need to pay my old source a visit, get some drugs back that they stole from me. Do you wanna come? I have a feeling you like danger." Brock was still holding my hand and leading me to the bedroom.

"Yep, I'll go with you."

CHAPTER 15

We pulled up at the side of a run-down apartment complex ten miles from the Brownsville & Matamoros International Bridge, Mexico. It felt more like a million miles away from the safety of the US border. The air-conditioning was pouring out the vents of our four-door rental car and blowing my hair back while my feet sweated on the floorboard.

"Let's go," I said. I opened the door and was accosted by the sweltering heat. I took the hair tie off my right wrist and wrapped it around my long blond hair several times. I heard Brock's door slam, and he walked over and stood next to me in his khakis and tank top.

"Get back in the car. In case you haven't noticed, we aren't exactly in Blond-ville," Brock said as he handed me the keys.

I put them in the pocket of my cutoffs and walked behind him. "In case you haven't noticed, you have blond hair too."

We were standing on a long colorless street strewn with garbage and gang graffiti. I had a dry mouth and a quick step as I perused our surroundings. It was one four-story concrete building next to another and then another. They were all the pale color of neglect, with clothes hanging over the balconies and the smell of rotting vegetables in the air.

"How do you know which one theirs is?"

"I've been here before. Hurry up." Brock was biting his lips and rapidly blinking his eyes. There was such familiarity to the nervous energy.

He led me up a narrow fire escape in the back of the building. We climbed three stories until we got to the apartment. The window was filthy, but I could see inside, and it looked like no one was there. Brock took one step back and kicked the window. The single-pane glass shattered, and there was a cacophony as the splinters hit the floor of the kitchen and some of the shards fell the three stories to the ground below us.

"Stupid, why didn't you see if it was open first?" I said.

"Shut up." It struck me as funny that he was whispering when we had just sent large shards of glass cascading down to the street. "Drug dealers don't leave their windows unlocked."

"*You* leave *your* windows unlocked."

"Shut up."

We bent down and climbed through the window, trying to avoid the remaining glass sticking from the edges of the window frame.

The apartment was small. There were two bedrooms, a bathroom, a living room, and a kitchen, where we had entered. The kitchen hadn't been cleaned since women could vote, and there was a poster of a half-naked woman in high-heeled black boots hanging crookedly in the living room above the couch. There were three guns on the kitchen table, along with several scales and empty beer bottles. Brock licked his finger, dragged it across the white powder residue on the table, and put it on his tongue.

"Bingo," he said.

"What am I looking for?"

"Two of the 'snack-size' bags I use for Pascal's stuff. They stole them from me. And three grand in cash. Move it, I want to get the hell outta here."

We split up, making our way from room to room.

The hallway used to be white, but now it was the color of smoke and smelled like mold. I stopped and opened the linen closet door. There were three black roller suitcases, one on top of the other. I leaned forward and picked up the first one, then rolled it to the living room. I was opening the third suitcase I had dragged into the living room, when Brock came in.

"What the fuck—why didn't you come get me?" Brock was staring down at the three open suitcases full of drugs, guns, and money.

"Oh, sorry . . . Hey, Brock, I found their stash," I said in my best smart-ass voice.

"Come on, let's get out of here," Brock said.

"What are you talking about? Let's just take the suitcases with the money and the drugs."

"You're kidding, right? Do you have any idea who these guys are? They'll hunt us down and kill us. I'm taking back what they stole from me. That's it. I don't have a death wish like you." He was stuffing money down his khaki shorts and eyeing the various bags of drugs for the right size and handing me two of them. "Come on. We've got to put these suitcases back." He was swallowing excessively.

"They're going to know, Brock. I mean, you did break their fucking window." I grabbed a brown paper bag that was lying on the floor and put the two ziplock bags of white powder in it. I'd feel fat if I put them in my shorts.

I heard a sound. My eyes darted to the front door and then to the guns on the kitchen table. Brock's posture went rigid. "Dammit. Move. Let's go."

"I know how to shoot a gun." I liked the adrenaline that was pumping through my veins.

"Are you fucking crazy?"

Brock's eyes were bulging, and he took off through the window. I followed. Brock had a quick, erratic pace. "Fuck," he said over and over as we made our way to the car. I was a few feet behind him. We got in the car, I handed Brock the keys, and we headed for the International Bridge.

I liked to stare out the window when the car was going fast. I glued my eyes to something blurry in the distance and stared at it until it came into focus.

"Do you ever have dreams?" I asked Brock, my head leaning on the window of the car. The adrenaline was gone, and I felt vacant inside again.

"None that I remember, really. Kinda glad, given the way you woke up screaming this morning. We don't need both of us screaming in the middle of the night."

I never uttered a word about the rape when I was fifteen, but in a way it was in every conversation and every dream I'd had since. Some were simple dreams: I was falling; my legs and arms didn't work. When I looked down, I had to choose who was going to catch me—my dad or Robert. Either way, I'd wake up screaming.

"Hello? Anyone in there?" Brock broke the spell, and I wondered how long I'd been out of the loop.

"What? Sorry, what?" I said.

CHAPTER 16

Alio came out onto her front porch and put a peanut butter and jelly sandwich and a tall glass of orange juice on the table next to me. Her hair seemed blonder than I remembered, but it could just have been me. She still had her apron on from her shift, and her eyes were hidden behind her sunglasses.

"You aren't leaving until you eat that whole thing," she said as she came around and plopped herself onto the wooden chair next to mine. "When did you start smoking Reds?"

"I think it was when I stopped giving a shit." It wasn't fair to drag her down with me. I had not had a night without a potentially lethal amount of drugs for over a week. "I'm sorry," I said in a low voice as I let out a deep breath.

"OK, now, what is going on? You disappear for over a week. No phone call, and all of your stuff is gone from your duplex. Logan and I were going mad. We were three seconds from calling the cops when Pascal told us that you were on a drug run with Brock. Have you lost your mind?" Her voice softened slightly. "Plus, sweetie, you look like I could crack you in two with my pinky. Skinny is one thing, but this is ridiculous." Alio was looking at me, and I was staring straight ahead at a bird that was making a nest in a tree.

"A hundred and three," I said.

"What?"

"How's Logan?" I asked without turning my head.

"He's a wreck. He found out you were using a different name at work, and he finally got ahold of your landlord, and he paid the damages from your last eviction so you wouldn't get in trouble for identity theft."

"Is he moving away?" I asked.

"Moving away? No, he is head over heels in love with you and wants to marry you. Moving away? Look at me." Alio was sitting on the corner of the chair, leaning toward me. She took off her sunglasses, picked up half the sandwich, and tried to hand it to me.

"Can I get some water?" I said. My brain was sluggish; the words sounded as if I had said them underwater. I thought, *Maybe I should take the night off from drugs tonight.*

"*No*, talk to me." Alio was in my face.

"I'm talking!" I didn't mean to say it that loud.

"We love you, and we're worried about you. Tell Logan how you feel; you can work it out. He adores you."

I was grinding my teeth, trying to hold back the tears.

"I can't, I'm so . . . Please." My head slumped and I stared at my body, which I didn't recognize. I wrapped my arms around my midsection to stop shaking.

Brock was going to be here in half an hour to pick me up.

"You are tearing your life apart. If you leave with Brock today, I have to say good-bye. I can't help you when you are making these choices." I could feel my organs throbbing.

"I'm not your charity case. I'm fine. I'm just tired." I couldn't even convince myself of my words. I just needed to go back to Brock's and sleep this off.

"Oh, Kath, you need help. Please talk to Logan." Alio turned her head toward the street and I did as well.

"You didn't! You told Logan I was here? Alio! No . . . ," I said as I watched Logan park his car and walk toward me. I stopped breathing and froze in place. He looked incredibly handsome in a pressed white T-shirt and jeans. His gait was different, not as deliberate. He came up the front steps.

"Can I have a hug, Mary?" he said, biting his lip. His smile was as brilliant as I remembered. I wanted him to yell and scream at me. I wanted him to threaten to leave me. Anything but his sweet, affectionate voice. I stood up, and he walked the two steps to me and hugged me. I let myself fall against his skin. I took a long slow breath of his smell and held it inside.

"You scared me, little one," he said into my hair.

"I'm so sorry, I . . ."

"Shh, you're OK. I'm here. I've got you. Let's get you home."

I squeezed him tighter and let myself fall further into his body. I wanted to stay in this very moment forever and ever until I died, and then for one minute longer.

"You're safe now," he said.

"I can't," I said.

"We can talk about all of it later. I'm just so grateful you're safe."

I pulled back, and Logan reluctantly let go of the hug but kept holding my hand. Alio was crying. She walked over to me and threw her arms around me.

"See?" she said.

Logan smiled at me, but I could see the pain I had caused him in his eyes.

I let go of his hand and backed away when I saw the blue Saab pulling up to Alio's house. Brock got out of the car, put his hands through his hair, and made his way up to the porch.

"Am I breaking up a party?" he said.

Logan looked at me; I looked down at the ground. I couldn't look at him. My arms were hanging at my sides, and I wanted to run.

"Kath?" Logan was staring at me.

"You aren't welcome here. Get off my porch," Alio said to Brock.

"Well, well, that's not a very nice hello," Brock said.

"You heard her." Logan squared his shoulders with Brock's and spoke in a firm voice. "You have caused enough damage."

Brock scoffed. "I've got a table waiting, babe," he said as he turned and started walking to his car. "I'll be in the car; hurry up."

I looked at Alio and then at Logan.

"It's OK, little one. He can't hurt you anymore," Logan said.

I looked at Brock, who was now sitting in his car. I could hear the distant sound of music coming from his stereo.

"Logan?" My voice was quivering. "I can't do this."

I gestured to the space between us. I knew I would just hurt him again, and I thought I should end the relationship while I could still feel the pain. "I can't do *us*." I was aware that my tears were giving me away, but there was no way to stop them.

"What are you saying? Don't. Come here." He stepped closer to me, and I took two steps back. I took off the ring from my left hand, put it on the table next to the sandwich, and walked to Brock's car.

I got in the car and closed the door to the Saab. I didn't look up.

"Well, *that* was fucking weird. What the hell is wrong with them?" Brock asked as he pulled a U-turn and headed downtown. I didn't respond, and we drove on in silence.

He slid the car into a parking spot at the top of a three-story garage. I didn't know if my legs would carry me down to the street; they were still numb from leaving Logan on Alio's porch.

We got out of the car. I was standing, that was a start.

"Let's move; I'm starving," Brock said, walking ahead of me.

I ordered two shots of tequila for an appetizer and the filet mignon for dinner. I ordered the filet mignon because it was the most expensive thing on the menu and Brock was paying. It was a relief not to have to pretend to eat; I just moved the food around a little. Brock never noticed if I ate or not.

"Aren't you a barrel of laughs tonight," Brock said.

"Fuck you," I said.

"OK, it's about time."

"You wish. Don't be an asshole tonight unless you plan to load me up on drugs. I am too exhausted to deal with you without them."

"You don't want dessert, right? Let's get out of here." Brock signaled to the waiter to bring the check.

I was dreading walking up the three flights of stairs to the car. Why did he always have to park on the top when there were plenty of spots on the first level?

"We need to get you some clothes that fucking fit; that dress is falling off you." Brock was behind me on the steps. "Cute ass, though. I've got a full shot from here."

I stopped at the landing, mostly to summon some energy to keep going. Brock kissed me; it tasted bitter and ugly. I wanted to bite his tongue off, but I kissed him back instead. He cupped my breasts through my dress and pushed me up against the landing wall. I kept my eyes open and stared at the rusted metal stairs in front of me. Brock's eyes were shut, and his mouth was tight and lustful.

"How about right here for our first fuck, huh, baby?" He was grinding on my dress, and I could feel his erection through his pants.

"Yeah, sure. Right here," I said. I was too tired to fight, too numb to care, and too weak to keep moving up the staircase.

He didn't ask again. He unbuttoned his pants, let them fall to the ground, pulled up my dress, and entered me while I stared at the hideous steps.

CHAPTER 17

Summer, 1993

The months passed and the drugs flowed, and I lived in a dingy, dirty place inside myself. I got out of the shower feeling filthier than when I'd gotten in.

This was going to be a "big night," as Brock put it. He was flying his new suppliers in from Mexico, and we were taking them out for a night on the town. I looked in my closet and chose the new black dress with the low back that I had charged to Brock's credit card, along with all my other clothes. I blow-dried my hair, which took way more energy than I had, put on some lip gloss, and headed to the kitchen for something to drink.

"Nice, babe," Brock said. "You are so fucking tan. Is that all you do all day?"

"That and entertain your drug dealers," I said.

"Well, if ever you needed to turn the charm on, tonight is the night. Bring it. I am so fucking stoked; it's going to be great." He was pacing the floor and slamming his second gin and tonic.

"What time does the limo get here?" I asked.

"Twenty minutes."

There were three guys, three hired female escorts Brock had hand-picked, and Brock and me.

The limo dropped us in front of the new, trendy Latin-fused-with-something restaurant. They all looked the same to me. We ate on the patio; it was dimly lit and full of candles that were now moving in circles when I looked at them. Brock had double-dosed me on the white stuff, and I was happy to engage with whoever happened to be in front of me. Brock caught my eye and gave me a nod, letting me know things were going well. He acted like he was the kingpin of the drug world, when really he was just a loser drug dealer in Omaha.

"Last call before we hit the limo and go dancing!" Brock announced. "We've got to move these bodies."

Two of the escorts were sitting on the guys' laps. They all seemed a little blurry, but I imagined they would say the same about me. Brock came around the table, paid the bill, and kissed me on the mouth.

"I've got another present for you," Brock said, smiling his boyish smile, and I looked down at his open palm.

There was a speckled pill in it; it wasn't white like the others. I tried to focus, but my eyes wouldn't cooperate. I took it from his hand and popped it in my mouth, washing it down with someone else's water.

"Now the party is started." Brock took my hand and we led our well-oiled crowd to the limo. I was holding on to Brock's hand a little tighter than usual; I needed him for balance because my liftoff was intensifying.

"What did you give me?" I asked Brock.

"Dunno. I got it from one of the guys."

"Did you take one?"

"No, you're riding solo on that one." Brock let go of my hand and turned to walk with one of the men. I teetered on one heel and caught myself.

The lights in the limo were multicolored. There were streaks of red, blue, and green racing around people's faces, and it was hard to distinguish who was who. Someone handed me a drink, and I put the glass against my face to feel the chill of the ice clinking around inside. My head was rolling a bit from side to side, and my eyes were going in and out of focus. A high-pitched piercing sound was coming from all directions, and I had to cover my ears. It was becoming increasingly hard to breathe, so I rolled down the window, but someone rolled it right back up. I needed to lie down—I had to catch my breath. But when I tried to inhale, a sharp pain sliced across my body and made me jump. I slid to the floor of the limo. One of the escorts was looking at me, and I tried to smile but my face was numb.

"She's fine. Just give her a minute," I heard Brock say from a distance.

I lay facedown on the carpeted floor and quickly realized that was a mistake. I rolled to my side in the fetal position and looked up at the lights. I had to get up, but I couldn't. The men began moving me with their feet to the rhythm of the music, stomping on my body. They were laughing. Someone poured a cold drink on me, and I could feel the ice cubes on my stomach. My body started twitching and I felt flames coming from inside of my chest. I tried to get my next breath. The breath wouldn't come. I could see only black tunnels when I opened my eyes, and the pain in my chest was unbearable. I was stuck to the wet floorboard below me, blinded and gasping for breath.

I played the somewhere-else game. I thought of the ocean and I let myself go. I heard the waves hitting the sand and saw myself sitting outside on the third-story balcony of my parents' house. Victorian. Then I stopped breathing.

PART THREE

mend (verb):

to repair something that is broken or damaged

CHAPTER 18

I didn't know that I didn't want to die until I almost did. But I didn't want to live either.

I was petrified to be on this bus, but it was the only shred of hope I had left. I was four hours north of Toronto.

"Anyone for Combermere?" the Greyhound bus driver with the frizzy hair yelled.

I had been staring out the bus window, thinking about Father Joseph Raya, the former archbishop of Galilee. He had stayed at my parents' house for a summer almost fifteen years before and had said to me in his magnanimous, beautifully accented voice, "Love is all we have."

He had a long gray beard and robes that dragged behind him on the ground. He was the only priest who ever made sense to me. Plus he had been exiled from Egypt for standing up for women's rights. I had never heard anything like that in my life. We would walk on the beach and talk. He didn't talk about God or rules; he talked about Marilyn Monroe and love, and he didn't dumb it down for me because I was a kid. He asked me questions about what I believed, and he listened. He gave me my first Communion under strict orders to do no such thing. He didn't care about rules; he cared about people. He told me about a place called Madonna House. It was a lay apostolate Catholic retreat center where people lived in the community for free and volunteered to work, largely in silence.

I needed a place to hide. Hide from the world and from myself. The worst that could happen was I would see the place and leave. I had exactly $243, which wouldn't get me very far. Now that the bus driver had called out my stop, I looked at the sweeping landscape and had a sense that I was putting myself away into a prison of trees and moss. It was surrounding me on all sides. *Where is the city? What have I done?*

"This is it?" I shouted to the driver from six rows back. I looked out my window and saw green terrain all around me. There was a small one-story log cabin with a sign in the left window that read "Café" and a sign in the right window that read "Post Office." There were two weather-beaten gas pumps in front, one for diesel and one for unleaded. I had never seen a town this exhausted.

"This is it, little lady. And you're the only one getting off," he said.

I had shoved everything I owned into two bags that I didn't bother trying to zip all the way up. I grabbed them and walked off the bus with one bag in front and the other behind me, trying not to topple down the steps.

This can't be my life. I slumped on top of an old horse post and stared at the back of the Greyhound bus making its way out of town.

"Howdy!" The billowing sound came from my left.

I jumped off the post and saw a tall, slender man, early thirties, with brown hair that wrapped around his head but didn't make it to the top. He had a full beard that was neatly trimmed, and he was handsome because of his eyes.

"Um, hi. I'm looking for a place called Madonna House. Am I in the right town?"

"You one of those? I would not have pegged ya for a religious type." His eyes drew me in; they were a deep green with a bit of mischief in them.

"Really . . ." I hadn't been to church in years, not since I had left my parents' house. "Truthfully, I don't even know why I'm here. I'm chalking it up to temporary insanity." I rummaged through the smaller of my two bags in search of my Marlboro Lights.

"Can I have one?" he asked as I pulled them out and opened the top of the pack.

I laughed as I handed him a smoke. "What's your name?"

"Wink." He reached out and grabbed the cigarette with one hand and shook mine with the other. "And you're in the right place. Madonna House is just a mile down the road. Do they know you're coming?"

"I didn't tell them. Hopefully, they won't be as surprised as me."

"The Madonna House van comes once a day, about an hour after the bus."

I stood up straight and pulled my jeans up over my hips where they had begun to sag. I nonchalantly stuck two fingers between my skin and my jeans; there was still ample room. I hadn't eaten since yesterday morning: one half of a hard-boiled egg from an earlier gas station. I smiled at Wink. "Do they have good food in there?" I asked, nodding toward the combination café / post office / gas station. He didn't respond but just took a long drag off the cigarette. I started to walk toward the door of the café.

"What about your bags?" Wink asked after me.

"I've got what I need," I said, holding my Marlboro Lights and my wallet above my head without turning around.

The café was clean, and it smelled like freshly baked cinnamon buns. I walked up to the white Formica counter and sat on a metal stool that was planted firmly in the wood flooring. It was a simple place, seven or eight wooden tables with matching chairs and a big mason jug in the middle of each table, which was filled with blue-and-white checkered cloth napkins and silverware.

A middle-aged woman came from the kitchen. She had on a red apron, and her blond hair was tied up in a bun with a small spatula stuck through it. Her walk was leisurely and confident.

"What can I get ya?" She had to be talking to me, but she was looking out the window behind me. She took a wet cloth out of her apron pocket and began wiping the clean counter in front of me.

"How about a Diet Coke, large?" I said.

She turned and walked back into the kitchen.

"Add french fries too, if you have them." I could fit way more than two fingers between myself and my jeans. I told myself that if she heard me, I'd get the fries; if not, I wouldn't get to repeat it. Somehow I would feel less guilty eating them that way, as if it were her idea to order them.

Wink strolled in and headed for the stool next to mine. His walk was so assured. "Hey, City, you change your mind yet? It ain't too late to get yourself out of here. We won't tell."

"Come on, Wink, it can't be that bad . . ." I was trying to remain playful in tone.

"Well, for starters, I hope you packed some other clothes in those suitcases outside. What you have on isn't going to fly down the hill."

"This is as boring as I get, Wink." I was wearing my coral-colored V-necked tank top, jeans, and ballet flats. I touched my ears and felt the gold hoops that were my staple.

"Well, they like ya a little more covered up, that's all."

"Are you kidding?"

"Like I told ya, the M-H van comes once a day to see who has landed on their soil for healing of the soul. That means you got about"—he checked the lopsided clock that hung over the restroom sign—"fifty minutes to get anything you're gonna need between now and Wednesday afternoon, which is when guests can leave for three hours and come to town if they want."

"Saved by the fries," I said as the woman with the spatula in her hair delivered my order. "Can you add two cartons of Marlboro Lights to my tab and bring the check?"

"Now we're talking, City. Can I grab another smoke?" I didn't need to answer, because he had already grabbed the pack I had from the counter.

"City, I have seen some of the most beautiful people turn ugly after getting in that van, and I have seen people who look like the devil himself come out of Madonna House singing like the angels on high. I guess I see myself right in the middle. You seem like a smart girl. Why you takin' chances?"

"I like taking chances, Wink, and besides, I've got a little devil in me I could stand to get rid of."

"Don't we all. Ain't that the God's honest truth. Put some of our special vinegar on those fries and eat 'em in local fashion," he said as he stood up, grabbed a few french fries, and headed for the door. "I'm sure I'll bump into you, City."

"My name is Kathleen!" I yelled as the door shut behind him. I opened the vinegar and gave the local flavor a try. I wondered how many calories were in vinegar.

I was standing outside, smoking my fifth Marlboro Light, when the van pulled up to the café. It was avocado green on the top half and cream on the bottom, with windows lining the sides. It was spotless—not a mark on it, even though it was more than twenty years old.

"This is a time warp," I said to the air. I dropped my cigarette on the gravel and put it out with my shoe.

A woman in her early forties stepped out of the driver's side of the van. Her clothes were the color of dirt, which matched the color of her unwashed hair. It looked like it was trying to escape the frenetic bun on top of her head. I couldn't tell if it was a skirt she was wearing or some sort of homemade take on 1970s culottes. Her tall, slender body had ample room inside her enormous clothes.

This woman needed "the talk"—the one none of us like to give, but that we do for the sake of womankind. This was the talk where you lied to her and told her not to worry, fashion faux pas happened all the time, and thank God hers could be over as soon as we'd burned the current outfit she was sporting.

"I couldn't scare her off no matter how hard I tried," Wink said to the woman as he came back down the street.

"Good, Wink, you're here. Let's go," she said. Her voice had a musical quality to it.

"This is Kathleen, but I think we should call her 'City.' And let's try not to beat all the feisty out of her," Wink said as he carried my two bags toward the van. "Kathleen, this is MK. She knows a thing or two about feisty."

"Got it, Wink. OK, kiddo, you're with me," MK said.

"Come on, City, let's go home," he said. An unfeigned laugh escaped my lips as he walked past me and winked.

Wink got in the front seat with MK. He didn't bother with the seat belt. His body was turned toward her with his long legs in the middle of the aisle and his eyes looking straight at her. "How are you holding up? This is your . . . third day home?"

I was so busy looking at her clothes and that manic hair that I hadn't looked at her face right away. I shifted to find her eyes in the front mirror. She was more striking than beautiful. She had a distinguished nature about her; it made me want to sit up straight. There were wrinkles around her fierce brown eyes that made me want to listen to what she had to say. I leaned forward enough to hear, but not enough to be noticed.

MK was ranting to Wink as she drove down the winding road, her sentences merging together. I was listening intently, trying to get the lay of the land. She had just gotten back from Liberia, where she had spent the last three years at the Madonna House field station. She was livid at the leaders of the community who had decided to close the station because of the country's civil war. Wink was trying to calm her down, but every time he tried to speak, she got louder.

"I can't stop seeing their faces, mostly the children's. They are being slaughtered, and I got on an airplane and left them there. I left them. I signed up for promises of poverty, chastity, and obedience seventeen years ago. Poverty isn't hard for me, chastity I won't speak of here, but obedience is my cross . . ." She paused. "And Liberia needs us now more than ever. Our mandate says, 'Take up their cross and follow Me.' It does not say, 'Take off when they need you the most.'"

We pulled off the pavement and onto a dirt road, where a sign read "Madonna House." There was a large white farmhouse on our right with a Byzantine cross on the top, and there was a lake sprawled out behind the house. The grass was thick and lush, and there were rows of tall flowers in a medley of colors in front of another large building next to the farmhouse. We parked on the left in front of another building with a sign that read "St. Germain's Dormitory."

"I'll pop your stuff inside, City." Wink was out of the van before I opened my door.

"Vespers are at five o'clock, so let's go and get you settled in beforehand." MK's voice went up an octave at the end of every sentence.

I followed her up the ten steps and grabbed the screen door from her as we walked in and Wink walked out.

"Thanks, Wink."

MK was standing next to me in the foyer, which had boot compartments from the ground up: small homemade wooden slots that had uniform name tags. It gave off the sour stench of cedar and sweat.

"No shoes are allowed in any of the buildings, and you'll find similar cubbies in each building. Pick one of these for yourself, and the labeler is there in the basket." She pointed to the corner where a wooden basket with a red cloth lining sat on the ledge in front of the window. "We ask for a donation to use the labeler if you're able. You'll need to sew a label with your name on it into each piece of clothing so that the laundry will get them back to you; otherwise, they go to our St. Joseph's clothing store down the street and we'll sell them. Tank tops are not allowed; shoulders and legs must be covered."

I gave her a once-over and said, "You'll sell them?"

I think she caught my subtle "Fuck you." I kept trying to tell myself that I could walk out any second, but it was starting to settle in that this was my only option—at least until I figured out another plan.

"Yes, we sell them." She started walking through a doorway. "No need to label the cubbies in the other buildings, since you are a guest; just use one that doesn't have a name tag. Follow me."

I slid my ballet flats off, threw them into an empty cubby, and followed her through the wooden door into the dormitory. I stepped into a long gray, wood-framed room with a large wood-burning stove in the middle.

Four rows of a dozen beds were lined up in rows with two feet between them. All the beds were twin-size with different metal frames. They had white sheets and different-colored blankets tucked in hospital-style, and each bed had an additional blanket identical to the others folded on top. There were two orange milk crates in between each bed. Each pair was topped with a simple piece of cloth and a mismatched lamp.

"Um . . . what is this?" I asked.

MK was halfway down the first line of beds when she turned around and said, "This is where you sleep."

She assigned me the fifth bed on the far right-hand side, against the wall. There was a small window behind the lamp.

I bent and looked out the window and saw someone walking in the distance, smoking, and my body relaxed a tiny bit.

"You are allowed eight hangers in that closet," she said, pointing back toward the front of the dorm. There was a closet with fabric instead of a door. "And any personal items need to fit inside these two orange crates." She was still singing her words, acting as if this weren't crazy, and she started making her way back down the aisle.

"Let me show you the bathroom." There was a wooden partition with entrances on two sides. "You are allowed to use these bathrooms only at night; the outhouses are what you will use during the day, and they are out the back door to the right. Everyone takes one shower per week. Let me know later what day of the week you would like to shower; there are buckets here, under the sink, for you to use if you would like to rinse off at night. Please do not run the water when you are washing your face or brushing your teeth; instead, fill the bucket with an inch or so of water and wash."

I looked under the sinks and saw three small old square Tupperware containers.

"Why don't you take fifteen minutes to unpack and get changed, and I'll come back and we can walk to the chapel together for Vespers."

She was gone before I could gather my thoughts. I walked back and sat on my bed, closed my eyes, and felt the stiffness in my throat. *Eight hangers and two milk crates.*

I changed my shirt, got my shoes on, and walked outside. I stood on the small landing at the top of the stairs and lit a cigarette. I sucked on it so hard, my ears popped.

I could see five other buildings and a parking lot from where I stood. Two were cabins constructed of unpainted dark wood, and the rest were painted white. I watched as people began to flood out of the buildings. They were all headed in the same direction, down a wide dirt path. I took off walking.

There were over a hundred people walking in silence down the long path. It was lined on both sides with tall, beautiful trees in the prime of their existence. I caught myself moving fast, then slowly. The faces I could see looked peaceful in the silence. I was used to chaos and noise, not peace and silence. The more I tried to calm myself, the more self-conscious I became. We crossed over the lake on a wide rustic bridge without a railing.

The light from the sun snuck in through the trees and landed on the bright gold onion dome that was on top of the dark-colored cabin twenty yards ahead of me. I moved to the side of the dirt road and let others pass. It was the chapel.

The chapel looked more like a beautiful old barn than a church. It was built in the shape of a cross, with stone wrapping around the bottom. It had an A-frame in the front, with a huge driftwood cross over the pine door and a slanted metal roof. I stuck my hands in my jeans pockets to avoid taking the olive branch this building seemed to be offering me. I hadn't been to church in a very long time.

I waited until the last person walked into the church, and then I went in.

The walls were the perfect color of honey, and ornate Byzantine icons of all sizes hung on the side walls and behind the altar. The altar was a simple, elegant, and inviting table with a white lace cloth flowing over both sides. There were no pews, and people were sitting quietly on the floor in their bare feet, with a few sitting on the built-in ledge that went around the inside of the church. There was a small room behind the altar, which could be accessed from three curved openings that were covered from the back with pleated green fabric.

I took my place in the very back right corner, hoping to be invisible hiding amidst the 150 pairs of shoes.

This was not the church of my youth: no leather kneelers, no ornate stained-glass windows, no solid-gold chalices or fancy covered hymnals. No one was speaking in tongues and dropping to the ground, slain in the spirit. And, oddly, I wanted to see what would happen.

The singing began, and it echoed through the room like the sound of angels. I leaned against the wall and closed my eyes. I was hearing with a different part of me. They were singing in Latin, and I was grateful that I didn't know what the words meant; I was sure that would ruin it.

A woman with white hair and piercing blue eyes got up from the ledge by the altar. She was solid and composed. She turned around, bowed, and kissed the icon of Mary holding baby Jesus, and then turned back around to face the crowd and headed straight for me. I was staring at her eyes, unable to move my body even as I commanded it to be invisible. She took my left elbow and gently guided me to an open spot in the middle of the church. She gestured to have me take a seat on the wood floor and went back to her spot on the ledge.

In a strange way, this music reminded me of the ocean, the melody soothing and fluid.

They sang in Latin for an hour. Afterward, I walked in the flow of the community toward the white farmhouse I could see from my dorm. I was feeling exhausted and raw, and I was happy that no one seemed to want to talk about what we just experienced.

When the crowd veered left toward the main house, I slipped out and went right toward St. Germain's.

"Kathleen?" MK's voice came from behind.

I kept walking, only faster.

"Kathleen . . ."

I turned to face MK and said, "Oh, hi."

"You need to come to the main house for dinner." She was standing straight, in the same confusing clothes she had had on earlier, and her unruly hair continued to do its thing on top of her head.

"Yeah, but I'm not hungry, and I'm really tired. So I'm gonna call it a night."

"No, hon, we're going to dinner. It is our duty of the moment." I would learn later that this principle was woven into the very fabric of the community. We were all there living with our promises of poverty, chastity, and obedience. MK held me by my elbow and steered me toward the main house. "And I asked you to wait for me to bring you to the chapel. Please do as I ask. Obedience will lead you to great peace," she said.

There was more shuffling of shoes as we entered the basement of the main house. I found an empty cubby and put my shoes in it. MK was already upstairs, and I contemplated heading back to St. Germain's. But I had a feeling she would round me up again, so I walked to the wooden staircase and headed up.

The dining room to my left was huge, with six tables lining both sides of the room and six straight down the middle. A lot of natural light streamed in from the windows that surrounded the room wherever there wasn't a bookcase. There were uniform white lights above the tables and two black runners on the floor, one on each aisle to protect the wood. Each wooden dining table had benches on both sides and chairs with slatted backs on each end. The eighteen tables were set identically with a plate at each of the eight settings, a mismatched teacup, and silverware. In the center of each table was a plastic container with toothpicks and salt and pepper.

The room bustled as some people took their seats and others headed to the door ahead of me, which opened into the kitchen. To my right was a beautiful paneled library, lined on one side with books and on the other with windows overlooking the lake.

Everyone seemed to know what to do except me.

"Sit with me, newbie." I turned to see an older woman with glasses perched on the edge of her nose. She took my hand in boyfriend style, interlacing her fingers with mine, and led me to the last table on the left side of the dining room. We sat with the windows behind us, facing the clock in the front of the room. "I always go for the window seats; I like the breeze. Plus, we get to people watch back here." She had short curly hair and skin the color of an Asian pear, and she was almost as round as she was tall. "I'm Laura. Now, who are you?"

"Kathleen. I don't really know what I'm doing here," I said.

"There is not a person in here who doesn't know exactly what you mean; we all had our first day here, sweetie." Laura went on to tell me that Marion, who had led me to my seat at Vespers, said being here was like stepping into outer space. Laura stopped talking and grabbed a toothpick. I sat in silence, watching 150 people settle in for dinner.

"Don't worry, you can stick yourself to me for a while. I'm staying in Germain's too, and I know the lay of the land. It's a lot to soak in, so just be gentle with yourself."

I had never even thought of the concept of being gentle with myself.

"I'll probably be leaving soon, so . . ."

Our table filled up with new faces. Laura introduced me, but I didn't remember a single person's name. I wanted a cigarette. The person at the head of each table by the aisle was the server. These people had to get up five or six times during the meal to fill up bowls of food, get more bread and water, and clear the table while everybody else just sat there and ate. *How do I get that job?*

Dinner was broth with rice on the bottom, and something off-white that looked like cottage cheese in a bowl, but I was pretty sure it wasn't.

"It's cheese curds, sweetie. Try it with the brown bread." Laura tapped my arm and passed me the bowl.

"Can I get a napkin?" I asked.

"If we don't grow it, beg for it, or have it donated, we don't have it, so napkins are scarce," Laura said. "We do get coffee on Sundays, though, and if the community doesn't drink it all, we get the leftovers on Monday morning."

I pushed the food around my plate, flattening it in parts.

"Can't leave it on the plate, sweetie. That's a no-no," Laura said, not so quietly.

"I can't eat this," I whispered to her.

The woman with the red hair who was serving our table was moving around a lot in her chair, which I took to mean she was antsy to get my plate.

"Here," Laura said as she picked up my plate and gave it to the young guy across from me. "Just this once. Here, Jeremy."

Jeremy smiled at me. He had thick cheeks and full lips that he licked a lot. His eyes were deep blue, a kind blue, with specks of yellow around the middles.

"Thanks," I said.

Dinner ended without a bell, but everyone must have heard something, because a flurry of activity started and I was lost again.

MK caught my eye and waved me to the front of the dining room.

"I guess I'm going that way," I said to Laura.

"See you back at St. Germain's," she said.

I made my way to the front of the room.

"See this sheet of paper?" MK said, pointing to a sheet hanging on the wall. "After every meal, all guests come up here. You look for your name, and it will tell you where to go. Let's see . . ."

There were more than fifty women's names on the sheet.

"Seems like a full house," I said as I looked for my name with MK.

"We can house as many as seventy women and eighty men, including the staff as we fill up for summer," she said. "But we get down to as few as seven or eight guests during the winter, and those are mostly applicants."

"What are applicants?" I leaned on the outside of my feet and added, "I'm probably just staying the night, a week at most, just so you know."

She wasn't looking at me; she was looking in the direction of the bustling kitchen. "Applicants are the people who are deciding whether they want to take promises of poverty, chastity, and obedience and become members of the staff here. They live at St. Germain's while they're deciding," she said as she looked at the list. "Tonight you're working in vegetables. You can head down the stairs and someone will tell you what to do."

I headed down the stairs and bumped into Jeremy. "Thank God, someone I know. What does 'working in vegetables' mean? Do I need to put my shoes on?"

He laughed out loud, a great and funny laugh, and said, "Come with me; I'm veggies tonight too."

"I love your accent. London?" I asked. He nodded.

We turned the corner into a tunnel of cement that eventually opened up into a large room with a taller ceiling and a dozen or so people standing around a very long, very old table. There were small bins of water on the table in front of each person and buckets of beets and carrots on the floor.

"Welcome to veggies," Jeremy announced as we entered. "Everyone, this is Kathleen. She just arrived this afternoon." No one spoke, but I got a few nods from around the table.

"Can I use the bathroom first?" I asked.

"Of course. The outhouse is through that exit to the left." He pointed toward a large doorway.

I walked out into the dark night, past the outhouse, and down the dirt road as I lit my cigarette.

CHAPTER 19

The air was moist and chilly, and I swallowed several times, adjusting to the thickness. I passed several other buildings that were modeled after the main house, all of which had a sign above the door that read, "I Am Third."

"I am third," I said out loud. I tried to translate it. My father was first, God was second, but I was very far from being third—maybe one hundred and third. I felt my step quicken when I thought of my father, even though he was five hundred miles away.

I found a thin path behind the main house. It was skinny, with footprints in the green grass, and I followed it. At the end of the grass was an old bridge with a railing on one side. It crossed a marsh of red-and-green brush that had grown of its own accord on one side and went into a forest of tall, lush trees like the ones on the way to the domed island chapel. The other side had a green railing, and a river flowed out from under it into a lake.

The rickety boards under my feet reminded me of the boardwalk in Spring Lake. I stopped halfway across, held on to the waist-high green railing, and took my shoes off. I put both elbows on the railing, held my head in my hands, and felt the wood under my feet. I was transported back in time.

When I was young, I would go under the boardwalk, sink into the soft, warm sand, snuggle my knees up to my chin, and listen to the conversations of the people walking above me. They would talk about their lives, tell stories of their day. Couples would laugh, their tanned hands clasped together. Often, kids ran around their legs playing tag. As soon as they got out of earshot, I'd make up the rest of their story, painting myself into their families. I prayed that I could have their lives. I wished I could have told them how scared I was to go home.

The silence was crawling up my body, making me sweat. I could feel the redness on my neck, making its way up my face. I opened the top of the cigarette box and then closed it again. I leaned over the railing and fought the emotion. I had taught myself to move, not think. Be defiant when I was afraid. But there was nowhere to go, and I couldn't find a shred of adrenaline to keep my mind at bay.

What am I doing here? My elbows were pressed firmly into the sides of my body, and I was breathing in bursts in and out. There was nothing but questions swirling in my mind. They were spitting at me, cutting me down, and cementing my nothingness.

What would happen if I let myself cry?

I heard footsteps coming from the opposite end of the bridge, and I stood straight, trying to smile to erase the moment. I looked out over the marsh, hoping whoever it was would keep walking if I didn't look at them.

"That cabin belonged to Catherine, our founder. She had many dark nights of the soul there," Marion said, pointing to a cabin standing alone in the distance. It was buried in the forest on the other side of the bridge.

"Peel the onion. You are here to pull the layers back and heal." She touched my back, and then she was gone, continuing her walk across the bridge. I wiped my face, shivered, leaned farther over the railing, and lit a cigarette.

I stayed for a long time, although I knew I was supposed to be cutting veggies or in the dorm by now. When I went back to St. Germain's, MK was waiting on the porch for me.

"We don't disappear."

"I am not part of your 'we,'" I said, and walked to my bed, which still had my unpacked bags on it.

She followed me, saying, "No one is keeping you here." She dropped what looked like a mass card on my bed. "If you would like to stay as a guest, you will need to embrace our way of life. All of it." The card was a copy of the "Little Mandate," which had been written by the Madonna House founder.

"Can I go to bed now?" I said, my back to her.

"Good night. Lights out at ten. For everyone."

I looked down the aisle to the bathroom, where there was a line at least six women deep on each side of the partition. I decided brushing my teeth and washing my face was overrated. I stuffed my bags under my bed, crawled under the sheet fully clothed, and pulled the covers over my head. I listened to the whispered prayers around me, and I said one simple prayer of my own before I fell asleep: *Please, God, tell me who I am.*

I felt as if I had just fallen asleep when I heard footsteps moving around on the wood floor. I could hear the faint sound of water running, which made me want to pee as I fell back asleep for a moment.

My heart raced, and I heard my father's voice in my head—*Feet on the floor!*—and I opened my eyes and reminded myself, as I did every morning, that he was not there.

I grabbed my bags from underneath the bed and rummaged for my toothbrush and some fresh clothes. I stole a look toward MK's bed on the opposite side of the room and saw her looking at me.

"You can't have your stuff scattered everywhere under your bed. That will need to be dealt with before teatime tonight if you want to stay here," she said.

I walked to the bathroom and put my face close to the cloudy old six-inch mirror that hung above the sink. "Well, if I can't shower, at least I can't see myself."

A woman about my age was standing at the sink next to me, filling her Tupperware with water. "I'm Betsy." Her thick black hair was braided into one long line down her back. "I wanted to say hi last night, but you went to sleep right away," she whispered.

"Hi. Yeah, I was wiped out last night. Why are you whispering?"

"We aren't really supposed to talk during the day. Only at meals and teatime. Do you know where you're working today?" I looked into her brown eyes; they seemed so uncomplicated.

"No idea." Did she just say we weren't supposed to talk?

"I'm in the laundry. Maybe I'll see you there," she whispered.

"Is that good?" I whispered back.

"Well, my favorite is to work at the farm, but MK moves everybody around a lot. Our last dorm mom didn't do that." Betsy never looked in the mirror. She finished with her Tupperware and headed out. Her small frame was swimming in her OshKosh overalls.

There was a line of eight women waiting for the sink, so I brushed my teeth and splashed my face with cold water (sans the freaky Tupperware), peed, and left the bathroom.

I hated the smell of coffee, because it smelled like my dad's breath, so cigarettes were my morning ritual. The August morning was chilly this far north. There was a slight breeze in the trees, as if they were trying to wake up the ground.

I leaned against the outside wall of St. Germain's and watched as people began to filter out of the other buildings and head down the dirt path that led to the island chapel. No one was talking. They were walking together, but I watched and their lips weren't moving. It made me suck on my cigarette harder. When the steady stream of people became a trickle, I followed.

I sat on the wood floor in the far back of the chapel for what turned out to be traditional mass. I knew every word, like riding a bike. I stayed motionless and silent and tried not to recite the prayers of the mass in my head. At least no one was speaking in tongues.

I closed my eyes when it was time to turn to the people around you and shake hands and say, "Peace be with you." No one tried to give me the sign of peace, and I appreciated not having to interact. When everyone stood up to go to Communion, I stood up and walked out of the church.

I sat at the same table for breakfast as I had for dinner the night before. So did many of the others from my table. Laura came down the aisle and took the seat on the end, the seat that indicated you'd be serving the rest of the table, with little time to eat. It reminded me to check the space between my jeans and my stomach.

"Watch and learn, newbie. You should serve one meal a day, and don't let MK spot you sitting in the same place too much or she'll fix that her way."

A priest named Father David got up and said grace, and then all the servers took off to the kitchen, which I hadn't seen yet. Jeremy and Betsy were the only other ones I knew at the table. There was very little conversation as the rest of the community filtered in. MK came in, stood at the top of the stairs, and perused the room. I watched her eyes find mine, and I smiled without showing my teeth—more of an I-saw-you-first kind of smile. MK made her way to the back and sat across from me, in between Jeremy and Betsy. I wished she would just leave me alone; it was hard enough to be here without her on my back. But on the other hand, it was the only adrenaline-producing thing I had in this place.

Betsy was talking to Jeremy, who had been living at Madonna House for over two years as a guest. Betsy was going on six months, and I had made a decision to steer clear of her. She was way too put together, and it felt authentic, which I found unnerving.

"How long do guests usually stay?" I had to ask.

"It really just depends, City," Jeremy said, with his fantastic British accent.

"Sounds like you've been talking to Wink. I like it," I said, regarding my nickname, which had already traveled through the community.

MK said, "I came as a guest, thinking I'd be outta here in a week. I met Catherine and Marion, and now I'm sixteen years in."

"Oh my God . . . really?" I said.

"Why aren't you going to the farm today?" Betsy asked.

"I have spiritual direction this morning, so Irene is going up to cook," MK replied. Her voice was so beautiful, but I got the feeling she really just wanted to cry. She shifted her weight to the left side of her body and leaned back on her hand. Everyone looked normal, as if she hadn't just said the weirdest thing I'd heard since I got here.

"OK, I give. What is spiritual direction?" I asked.

"You pick a priest, tell him the scariest stuff about yourself, and ask him to help you know what to do with it." MK was using her arm to stretch her back on the wooden bench.

"MK, don't scare her." Jeremy was all smiles. "Really, it is a gift. Spiritual direction guides you closer to God, helps you discern your calling in life."

"It doesn't scare me; I would just never do that," I said.

"You will if you want to stay here," MK said.

"Here we go, kiddos, breakfast is served," Laura said as she laid the bowls in the center of the table. I felt my stomach growl, which gave me a sense of control over my own body, because it meant I had resisted the urge to eat for quite a while.

There was brown bread, some kind of pinkish gravy-looking thing that Laura said was cooked rhubarb, and unsweetened yogurt. When the bowls came to me, I passed on the bread—even though it was fresh from the outdoor oven and smelled delicious—and put two bites of yogurt mixed with two bites of rhubarb into the bowl and took my time mixing it up. I took my one allotted bite; it was so tart my face puckered. I got the eye from MK as I pushed the rest of the food around the bowl.

"Madonna House asks that you eat a little of everything at every meal," Betsy said, smiling at me.

"I've heard," I said, almost without opening my mouth. I wanted to say, "Wipe that fucking smile off your face and look around. Smell the coffee—or lack thereof—and realize we are sitting in voluntary lockup." Instead, I sat there waiting for the meal to be over so I could see what my job for the day would be.

I was passing the main house on my way to St. Germain's to use the indoor bathroom and have a cigarette to fill my belly, when a peppy woman's voice stunned me out of my mission.

"Welcome. I am Patricia." She was standing at the top of the landing of one of the other the buildings adjacent to the main house, holding open the screen door; above the doorway there was a sign marked "Laundry," with the "I Am Third" sign hanging just below it.

I looked up as I passed by and said, "Hi."

"Let's get started."

I wasn't ready to "get started" yet, so I hoped she wasn't talking to me and just kept walking toward St. Germain.

"Kathleen . . ." *Shit.* I stopped.

"I'll be right back; I forgot something at my dorm," I said, and kept walking.

"I'd rather you came now. It is time we all pray with our hands," she said, making her way down the stairs behind me with her arms out in front of her, embracing the air.

"I'll just be a minute," I said.

"Come, dear." She kept walking toward me with her outstretched arms, and I guess I was more scared of her hugging me than getting to work. After a moment's hesitation, I walked around her and back up the steps to the laundry.

This was not your usual laundry room. It looked like a well-oiled machine of cleanliness. There were two industrial-size washing machines on one wall, with matching dryers next to them. In the middle of the room, there was a smooth, dark piece of wood three feet wide that ran almost the whole length of the room. It was piled high with dirty laundry, which two women were sorting into different buckets on the floor. Another woman was in the corner behind a sewing machine with a pile of socks next to her, mending. Three other women were dumping endless buckets of dirty clothes on the center table as they were dropped at the front door by other community dwellers.

Patricia began speaking, her voice stern even in a whisper. Her face was so red, she looked like she had a fever.

"We do little things exceedingly well for the love of God." I stared at the little red dots of broken capillaries on her face. "We clean laundry while our brothers and sisters are doing other work to serve. We work in silence. Only necessary words are spoken. Follow me." She walked to the far end of the room in her khaki pants, which were two inches too short, and stopped in front of a double sink by the window in the back.

She explained laundry like Machiavelli described the art of war. She launched into a monologue about how laundry must be "expressly defined." I couldn't help but begin reciting in my mind what I had memorized in my days at university as Machiavelli's purpose: *To honor and reward virtue clean laundry, not to have contempt for poverty dirty laundry, to esteem the modes and orders of military discipline the laundry room, to constrain citizens to love one another, to live without factions dirty laundry, to esteem less the private than the public good.*

"Put the gloves on your hands and pull them up as far as they will go on your arms." She came around and stood behind me and waited.

"Please take one handkerchief out of the water, and I will walk you through how each one needs to be cleaned in your duty of the moment." I could feel her warm breath on the left side of my neck, and I took a step to the right.

This "duty of the moment" was starting to have a life of its own. People talked about it with such acclaim, as if it were the answer to the world's problems.

"Clean it thoroughly. Make sure that all of the debris is picked off. They've been soaking since before breakfast, so there should not be too many that are hardened. You may use the bar of soap in the dish to your right sparingly."

"Debris?" I asked. I looked into the sink and saw dozens of handkerchiefs with green and brown boogers on them in the water. Hundreds of boogers had floated to the surface of the water, pooling toward the sides of the sink.

"No need for chatter," she said, stepping to the right and staying behind me.

My lips turned down and my nose wrinkled as I put the rubber gloves on. They felt like a liquid coating of sweaty plastic on my hands. I cleared my throat loudly and leaned back.

I was trying to find a tactful way of saying, "Throw these mucus-infested things in the trash, and buy some tissues. Hell, I'll beg for them for you! Just don't make me stick my hands in that foul water."

I started to take the gloves off and said, "I have to go to the ladies' room," swallowing the throw-up that was making its way up my throat.

"After we walk through a cleaning, you may go to use the outhouse," Patricia said, moving to the side of the sink, taking my gloved hand, and putting it in the water.

I closed my eyes. Machiavelli's mistress led me onward: "Let's begin. Remember, while you are here cleaning these handkerchiefs, someone is sorting beans for your lunch and another is tending to the wood needed to keep us warm this evening."

My head was turned to the right to avoid looking in the water, and I blurted out, "How do I get those jobs instead?"

"We live the humble life of Nazareth here. Listen for God in the simple tasks of the day. Be silent and make your duty of the moment a prayer."

"I am not kidding—I can't do this job. Please, can you reassign me to something else?" My arms were straight forward, dripping the nasty water back into the sink.

"We work in complete silence." She turned and walked to the cubby with all the irons in it. "Please let me know when you've finished cleaning your first one so I can have a look."

I didn't know why I'd come here, but I was sure it was not to clean other people's foul handkerchiefs. I had just under $150: Surely that could get me somewhere other than here? I closed my eyes, put my hands in the warm water, and pulled out a handkerchief.

I gave it a one-two scrub and threw it on the table next to me. The handkerchief made a splat as it landed and sprayed water six inches in every direction.

Patricia made her way over to the table and picked up the handkerchief.

"Please wash it again and do not throw the garment. Place it on the drying rack." She turned and walked to the ironing board and resumed ironing the cream-colored shirt.

"You're kidding, right?" I stomped my foot and began to take off the gloves.

"God's work is not a joke. It might help you to meditate on a phrase as you wash. Meditate on 'I am Third' and see what God is trying to teach you." She was poised, unfazed, and totally fucking annoying.

After six washes, Patricia was satisfied with the result.

"Beautiful," she said in the exact same tone that she had repeated five times. "Please wash the next one."

I looked up at the plain white clock that sat flat against the wall above the door and calculated that it had taken me twenty-five minutes to wash one handkerchief. I tried to do the math on how many more were in the begrimed basin. There must've been at least five dozen. I reached into the basin for my second handkerchief.

Lunch was not much of a respite except for the fact that MK showed me how to serve the table, so I didn't have to eat very much. I couldn't have eaten anyway: the disgusting morning of boogers was etched in my brain.

Back in the laundry, I looked at the clock: 2:10 p.m. I would have thought that almost five hours of scrubbing handkerchiefs would make my insides feel cleaner. But it didn't. To the contrary, the more silence there was, the dirtier I felt inside. Maybe I needed to stick my head in the basin and scrub my brain until I could make some sense out of how I had gotten into this laundry room in the first place.

CHAPTER 20

Every day, after every meal, for the next two and a half months, I walked to the front of the dining room and checked the guests' "duty of the moment" list. Every time, it had the same letter next to my name: *L* for "laundry." I swear, MK had it in for me.

The days were made up of torture, silence, dirty handkerchiefs and underwear, silence, more silence, endless numbers of shirts that needed to be ironed, and more silence. I was exhausted to my core, yet I stayed. I had nothing left in Omaha, I had no contact with my family, and being homeless sounded only slightly worse than suffering though the days here.

I lay in my creaky twin bed night after night staring up at the wood rafters above, trying to organize the chaos of feelings that were coursing through me. I was scared to go to sleep because I knew my father would be there and hated to be awake because I would still feel vacuous.

There was little information about the outside world here. There was no TV; there were no newspapers. I made two collect calls to Logan; they felt desperate and selfish on my part, an attempt to cling to someone who had moved on. I wrote to Shirley every week, but it was becoming increasingly hard to find things to write about besides the laundry.

Along with everything else, the gap between my jeans was closing in. I was down to one finger between my skin and my pants, and I dreaded getting dressed in the morning. Every time I tried to skip a meal, MK would find me, no matter where I hid. Even the outhouse.

There was no chance that it had only been eight minutes since I last looked at the clock. I stopped sorting the endless white socks in front of me and looked around the room to see too many unfamiliar faces.

Guests at Madonna House came and went. Some stayed a week, some a month. Two of the guests in the laundry today were particularly annoying. They had just gotten here in the last few days, and they both had constant grins on their faces. They were in Patricia's good graces, which I never was. Their upturned lips and peaceful eyes aggravated me. I kept my distance.

I moved toward the door, mumbling, "I have to go to the bathroom."

"Of course." Patricia moved closer to the door. "Teatime is in an hour."

"But I have to pee now." Of course, I had no intention of peeing. I was going to sit in the outhouse and have my rationed half a cigarette for the morning. Patricia slowly moved with her ironing board to the front of the door and continued to iron the flowered dress shirt like a benediction to forced obedience.

Bitch, I thought. I went back to the socks. There was a ringing in my ears from the silence, and the room lost a little of its focus. I took one sock with the mandated label inside: it said "Jeremy Davey." Instead of looking for the match, I looked for a woman's sock to match with it. I found Betsy's sock, put the two together, and threw the pair into the clean bin. Take *that*, Patricia. Exercising my power to . . . mismatch socks.

I knew three things to be true: these people were unbearable, the silence was maddening, and I had nowhere else to go.

I sat as close to the door as I could for teatime.

"With the gift of listening comes the gift of healing," Patricia said, leaning on the ledge in the laundry room while reading from the book by Catherine Doherty, the founder of Madonna House. "Our founder left us with so much. One day she told me that all I needed to do that day was to be grateful for tea, for every intricate sip, and to know how blessed we are to be alive."

"Now I really have to go to the bathroom," I said, and put on my borrowed boots and hat and opened the door to go to the outhouse.

I was accosted by the blowing wind coming off the lake. The cold late-autumn wind cut through my skin and chilled my organs. I practically ran to the outhouse, holding my coat with the broken zipper shut. I opened the door, which was immediately flung open by the wind, and went inside without bothering to close it. I lit my cigarette and sat on the cold toilet seat with my pants on.

The smoke felt comfortable. I watched it billow out and surround me before being swept out by the wind. I was losing feeling in my fingertips, but that didn't stop me from sucking on the cigarette until there was nothing left to inhale. I pulled my pack of Marlboro Lights out of my coat pocket and counted them. I only had six left. Six. I counted them again in hopes that they had duplicated in the past few seconds. Six. My throat tightened. I was only allowed to leave the compound for a half day each week. When I'd gone to town last week, the café had only two packs left, which of course I bought. My half day off wasn't for two more days. I made a mental note to steer clear of Wink, since he was constantly bumming smokes.

"Who's smoking in there?" I could hear MK's voice approaching.

"Me. Why? Is it a crime?" I stood and threw the butt into the disgusting pit below and walked out.

"That is not taking care of your temple," MK said, rubbing her hands together to create some warmth.

"Yeah, the your-body-is-your-temple thing isn't really up my alley. Gotta get back to sorting socks." I could feel her eyes on me as I started to walk in the direction of the laundry.

She called after me, "After lunch today, you and I are going shopping."

I turned and took a few steps toward her. "Really? Shopping? Are we going to bond?"

"Your pants are so tight, you look like the back of a horse," she replied, then turned, opened the outhouse door, and went in.

My legs began to twitch, and I froze in place. My hands shook as I put my fingers inside my size-two pants. One finger fit, but barely.

The secret was out: everyone knew how ugly my body was. Since the night I was raped, I had rules I followed to keep the secret; if I had a shape like a woman, I would be raped again. If I was hungry, I smoked. If I had to eat, I cut the food into tiny bites and ate only a few of them. I moved the food around a lot on my plate without taking a bite. I poured condiments onto the plate so it looked like a full plate of food. I knew how to have a Diet Coke and tell myself it was a meal. But Madonna House didn't have condiments or Diet Coke, and now I was fat, and MK and probably the rest of this godforsaken community knew it.

I heard Patricia's voice in the distance: "Back to the duty of the moment, please."

"Fuck this place," I said under my breath.

"You are what you eat," Wink said as he watched me play with the three bites of food on my plate during lunch.

"So, I'm *nothing*," I said without looking up.

"Come on, City, you need to put some meat on those bones. You can't survive a whole winter up here with that beanpole body of yours. Eat up."

My eyes went wide and darted to his. "All winter? Are you nuts? It's November. I'm out of here in, like, a week." My voice quivered, and the tears stung as they rolled down my cheeks.

Betsy piped in: "You know, your dad called twice this morning. Maybe talking to family would help."

I asked the community not to tell me when he called. I had been dreaming that he showed up when the whole community was in church and forced me to leave with him at gunpoint.

I looked down at my thunder thighs and let the tears, one after the next, soak into my jeans. I was grateful. Everyone at the table knew I was crying, but no one interrupted my pain or tried to make it better. They didn't need to fix it; they just allowed me to let it out, to feel the weight of my sadness. And I cried harder as they continued to talk.

After lunch, I followed MK out of the dining room, making sure to stay behind her so she couldn't see my body or my tear-streaked face.

"Where are we going?"

"You'll see. Hurry up."

She walked so damn fast that it was annoying, as was everything else she did. I stared at her hair and hoped it might spontaneously catch fire.

"Why are we going to the dorm?"

She didn't answer. She walked up the steps, opened the door, and kept her pace through the shoe room and into the bedroom. She took a hard left inside the door and walked past the wood-burning stove and to the wall on the far side. There was a door I had never noticed. She opened it and gestured for me to go first. I stood there, eyebrows raised, and mirrored her gesture. She sighed and walked forward, and I followed her through the doorway. My nose filled with mustiness. When I got to the top of the stairs, I looked around and saw boxes and boxes of clothes, all sorted by gender, article, and size. "Women, Long Pants, Size 10."

"What size are the pants you're wearing?"

"I don't know."

"You're lying."

"Two."

"Oh, sweetie, your body doesn't want to be a size two." She took two steps toward me, and I backed up. "I want you to look through these boxes and see if you can find something that fits." She started sliding boxes across the wood planks.

"Ah, here. Size six. That should work."

"Are you fucking kidding me?"

"Language."

I swallowed, trying to hold the tears back. I could feel my face turning red, and I felt the room closing in on me. I swallowed again. I could feel the tears making their appearance.

"I will not . . . ," I protested, and my voice shook. I looked at MK and the floodgates opened, tears pouring down my face in complete humiliation. "I can't." My clothes were suffocating my body; the taste of vomit was in the back of my throat.

She came closer, and this time I didn't back away.

"You can't keep this up. You're killing yourself one unfinished meal at a time."

I stared at her. She had noticed my attempt to retreat, to quietly disappear. She saw, and I was frightened by my failure. My eyes filled with tears, and I tried to blink them away, but they cascaded down my cheeks, falling to the floor past my shell of a body. I wiped my face with both sleeves, but the tears kept coming.

"I know. I know you feel like this is the way to keep people from seeing you, from getting close, but you'll see, trust me. Just try for one day: one day to eat all three meals and wear"—she looked around the room, found the "Women, Long Pants, Size 6" box again, took the top three pairs of pants out of the box, and walked over to me—"one of these."

She pulled my hands from my side and placed the pants in them. They weighed a thousand ugly pounds. I stood there quietly, beaten.

"Come on. Time to get back to our duty of the moment." MK turned and headed down the rickety steps, and I followed with the size-six pants folded in my arms.

I woke up before it was light out and snuck up the stairs to the room with the clothes. I just couldn't put size-six pants on my body. It was dark, but there was one window through which the predawn light was shining its rays. It was warmer up here, and I was tempted to just lie down and go back to sleep. No one would ever think to look for me up here. I regretted leaving my cigarettes under my pillow but made a mental note of my new smoke spot. I knelt down and tried to see the writing on the boxes.

"Dammit, I can't see a fucking thing in here."

I moved to the boxes by the window. "Women, Long-sleeved Shirts, Size XL." I nearly dropped it out of fear. Second box: "Women, Culottes, Size L."

Dear God, now I'm back with the Disciples of Light. Shit.

I remembered that MK said they didn't have size two, so I was desperately hoping that they did have size four. Another box. "Women, Skirts, Size 12."

Fuck.

"Women, Pajamas, XL."

"Women, Skirts, Size 10."

"Women, Short-Sleeved T-shirts, Size L."

I was beginning to lose hope. I quietly dragged the next box to the window so I could decipher the writing: "Women, Bathing Suits, Size XL."

Oh my God, bathing suits? I kept moving.

I dragged another box out: "Women, Long Pants, Size 6." I cursed that box and moved on.

And another: "Women, Long Pants, Size 4." *Bingo!*

I grabbed the top pair, ripped off my pajama pants, and slid the jeans over my ballooning body. One foot at a time. A secret prayer—or something that might resemble a prayer—slipped through my lips.

"Please fit. Please. I need at least two fingers."

I pulled them up my waist, gingerly zipped and buttoned them, and placed my fingers on my skin.

"One. Two. Three. OK, two. Maybe two and a quarter."

There was a certain celebration that I was back to two fingers, but I quickly reminded myself that this was a size four and there was absolutely nothing to celebrate. I would put myself on full food lockdown. Cigarettes only. No matter what and for as long as it took to get two fingers into my size-two jeans. I hated that MK was privy to my secret. I told myself that this was an all-or-nothing game and I was going to win.

I took four pairs of pants off the top of the size-four box. I couldn't have cared less what they looked like, what color they were, or what the brand was. All I cared about was that they were not a size six. I walked back down as quietly as the rickety stairs allowed, put the pants in the orange crate next to my bed, and climbed under the covers. I glanced over at MK's bed and smiled. I had won that round.

I turned over in bed and looked out the window. The sun was just rising. I stared at the pink and purple light bouncing off the trees. I couldn't see the sun, but I felt it. I felt the power of the day. I felt gratitude oozing from the fall landscape. I stared at the vibrant colors and was strangely grateful to be here. As my eyes began to close, I thanked whoever was in charge of all this beauty and my slight feeling of contentment.

When my eyes opened again an hour later, I pulled my clenched fists apart before I got out of bed. I didn't remember the specific nightmare, just the feeling of fear. I was sure it was one of the three consistent ones: I needed to move or else I'd be beaten—but I couldn't walk; my dad was coming toward my bed while I was sleeping; or I was falling from a very tall, nondescript building. I massaged my hands to wake them up. The air was getting noticeably chillier every morning. I thought about the winters up here: they must be miserable. I didn't want to find out.

CHAPTER 21

The next day was no different from the day before. Or the two months before that. My days consisted of shuffling silently from the dorm to the church for Vespers, to breakfast, then to the laundry, back to the main house for lunch, more laundry, back to church, dinner, dishes or veggies, teatime, and then bed. I was an angry, bitchy robot caught in the arms of a loving community.

I was four straight hours into ironing dress shirts in the middle of the silent room. There was a dual purpose here when you ironed. To save on electricity, dress shirts got only fifteen minutes in the dryer and then were handed to me to be fully dried and pressed.

I had to speak; it was so dark inside the quiet. It made me feel submissive, like my mother. I felt a rousing, angry roar making its home at the bottom of my voice box. I tried to stick two fingers between my size-four jeans and my skin to remind myself that I was still in charge, but they didn't fit; I was down to one finger between me and a complete meltdown.

I looked up and saw two young guests I had never bothered to meet, both in their twenties, peacefully folding underwear on the far side of the same counter. One had red hair in pigtails and jean overalls and looked like she was singing a happy tune inside her head; the other had short dark hair and a huge smile that showed too many teeth. I moved one step toward them, longing to break the silence.

I looked down at my shoes. The laces were untied and my feet were bouncing in rhythm—my heels coming off the ground a half inch, making my whole body go up and down—and my thighs were twitching. I was fidgeting now more than normal; I wanted to talk, and I needed the silence to end. *Say something.*

The two guests raised their heads at the same time and looked at me as I crept toward them, bouncing and shifting in my shoes. I shook my head and looked down. I tried to stop my body from moving up and down on its own.

The memories came flooding in. My dad coming toward me with his belt, and I flinched. My body felt wet from the bathtub my mother had abandoned me in. I touched my hair to see if I was underwater. Where was my mother? I could see Robert raping me as if I were watching from above. My dad killing my innocent Irish. I recognized the voice in my head but couldn't place it. The redhead was looking at me. "Whose voice is that?" I said out loud.

You are shattered, weak, unworthy. You will never be safe, never be loved. Oh my God, this was my internal voice—and it was center stage. That was me. *How old am I? Nine? Twelve? Fifteen?*

"Duty of the moment," I heard Patricia say from a distance.

"Duty of the moment?!" I said loudly. "No. I can't. Fuck this." I let my shoulders slump and clasped my hand over my mouth. I had said it out loud and with a spitting force.

I darted past the two peaceful guests and past Patricia, who was next to the cubbies, staring at me with her mouth wide-open. I stood on the landing, spit the breath out of my lungs, and coughed. I stretched my arms out to the side and shook them, trying to get out of my skin.

"Keep moving," I said out loud. "Keep moving."

I ran down the stairs and didn't stop until I got to the pay phone in front of the parking lot by St. Germain's. I picked up the receiver and dialed the number collect.

Logan accepted the charges. His voice was raspy, as if he were getting over a cold. I cannon-fire exhaled through my mouth when I heard it.

"I need to see you," I said.

I drove well over the speed limit with the window down and the radio volume up, attempting to calm myself with the noise.

I stole Betsy's light-blue Ford Taurus and left a note on her bed saying I'd try to find a way to get it back to her, knowing I wouldn't. It was the first time I was grateful we were only allotted two milk crates for all our stuff: the keys were in Betsy's top crate.

I would have loved to have seen MK's face when she realized I was gone. I wished I'd left a note for her too that said, "How do you like that duty of the moment?"

I had been on the road for close to six hours and was almost to the cabin in the Finger Lakes where Logan had told me to meet him. Since I'd moved to Madonna House, he had moved to New York City, so it was about the halfway point between us.

My elbow was on the center console, and I was obsessively twirling the hair behind my right ear. I moved my left heel up onto the cracked leather seat, but it didn't help with the fidgeting.

"New song," I said out loud as I gave my fingers something to do besides twirl my hair. I pushed the fluorescent scan button on the radio until I heard the applause blaring in my ear. Elton John and George Michael filled the car with "Don't Let the Sun Go Down on Me." I eased up on the gas and listened. I had heard this song so many times, but today the words were clear, and I listened with my whole heart.

Being away from Madonna House even just for these few hours was making me realize that the silence of being there had gotten in and changed me. Without the constant adrenaline rush I was living with in Omaha, my mind had cleared away some of the chaos that had made me such an emotional anarchist for so long.

My tears wet my cheeks, and I didn't try to stop them as they rolled into my mouth, questions about how I had let myself become so unraveled attached to each one. I couldn't figure out if I was happy, sad, or angry, but I was surprised to have found a glimmer of hope in the exploration. I was not the same person I had been in Omaha, and being at Madonna House had possibly saved my life.

I looked out the window and saw thousands of tree leaves surrounding my car, starting to say good-bye for the winter. The orange ones caught my eye: they had the most fire; they were the ones that still had the most to lose.

I pulled into a dirt driveway and saw Logan's black Bronco parked in front of a cozy wood cabin with a wraparound porch. It was barely four o'clock, and the sun was sparkling on the lake that the cabin was built on. The lake was long and skinny, with hills on both sides dense with colorful trees showing off their autumn brilliance.

I turned off the radio, parked the car next to Logan's, and stared out the window at the array of color. My heart raced, and I rubbed my hands together to move the moisture that was on my palms.

He walked through the screen door and toward the car. He had a black T-shirt tucked into his Levi's jeans, and he was barefoot. He quickened his pace and bit his lip as he came toward me, past the last of the autumn flowers that lined both sides of the walkway off the porch. I jumped out of the car, quickly slipping one finger between my jeans and my skin, silently hoping he wouldn't notice the weight gain, and shut the car door before moving to him.

"You," he said as he picked me up off the ground and held me chest to chest. I put all ten fingers in his hair and laughed out loud.

"You," I said.

"Can I kiss you?" His body tightened slightly and he squeezed me.

"You can kiss me," I said.

I could feel his body loosening at the seams with the permission granted. I became aware of how often he had to ask permission to come close to me, and the toll it had taken on him. His lips were soft and tentative.

I had placed so many rules between us in the past, as I was constantly looking for reasons not to accept his love.

"Come on," he said. He looked into my eyes, kissed me again on the lips, and took my hand in his. We walked hand in hand up the walkway and into the cabin.

I stopped just inside the door. There was a two-story river-rock mantel with a roaring fire in the fireplace and stacks of firewood on each side of the wood cutouts next to it. The color of the inside walls was the same stunning color as the inside of the island chapel, and I turned my attention to the large glass doors that opened onto the wraparound balcony in the back. It overlooked the stunning autumn trees and the reflecting water.

"You have no idea . . . ," he said, and bent to kiss me again. His lips were parted and wet, and I moved closer to him. It felt different with Logan now: a layer of protection had been removed. I leaned into him, melting into his safety and love.

"No, *you* have no idea . . . ," I said playfully. "Wait until you hear where I've been for close to three months."

He pulled me in for another kiss and said, "God, baby, I missed you."

"I've been living in one room with fifty women and two milk crates carrying everything I own."

Logan left my side and moved around the kitchen as I told him about MK and the nasty handkerchiefs in the laundry at Madonna House. He grabbed appetizers from the refrigerator and a bottle of wine with two glasses. "Oh my God, wine. That looks like pure gold." He poured us each a glass, and we clinked them together.

I leaned in for a kiss; it was different to be the initiator. I took a sip of the wine. The liquid stung the back of my throat; it had been a long time since my taste buds had been alive. "Wow, that tastes so good."

I sat on the stool at the counter as he laid out a beautiful spread: olives, salami, cheese, and crackers. I studied his face as I nibbled on the food.

"Look at my girl eating."

"Oh, yeah, right. Sorry."

"Sorry? Baby, I love seeing you eat, and you look healthier than I have ever seen you." For a moment, I felt genuinely proud of myself, and then I dropped the cracker back onto the plate.

"Isn't that just code for 'fat'?"

Logan moved around to my side of the counter and hugged me.

I was stiff again but kept the conversation going. "Tell me about your place in New York and the job and your mom. Everything." My tight posture felt ugly but familiar.

He didn't say anything in reaction to my rapid-fire questions in an attempt to change the subject. Instead he took my hand and led me down the hall to the bedroom. It was cozy, with another smaller fire warming the room. "Will you just lie with me for a bit?"

I walked over to his suitcase, which was open on the floor next to the bed, and picked out a white button-down with tiny blue stripes. I could feel his eyes on me. I wanted to undress in front of him, but I suddenly became self-conscious and walked into the bathroom and closed the door. As I undressed, I held his shirt to my face and breathed in his musky scent.

I came out of the bathroom wearing his shirt but realizing I really did just want to lie with him too. "Logan, I don't want to make love to you tonight." I couldn't believe I had said it. I could feel a smile on my face, and then I waited for the reaction, the anger or disappointment to come. I was scared and could feel myself bracing for an impact.

"OK." He smiled at me. "I'll grab the wine and we'll talk." That was it? I took three breaths in and let three breaths out while Logan went and gathered our wine from the kitchen.

We lay by the fire and talked late into the night and the next day. We left only to take a walk outside in the autumn beauty, holding hands and stealing kisses. I told him more about the silence at Madonna House, the stillness of the work, and the quirky people who were housed there. I told him about the beautiful chapel that didn't feel like a church and the simple tone my life had taken on. He told me about his move to the big city; his new job, which he loved; and the crazy neighbor who lived below him. We talked about his mom and how much she missed him and what it felt like to be one man in a sea of millions, trying to make his way.

We slept by the fire again the second night, and Logan held me so tight as he and I drifted into sleep. There was a stirring in my heart. And for the first time in a long time I wasn't afraid of my dreams. I woke before dawn and snuck out of our makeshift bed, grabbed a blanket, and went down to the water. It was chilly and calm. The water seemed to sleep at my feet, and I tried to enjoy the moment, but I began to nag at myself about the situation I was creating. Who was I kidding, sitting there, taking Logan's love and pretending with my sweet words to know what love was?

For so long I was unconsciously trying to kill myself, and I was free to do that because I had pushed away the people who I thought might stop me, and the ones I surrounded myself with wouldn't care if I succeeded.

I put my feet in the freezing water up to my knees.

I had looked my father in the eye when he hit me. I had tried to plead with him that I was just a little girl, but the hits just got harder. My legs felt numb from the water as I stepped in deeper.

Logan had walked up behind me. "What are you doing?"

I paused and took in a whole breath of the crisp air.

"I have spent almost three months being silent up there. Partly because I had to get away from Brock, but partly because I thought I might figure out who I was—or who I wanted to be." I wrapped my arms around my chest and stared out into the lake. "All I've learned is I'm a fraud, Logan. I'm a nobody."

"Let's go inside and talk. Get out of the water, Kathleen. Come on, you've got to be freezing to death." He motioned toward the house as I turned to face him, my legs turning a pale blue in the water beneath me. I shook my head, first slowly and then faster as I threw my head back and yelled at the sky.

"Don't you get it?!" I slumped forward and splashed the water in front of me. My voice echoed off the lake, and when it was quiet again, I looked up into Logan's stunned eyes. "I'm already dead . . ."

I shrugged my shoulders, tears welling up in my eyes.

"I can't do this again," he said, and turned and walked inside.

"I know," I said to myself.

CHAPTER 22

The window on the driver's side had been down for hours, and the wind was slapping my hair into my face, reminding me that I was still alive and not dead, like I felt. I pulled the black hair tie off my wrist, scooped my hair on top of my head, and wrapped it up. I wiped the tears from my cheeks with both hands and felt the heat from the sun settling on my face through the windshield.

I turned left into the Madonna House parking lot and parked Betsy's car in the farthest spot from the main house. I know I didn't fit here any better than I did with Logan. I wasn't worthy or holy. But I didn't fit anywhere else either, and I had a bed here, so I had come back.

It was five thirty, which meant the community was in the island chapel for daily mass. I had half an hour. If I walked away now, no one would know I had returned. I could leave the car and hitchhike somewhere. My hand shook as I lit a cigarette. My lungs ached from the smoke, and the only thing I could taste was heat. I threw the cigarette on the ground and crushed it with my left foot as I stepped out of the car.

I walked in the direction of the main house, with no intention of going in. I read the sign above the door: "I Am Third." I had learned what the phrase meant: "God is first, my neighbor is second, and I am third."

I walked under the sign and into the basement, threw my shoes into an empty cubby, and walked up the stairs without a plan. My feet were so heavy. I turned around at the top and looked down the staircase, still holding on to the railing. I could still turn around. I could still sneak away. I tried to bring the music I had been blaring in the car back into my head so the silence wouldn't be so loud, but I couldn't remember one song I had heard in the last several hours of driving—not one. All I could hear was my heart beating in my ears. A massive *thump . . . thump . . . thump . . .*

I turned back around and stared at the long empty room with the tables dressed in their uniforms that never changed. I had never been alone in a room here. I wanted to grab the mismatched teacups and pathetically old salt and pepper shakers and throw them to create some noise.

"Well, well . . ."

My head jerked, and I gripped the wood floor with my toes. I didn't need to turn around to see the smile on MK's face behind me. She had such a beautiful voice, but I didn't want to give her the satisfaction of eye contact.

"Hey," I said.

"Why are you back? To return the car? You're lucky Betsy hasn't pressed charges." As usual, her tone went up at the end of the sentence, which further infuriated me.

"Why aren't *you* in the chapel?"

She took the six steps to stand directly in front of me, and I felt the wind on my back from her brisk walk. I wished we were the same height: I didn't like that I had to look up at her. Her neck looked as if she couldn't turn her head from side to side, and her bun was as pissed off as ever.

I smiled without parting my lips, stood as straight as I could, and kept my eyes on her bad Christmas sweater. The sweater was green, red, and black, with snowflakes and Christmas trees wrapping around her body.

"It's October, MK," I said, pushing my shoulders back and moving my gaze to her eyes.

"You can't stay here," she said, without acknowledging my comment.

"That isn't up to you," I replied, clenching my jaw.

"You aren't ready; you need to leave. Come back when you can face yourself."

I put one hand on my hip and stared at her.

"I am not your enemy. You need to look in the mirror, little girl. I know you're scared. You can barely breathe. You're pure fear inside that shell. You don't eat, cigarettes are your lifeline, and you have been trying to kill yourself in all the socially acceptable ways for years. But until you break it all down, until you itemize your life with all its pain, you will always just be running from yourself. *You* are your enemy, not me," she said, her eyes matching mine in their fire.

My body started rocking in place, my shoulders curled, and my arms fell heavily at my sides. I stared at her eyes, not able to focus on the deep-brown color but instead watching the roaring fire inside them. The flecks of orange danced with a recognizable darkness.

"You . . . don't . . . know . . . me . . . ," I whispered and looked at the floor, tears streaming down my cheeks.

She put both hands on my shoulders and leaned into me. "Maybe not, but I know me," she said, "and you look an awful lot like me when I got here."

She took her hands off my shoulders, and I caught myself as I fell forward.

"If you want to stay here, you will do your duty of the moment without complaint; pick a priest to be your spiritual director and see him every week; be silent; and live the life of poverty, chastity, and obedience. The decision is yours."

I wanted to keep talking, arguing—anything to keep our voices filling the space—but when I opened my mouth to reply, she had already turned the corner into the kitchen.

My skin was hot and prickly, but my fingers and toes felt like ice cubes. I walked the three steps into the library and sat on the wooden bench in the corner. I pulled my knees as tightly as I could into my chest and circled them with my arms. I could hear footsteps downstairs: the community was on its way in for dinner. I put my hands over my ears and firmly planted my head between my legs, hoping for more time.

"Breathe." I heard myself say it as an echo. I said it again to make sure it was me saying it: "Breathe." The sound was muffled, and I pushed my palms harder on my ears, then softer, then harder again, finding a cadence for the word, reminding myself that I wanted to be alive. I had come back. I was back.

I was light-headed from inhaling my own breath, so I lifted my head to get some fresh oxygen while repeating the only word I knew: *"Breathe."*

My legs hit the floor when I noticed that Wink had come to sit next to me. He was relaxing on the bench, legs outstretched. He had his green button-down shirt on, rolled up to his elbows on both arms, and he smelled like hotel soap.

"My God," I said, "you scared me."

He leaned forward. "Oh, I thought MK had already taken care of that," he said, putting his elbows on his knees and looking me in the eye. "That was a boneheaded move," he added, smiling as if he knew the answer to a riddle no one else knew the answer to. "Make it right and stay here and do your work." He paused only for a moment. "Come on, we're going to dinner." He took my hand and gently guided me to the third table on the right side of the dining room. I sat next to him on the bench, looking at the last few community dwellers coming up the stairs for dinner.

"Wait," I said, "I'm not sitting at this table. I've never sat with her before."

"Nope, stay here," Wink said as he put his hand on my shoulder.

"Wink, no, not this table, and of all nights, not tonight." I moved one leg around the bench to stand up, and as I did, I took both hands and swiped the fresh tears on my already watery face.

"City, stay," he said.

Marion walked into the dining room dressed in khaki pants and a black turtleneck that made her eyes look like blue sapphires. She always sat in the same seat at the same table, and I was in the seat next to hers. She sat down, did the blessing for the meal, and then turned her gaze to me.

"You came back? Why?"

"I don't know."

I felt her complete presence, as if she were roaming around inside me.

"What does your heart say?"

"I want to find a home." My palms were sweaty, and I wasn't sure where the words had come from.

"You want to find yourself—who you are without the fear."

I looked in her eyes, and I could feel something, a lightness. I felt hope.

"That is all any of us want. To know who we are and to act without fear. Come with me after dinner. It's time for *poustinia*."

"What is that?"

"It's the Russian word for desert."

My body fell slightly forward when she broke her gaze with me and turned her attention to the meal. Wink put a spoonful of beets and a larger spoonful of lentils on my plate and then passed me the basket with the brown bread in it. To my surprise, I took a piece and slowly scooped bites of the lentils and the beets into my mouth until the plate was empty.

After the meal, I followed Marion through the kitchen, grabbed a community coat off the hook, and headed out the back door. It was cold, and my belly had a very foreign feeling of fullness. I chastised myself for eating and recommitted to starving myself tomorrow.

Marion led me to a tiny cabin that stood near the main house, surrounded by other buildings. She walked up the two steps, opened the door, and gestured for me to follow. There was a tiny bed, a desk, and a wood-burning stove, with a pile of logs neatly stacked along the wall. One shelf had a pitcher and a glass on it. It was crowded with the two of us in it.

"Here is your *poustinia*, your desert. Be alone with God. I will pick you up for Vespers in the morning." There was warmth in her words, a kindness, an empathy. Normally *poustinia* was twenty-four hours long; clearly she didn't think I would make it out alive if I had to do the full time. The only food was brown bread and water, and there was nothing to distract you—nothing but a Bible.

"Thank you," I said, but she was already walking back toward the main house.

I lit a cigarette and smoked it to the filter. I hated being alone, but I felt some peace in the fact that I was just steps from the main house and the surrounding buildings where others would be sleeping. I stoked the fire, walked the three steps to the bed, covered myself up, and fell into a fitful sleep.

CHAPTER 23

I was grateful to have slept. I woke the usual way, my body twitching and my fists clenched. The nightmare of my father coming toward me while I was sleeping was winding around in my brain.

"You're OK," I told myself. I was always embarrassed that I talked to myself, but hearing the words out loud was much more effective in calming myself down than keeping them bottled up. It was a reminder to myself that he wasn't in the room; he was thousands of miles away.

I rolled onto my right side—almost falling off the bed—sat up, and put my feet on the cold wooden floor. Out of the ether, the memory of my father's voice echoed: *Feet on the floor!*

Ugh, will that ever go away?

It was freezing in the tiny cabin, because I hadn't gotten up to stoke the fire in the night and it was completely out. I cupped my hands and blew into them. There was a knock on the door, and I opened it to find Marion standing on the porch, bundled up in a down coat.

"Good morning. May I?"

"Of course," I said. I stepped aside to let Marion in, and she made her way to the bed and sat down.

Her short white hair was combed to the side today, which made her blue eyes stand out even more. She asked, "What are your thoughts this morning?"

I knew what she meant, but I had nothing to say. "Thoughts?"

She nodded and waited. I tried matching her stare and waiting for her to speak, but it was as if her silence were pulling words out of me.

"I don't know why I'm here. I just know that I'm angry and I'm scared. Petrified, really. I'm losing control."

"Are you sure you haven't already lost control and you're trying to get some semblance of control back?"

I wasn't using my usual defense tactics.

"Give in, look at the pain you're in, and ask what you're supposed to learn from it. Live in the questions for a time. Don't look for the answers right now."

My muscles relaxed just the slightest bit on hearing her words. I was suddenly aware that I was tired to my core. I was tired of trying to be OK. Tired of faking it. Tired of keeping up my tough exterior while my insides were shattered.

"Stop running from yourself. Take the time you need to learn who you are. Embrace the silence, the stillness. You are here for a reason."

It was useless to fight against her words. I was fragile to my core. I stepped back to lean on the wall, and the icy coldness of the wood soaked into my back. But I wasn't cold. I was waking up.

Marion and I walked to the beautiful church in the woods in silence. I sat on the wooden floor and listened to the melodic voices all around me singing in Latin to a God I had hid from for so long.

At breakfast, I allowed myself a few bites of brown bread and jam before I measured the space between my pants and my skin. In the past, my rule was to check first so I could limit how much I was allowed to eat, but today felt different in every way. The time was just passing. The world felt still.

I put my fingers between my size-four pants and my skin; there was only room for one finger. I swore that there had been room for two just yesterday. I checked again. One finger. I could feel the panic, the loss of control, and I cursed the jam that I could still taste on my tongue.

"Not hungry this morning?"

I looked up to see the man who was serving our table. I had noticed him before—he was the one with the loud laugh—but I had never talked to him.

"I'm not feeling well," I lied.

"Never stops me from filling my belly. Pass me the rhubarb? I'm Father Jim, by the way."

"You're a priest?"

He didn't look like a priest, and he didn't dress like one either. He was wearing jeans and a blue flannel shirt that complemented his light eyes.

"In the flesh."

As breakfast was wrapping up, I turned to Father Jim and asked, "Are you a spiritual director? MK says I have to have one if I want to stay."

"I am. There are a bunch of us here," he said. "You need to pick someone that you feel is right for you. It's more of a feeling than anything else."

"Can I tell MK that you're mine so I can get her off my back?"

"Sure, you can tell MK that I'm yours," he said.

"Oh, I mean . . . Sorry."

"No need to be sorry. No better time than the present. Let's take some time right now; there are plenty of people to help with the dishes. I'll go tell MK, and I'll meet you outside at the picnic table."

"It's pretty chilly out there," I said.

"Chilly? Wait a month: we'll have six feet of snow around here. We're havin' a mild fall."

I made my way outside, lit a cigarette, and wondered what the hell I had just gotten myself into. Father Jim joined me a few minutes later and sat across from me on the picnic table, his black hair blowing in the wind.

"I like to start with confession, but what did you have in mind?"

"I don't have anything in mind," I said, shifting my legs under the table. "But I would rather not start there; that feels like a million miles from anywhere I want to go."

I pulled out my cigarettes and offered him one, but he declined. I was glad. I lit another and left the pack on the table between us, opening and closing the top of it as we talked.

"How's your stay been so far?"

"OK," I said.

"What does 'OK' mean?" he asked, and leaned in closer. I looked at his eyes, and he looked at my mouth.

"I am figuring some things out here, and sometimes it's hard for me to say what I'm thinking because I can't really hear myself very well yet."

Father Jim asked, "What do you want to get from spiritual direction?"

"Um, I don't know. I didn't plan on any of this, so I don't know what to expect," I said.

He asked about my childhood and I told him it was fine—normal, really. I talked about the ocean, my beautiful house, and Shirley. It was easier not to dive too deep.

I changed topics as soon as I could and asked about his life. His story was simple, like a song I knew all the words to: grew up in Michigan, one of a whole bunch of kids, etc.

I just needed to keep the focus on him. "How did you get to Madonna House?"

"I was here for seventeen years as a staff member before I became a priest. I always figured I was too sinful to be a priest, but it turns out priests are sinners too."

He talked for the better part of an hour, and we made a plan to meet at the same time the next week.

CHAPTER 24

The days blurred into a month. Another breakfast was finally over. I had eaten again, so I was in a bad mood, same as the day before. I would feel proud of myself for eating and then immediately beat myself up and recommit to not eating. The next day the cycle would start over again.

I got up to go to the laundry, not bothering to check the chore list. When I got to the front of the dining room, Jeremy was staring at me and smiling. I smiled back, staring at his chipmunk cheeks, in which it looked as if he had stuffed part of his breakfast for later.

"What are you up to?" I asked. The color in his eyes looked welcoming, and he licked his bottom lip.

"Well, unless you think someone is playing a rotten joke on you, you're going to the farm. That's right: says so right bloody here," he said, pointing to the guest list. I leaned forward and put my hands on either side of the chore list that was pinned to the wall, in search of a capital *F*—and there it was. A beauty of a letter, infinitely better than the letter that would remain nameless for fear of its reappearance.

I was in the fourth row of the van with Jeremy and two new guests from Colombia, Claudia and Silvi.

"No need to be crowded back there. Kathleen, come sit up here with me," said MK, the wrinkles around her brown eyes softening in a smile as she pointed to the passenger's seat and stared at me in the rearview mirror.

"I'm good—thanks, though."

"Come on up."

Jeremy tapped my leg. I shot him a dirty look and moved over the multiple pairs of legs and supplies to get to the front.

"Seat belt, please," she said nonchalantly, while hers remained at her side, unbuckled.

MK was busy explaining my new job working with her in the farm kitchen. The farm was five miles up the winding road. A handful of the men from the community lived up there full-time to take care of the animals, so we'd be cooking dinner for them and lunch for the sixty or so helpers that came up to harvest and can the fruits and vegetables every day.

"It would be great if we could grow bananas here; I have some great recipes. Have I told you how many different varieties of bananas there are in Liberia?"

I turned my head and stared out the window. I realized how beautiful it was here. The trees had all but lost their leaves, but a few colors clung on. The evergreens were a lush green and surrounded the road to the farm on both sides. It was a gorgeous day, chilly but sunny, which gave it a lighter feel. None of the long-timers could believe we weren't buried in snow; they said this was the warmest winter they could remember.

We hopped out of the van, and MK assigned the three vans of people to their tasks for the day as I stood watching the sheep in the pasture.

"Let's get a move on . . . Take this list and that wheelbarrow"—she looked at me and then pointed to the first wheelbarrow ever created, sitting like an ancient artifact by the front door—"and head to the root cellar and collect what's on the list. Don't dally." She turned and walked toward the farmhouse.

"What's a root cellar?"

"Oh dear . . . over there, before you get to the slaughterhouse, on the left." MK pointed and then opened the farmhouse door and walked in.

I found the slaughterhouse first, with three dead cows strung up on rope inside of it. I ran out the door and swore off meat. A few feet away, I found a small wooden door lying almost in the ground with grass and big rocks around it.

I had the sensation of opening a grave as I pulled on the heavy wooden handle of the root cellar door. I stood carefully to the side in case it had a will of its own and decided to slam shut. Peeking into the darkness, all I could see were stairs that looked like they led to the abyss.

"No way . . . I am not going in there." I let the open door drop flat on the ground, and sat on a tree stump to the side of the root cellar.

"Have you lost the plot?" I jumped when I heard Jeremy's voice. I thought it came from the root cellar. "She'll kick you outta here, you know. Get down there and get the lot for lunch before she sees you." He touched my shoulders and kept moving. "There's a flashlight on the first step."

I stood up and moved a little closer to peer in. I walked to the top step, quickly grabbed the flashlight, and stepped back by the door. I shone it down the stairs and said, "Why can't they be normal people and have refrigeration? I mean, it is almost the twenty-first century, for God's sake . . . Great, I'm talking to myself again."

As I tentatively walked down the steps, I shone the flashlight to the left. There were huge bins lined up one after the other, built into the dirt and filled with vegetables. Beautiful, colorful vegetables, unlike any in the grocery stores. They were rawer, more gorgeous, still covered with dirt and grass. The colors were more vibrant. The purple eggplants were rich, like royalty, and the onions looked like gemstones. The root cellar was half a football field long—it just kept going and going—and I was awestruck by both its contents and its function. I touched the bright orange carrots, and they were cold, colder than a refrigerator would keep them. There were shelves all along the right side of the cellar, well stocked with other supplies.

I grabbed one of the straw baskets from under the shelves and pulled the list from my pocket. I carried three baskets of beets, parsnips, carrots, sweet corn, and melon up the stairs. The ancient wheelbarrow had turned into a chariot for the produce. There was only one thing left on the list: lard. I had never heard of a vegetable called lard. The bins were meticulously labeled, and I looked at every one, but no lard. As I was making my last trip up the steps, I saw a painter's bucket by the door. "LARD," it said in big bold letters. On top of the bucket, there was an old metal chisel with a flat head on the end sitting next to a handmade hammer.

I walked over and stared at the sign. *Is this . . .* lard *lard? Like* animal fat *lard?*

After several attempts at opening the bucket with the chisel, the lid flew off and landed in the onion bin. There was a hard, white, greasy substance inside the bucket, and I screamed, *"Oh my God, is this what I've been eating?"* I chiseled a sliver off the top, plopped it in a bowl that was next to the bin, and left the lid open, hoping it would go bad. I closed up the root cellar and headed for the farmhouse.

"You smell like smoke," MK said, fanning the flames in the wood-stove that we would be cooking on. "I won't say it again: no smoking during work hours."

The kitchen was a good size, with a large pantry. All the ingredients were in matching glass containers with lids and their contents printed in bold. There was a farm sink large enough for me to sit in and a big wooden table in the middle for preparing. The stove was a hundred years old and black as night, with hefty silver handles. There was a neatly stacked pile of firewood next to the stove, and pots of every shape and size hung above the table. I thought of Shirley and how much she would love this orderly kitchen.

"We cook on that?" I asked.

"We work in silence; only necessary words, please," MK said. She looked at the beets and nodded in the direction of the cutting boards.

"Oh my God, there's a bathroom in here? No outhouse? Whoop. Whoop."

"We work in silence," she said again. She was flying from the pantry to the table in the middle of the kitchen and back again, whipping out ingredients and mixing them with cheese curds. I walked into the bathroom with awe.

"Shit," I whispered when I saw the scale next to the sink.

"KATHLEEN!"

"Sorry, OK, got it. Working, see . . ." I walked out of the bathroom and grabbed a knife to start cutting.

My fingers were raw by lunch. I chopped onions, carrots, and beets for hours in complete silence. My head hurt from thinking, and several very bad memories made an unwelcome appearance. I tried counting my breaths to get more comfortable with the silence, which was a complete joke. I was still so afraid, but I was trying to live with the questions, as Marion had suggested. But really, I just wanted the answers.

Finally, it was time to set the table for lunch. There was a long dining room off the kitchen, with one extremely long table and benches tucked underneath. It looked like it could fit about thirty people. A large greenhouse was attached to the dining room, and I peeked my head in. Green, gold, purple, red, yellow, and orange—the colors were brilliant and coming from every direction, including the ceiling. It smelled delicious. I quickly closed the door before MK could see that

I was off task. She walked into the dining room and said, "Outside," then walked back into the kitchen.

I walked outside and saw Jeremy, Wink, and another man setting a table down on the grass. Five others were already there. Jeremy raised his head in greeting, so I stuck my tongue out at him and smiled. "I guess we're eating out here," I said, and started to head back inside to get what I needed. I thought it was damn near freezing outside, but apparently I was the only one.

"Tell MK Father Jim is here," Jeremy said.

"Got it."

As I walked around the tables, I listened to my breath. I felt the air hitting my cheeks, and I tried to identify the different smells: clean dirt and the perfume of a harvest. Steam was coming out of one of the buildings close to the tables, and it smelled like a candy factory. I could see Claudia and Silvi through the window, stirring a pot that was bigger than the two of them, giggling and tripping over each other. I thought about going to check it out, but then I glanced at the farmhouse and knew I should keep walking.

I guessed that Father Jim was the youngest priest at Madonna House. He said he was going to celebrate the mass outside, which was a very rare treat. The only time I had ever been to mass outside was when Archbishop Raya once said mass on the beach in Spring Lake, which was a real no-no, but he did it anyway. He said God didn't care where you worshipped Him.

It was nice to be surrounded by nature while I watched people pray at mass. Father Jim had a casual way about him. He was standing at the head of the table outside, and he picked up the Bible that was lying on the gold-and-white cloth. I stared at him as he read the Gospel according to Luke.

I had heard the parable a hundred times in my youth, but there was something different about the cadence of his voice. It struck me that he was really reading it as a story. He was reading the part where the son comes back to his father's home from a trip of sin and debauchery. He stopped reading, came around the table, and walked slowly up and down the length of it. He was white-knuckling the Bible, and his eyes were welling up with tears. I held my breath, having never seen a priest have emotion except to chastise sinners.

"I am the prodigal son. I cannot preach to you pretending that you are the sinners. I am a sinner. I have left my God; I have hurt others. I have wandered so far from my path and always—always—you, my family, and my God have welcomed me back with celebration." He walked back to the front of the makeshift altar, turned toward the community, and began the Apostles' Creed. The community, except for me, stood and said the words along with him.

Lunch was actually delicious, and I let myself eat until I was almost full.

I sat with Claudia and Silvi, and they told funny stories about making the jam that morning. They were welcome company. Father Jim was close by, and he asked the girls where in Colombia they were from. Then, without waiting for an answer, he started telling a story about when he was in Colombia in his twenties and how freely people did drugs there, himself included.

Father Jim and I had our weekly spiritual direction session after lunch. It was the usual: I asked questions; he went off on tangents. There were some things that I wanted to share about my past, but I couldn't find the words, so I tried to soak in the nature around me and let it inspire stillness. I wanted to tell him that I wasn't as angry as I used to be but that the restlessness was still a dark cloud over me. By the time the hour was up, I was annoyed by how much he talked, even though I was filling the time with questions. When we got up to leave, I promised myself I would try to open up more next time.

MK broke her own silence when I walked into the kitchen. "It's OK to change spiritual directors."

"No, he's fine."

The afternoon was mentally exhausting. My head was pounding from the negative thoughts that were running amuck in my brain. MK was mad because I broke a large glass bowl that was full of the beets I had just spent an hour cutting, and we had to throw the food away.

"Glass bowls and beets are gifts; please be more careful," MK said. I followed that up by breaking another glass bowl, empty this time. I saw it falling off the wooden table in slow motion, heard the sound of the glass shattering into pieces on the floor.

My life was that bowl falling in slow motion, fracturing. MK didn't say a word; she just handed me the broom.

I was left with nothing but inner voices of complete unworthiness. I was utterly alone, and I was scared. There wasn't an ounce of adrenaline involved in cutting vegetables, so there was nowhere else for my thoughts to turn other than the void, the blackness. There was no one waiting for me, no one wondering how I was doing. I officially belonged nowhere; I was nothing. I cried into the third glass bowl that I needed to fill, surrounded by more silence. I was grateful for MK's presence, even though she was silent. At least she was there in case I really did break.

I made four trips to the bathroom to try to get the guts to stand on the scale, but I couldn't do it.

When we got into the van to drive back to the main house, I voluntarily took the passenger's seat because I figured MK would make me sit there anyway. I watched the world go by outside the window as MK slowly drove the five miles back home. MK and the structure of Madonna House were predictable. I sunk deeper into my seat.

I was grateful for the slow movement; some of the trees looked as if they were singing as they moved in the wind. I could see the tiniest of changes around me. I glanced at MK. It was interesting that, everywhere she walked, it was as if she were chasing a bad guy; but when she drove, she was a ninety-year-old woman enjoying the scenery. She had her seat belt off and was resting her right hand leisurely on the steering wheel. Her left arm leaned against the window, with her palm on her bun. I wondered if she was thinking of Liberia.

CHAPTER 25

Winter, 1994

We were down to just eight of us in the guest dorm, including MK; apparently, all the smart ones had left. I didn't know that this level of cold could exist in the world. It was late February, and the windchill coming off the lake felt like shards of glass cutting my face as I walked to the main house. The snow was piled so high on either side of the walkways that we had to make our way single file through the pathways from one building to the next, following whatever puffy coat was in front of us. If someone had taken a picture from a helicopter above us, we would have looked like a white-ant colony without a roof.

I wasn't enjoying Wednesdays as much I had the first few months. Wednesday meant the afternoon off, and lately I didn't know what to do with my four hours of freedom. It was unnerving to be in charge of my own decisions; I'd gotten used to the boundaries of community living. I had learned to trust these people and the consistency of their days. I had enjoyed the last few months working at the farm. I had become well versed in the art of sorting beans, making large vats of jam, canning all kinds of different things, chopping veggies, sorting through the root cellar, and keeping that awful stove at a consistent temperature. I wouldn't go so far as to say I liked it, but there was a calmness that I'd never experienced before.

I was also off-kilter because it was my weekly night at the *poustinia*. The stays at the *poustinia* had gotten a little more intense. I would try to sleep the time away, but that didn't work every time. I smuggled books and such in with me, but there was something about just being with myself for that long that really made me uncomfortable. I would spend hours looking out the window, watching people go by and making up stories about their lives. It reminded me of when I sat under the boardwalk wishing the people above would take me home with them.

MK often took her *poustinia* on the same day, in another of the cabins, and when she did, I could skip mine—and she'd have no idea. She hadn't caught on to that trick yet, and I was hoping she wouldn't tonight.

I only had an hour before dinner, and I was on a mission to find someone to drive me into town so I wouldn't have to deep-freeze my body like I had last week when I had walked the half mile or so to town for a carton of cigarettes—only to find that the shipment of cigarettes hadn't come in yet. It was a very depressing walk back.

I was smoking less now because I had to ration my cigarettes and because I had to smoke outside, which was miserable. My fingers would freeze in an instant. Smoking less meant eating more, and it was becoming a dire problem. Last week, I'd had to sneak up the rickety steps and trade my size-four pants for the wretched size sixes.

I walked into the basement of the main house and bumped into Wink.

"How goes it, City?"

Shit, he's going to ask for a cigarette, I thought, but I said, "Hi, Wink." I tried to move quickly around him, but he kept pace with me. I got to my boot cubby, took off my boots, and pretended that he wasn't there.

"I've got a trade for ya. One cigarette for this here thick envelope that just came in the mail."

I looked up to see him holding a manila envelope addressed to me. "What?"

"Can't say I never gave ya nothin'." He spun around on his socks and then held out the envelope.

I saw my father's handwriting. My body stiffened, and I could hear my heartbeat racing in my ears. I could feel him in the basement, and my eyes darted around the room for an escape in case he materialized.

"You look like ya seen a ghost. You OK?"

"I'm OK. I'm OK . . . here." I handed him my pack of cigarettes without thinking and grabbed the envelope out of his hands. I held it away from my body and stared at it. *What does he want from me? Why would he be contacting me?* I was twelve again in an instant. Afraid. My body was weak, and I needed to sit down. I was murmuring, "I'm OK, I'm OK . . ." under my breath.

"Come on, let's get you a seat," Wink said, taking me by the arm and walking me upstairs to the little library. I didn't want to open the envelope, but worse than not opening it was not knowing what was in it.

I opened the envelope and looked inside before I put my hand in it. I grabbed the piece of paper first. It read, "You will be coming home on March 30th. See you then." There was a plane ticket and a hundred-dollar bill in the envelope.

There wasn't a decision. I had to go back there—he said so. My time of pretending that I was anything other than his daughter was over.

MK walked into the little library and came and sat next to me. Wink was holding the envelope now because I had dropped it on the ground.

"What's going on here?"

"Someone got a package she didn't like," Wink said as he gestured to the envelope in his hand.

Their voices sounded so far away, and when MK touched my shoulder, I jumped to my feet.

"I'm OK . . ."

MK stood as well. "You're not OK. What's going on?"

"I have to leave March thirtieth," I said.

"Says who?" MK gestured to Wink to give her the envelope.

My body felt heavy. "He does," I said, pointing to the envelope.

MK sat with me in silence until it was time for dinner. She walked me to the dining room and sat me at Marion's table. I didn't fight her and sat silently, watching the community filter in.

Marion came out of the kitchen dressed in a red sweater and black pants and walked to our table—*her* table. She looked like she had seen a ghost and beat the shit out of it. She was pale, with red blotches on her face and neck, and both of her hands were so tightly balled into fists that I could see the whites of her knuckles. Her signature quiet glide across the floor had been traded for an angry pounding of determined steps. She passed behind me and took her usual seat at the head of the table across from Jeremy, who had just returned from the kitchen with our food. Marion's eyes were glued to the air six inches above her. Her eyelashes stuck to the skin above her eyes, and her mouth was set between a straight line and a frown.

The silence had a foul scent. The air was thick and wet; it made my nose crinkle and my eyes burn. I looked around the room, and it was as if she had petrified it. Jeremy was holding a bowl of beets in the air with one hand while his other was frozen in the act of pulling the chair out. Laura held a pitcher of water suspended two inches above a glass. Wink had a straight back, legs casually stretched in front of him, with one hand reaching across the table for the tea and the other on his knee. And Betsy, who was straight across from me, had her mouth open as if she were about to say something.

Marion put both of her fists on the table. Her white hair was prickly and standing on end as if she had just pulled her finger out of a socket. But she was staring far away from here. Her red sweater was disheveled, and the white turtleneck under it was tight against her neck, standing at attention. She stood up, and the dining room shook. I heard a glass break somewhere in the distance, but I couldn't take my eyes off Marion.

"I HATE YOU, GOD!" she screamed. Her arms were extended in front of her, one held higher than the other, like a boxer in a ring, and the red blotches on her face were spreading. "In twenty-three years, I have asked You for exactly one thing—ONE! I had a plan for my life, and I gave that up because YOU asked me to. One thing I asked You for, ONE THING: to protect him." Her voice ricocheted off the walls. "To protect him." Her head was raised to the heavens, and I could see embers of hatred fanning the fire in her eyes.

She looked up and her fists followed. "Do You hear me?" I couldn't take a breath; there was no oxygen in the room. She willed the sun behind a cloud, and the light in the room darkened. "Did You bother to whisper in his ear when he was buying the gun? Were You AT LEAST with him when he pulled the trigger and bled to death in his apartment? Alone. You didn't stop him. You weren't even there, were You?" Her voice was shrill and her eyes were shattered. "You broke our promise, and I WILL NOT forgive You." She shifted her weight to the right side of her body, put one hand on the table, and looked down.

"You abandoned me. How can You call Yourself a merciful god when You stood by and watched Brad in so much pain that suicide was the only answer? Where is Your end of our bargain? I kept mine: I have been living my promise every day. In every duty of the moment that You asked of me, I gave my yes. 'God's will'—HA! All these years, I have surrendered to that notion, and now I am a pawn in Your big lie."

I tried to stuff my head into my shoulders, waiting for the impact. I stared at her, and I felt . . . power. Red-hot holy power. She was dancing with the divine, and she looked unafraid. She was upright, with her chest thrust out and her legs firmly rooted on the floor. She wasn't bracing for impact: she was delivering it.

Anger would normally get me moving, set me off on a plan of attack, but Marion's anger was drawing me in. It was taking hold from the inside and organizing this particular emotion in a different way. Her anger felt useful. My dad was the only person who was "allowed" to be angry in my old home; seeing a woman I trusted get angry shifted the world on its axis.

I was light-headed and dizzy, and I wanted to tell her she was right, she should want to abandon God and the rest of us should go along with her. I took a long, purposeful, deep breath, and I liked the feel of her anger in my body . . . I could feel it wandering around, hot lava gushing through the sadness and fear in my soul and melting everything in its path. God wasn't striking her down—my childhood God would have, but her God must be bigger, stronger, able to take the emotion. I breathed in again, and the fire settled on my tongue with a strange whisper of hope.

She went on: "I don't hear You; I don't feel You. Have I ever felt You? When did You abandon me and my brother? Have I been planting Your voice inside my soul all these years, telling myself what I wanted to hear instead of knowing the reality that I am really just alone? You walked away years ago—if You were ever even here." She was ferocious. Her words were hitting the air hard in a one-way conversation with her God. Her body moved freely from side to side, and the tension in her hands was gone, her knuckles no longer white but instead glowing with the rest of her body, illuminated from the inside.

I wanted God to appear in that modest dining hall so Marion could take him to task with her questions and her anger. I wanted God to be forced to explain himself. *Why did her brother have to die? Why did she have to sacrifice so much? Why did I have to be raped? Why did my father want to kill me? Why did my mother do nothing?*

It was so quiet. I wanted Marion to scream so I could scream. I could feel the forbidden Pandora's box opening in a deep place inside me, and I was very purposefully peering inside the tiny cracked lid. I put my hands on the table to stabilize myself in a room that had started to spin out of control.

Marion's back slumped just a fraction, and she felt for her chair behind her and sat down, keeping her eyes to the sky beyond the ceiling.

"I hate You," she said with a whisper, and looked down at her hands.

Betsy and I were the two closest to Marion. Betsy looked like a tiny corpse, cold and embalmed except for the constant tears that were hitting those already gathered on the table. Both her arms lay limp at her sides, and her head hung over the table with her hair closing like a curtain over her eyes. Her pain was sticky; I was afraid to get too close to it, and yet I wanted to move toward her and toward Marion.

I slowly scooted myself down the wooden bench closer to Marion. My movements shattered a nonverbal agreement that we had all made to stay frozen in time. Marion's skin was bunched around her eyes, and her eyebrows held her anger.

I reached out and slowly wrapped my five fingers around her right hand, never looking away from her eyes. I could feel her heartbeat, steady and convincing, through her skin. Her eyes were glassy but still full of blue fire. She exhaled deeply and closed her eyes for several seconds. I took my other hand and placed it palm up in the middle of the table. A moment later, Betsy's hand was in mine and our eyes met. The bones in her face looked broken, and she squeezed my hand tight. Wink placed one hand on top of mine and Marion's and one on top of Betsy's. Laura scooted next to Betsy and did the same. Jeremy had both of his arms on top of Laura's. Jeremy and I looked at each other, and our eyes locked for a moment, which gave me a warm feeling.

The community slowly and organically began to build a cocoon around our table. Some of the bodies were warm; some were like a draft of cold air, as if someone had opened a freezer behind me. We flowed left to right with tears and arms and hands interchanged, layers building and peeling away. People moved slowly, some taking their turn to walk behind Marion and lay their hands on her shoulders or her head, others just staring at her from a distance, looking for the woman they knew.

When MK made it through the layers, she placed her hands on my shoulders; their softness permeated my T-shirt and relaxed my shoulders with experienced and subtle pats. She leaned over and laid her hands on top of ours, then rested her body with a deep breathing in and out, as if she were reminding the rest of us to breathe. She stood and moved behind Marion, placing her hands on Marion's head and closing her eyes. Marion's body rocked slightly from side to side, her eyes still fixed on the sky. People began singing in Latin, a melodic tune that brought more emotion.

In the middle of the third song, which was being chanted in different harmonies, Marion squeezed my fingers and slid her hand out from under mine. She stood, shook her head slightly from side to side, and walked into the kitchen. We sat immobilized until we heard the back door open and close.

Our hands disengaged and we began to move on our own again. I pulled my hands close to my chest, not wanting to lose the connection to something much greater than myself.

The community was in a war zone of disbelief. Betsy had her head down and was crying, her hand still on the table. A dozen or more people began buzzing around, removing the unused dishes, sweeping up the broken glass, and clearing away the food. There was a pungent smell of incense in the air. The room felt raw with the beliefs of 150 people exposed, vulnerable.

"Wink, are you OK?" His back was straight as a board, and his legs were no longer stretched out. Instead, they were at ninety degrees, and both of his hands were on the bench, keeping his back upright.

"No," he said. He was breathing out of his mouth, and his eyes were wide-open, staring at the crucifix over the doorway. He got up and walked into the kitchen.

The cool air enveloped me as I walked out of the basement. I took a deep breath, allowing the smell of dense wood mixed with incense to rest in my lungs. Marion's words raced around inside my mind as I walked slowly around the grounds, following this path or that. I walked to the island chapel, wondering why so many people go to church when they need answers. Leaning against a tree, I watched the community gathering inside, candles flickering in the darkness. I stared at them. They were standing, kneeling, prostrating themselves, and kissing the icons.

I found myself at the bridge. It was freezing, but I needed to be there. I stood in the middle, overlooking the marshy Madawaska River below. I planted my feet on the cold, well-worn timber and rested my head in my hands on the green railing. I was in a trance but aware of my surroundings.

I needed to purge the wreckage inside me. Each memory felt like a sharp piece of glass that I wanted to dump into the lake. I could feel all the pain in my core, and so I let the memories surface one by one.

The first pieces came from the wall I had built to separate myself from the world. These memories felt thick around the edges but hollow in the middle. They were full of disguises and smiles that had never been true. I could see that the veneer had been cracked in a hundred places, and it was just barely holding together with adrenaline and a false sense of control. Other memories came camouflaged, and I couldn't see through to the middle. But I could feel their weight; it was my worthlessness.

I held each of them with reverence as I turned them over in my mind, blessing each one of the tragedies, letting the edges crack and dull before casting them out, with a strength that came from my very center, into the water, knowing that each one had a part in making me who

I was. I imagined them floating on the surface until the water realized how heavy they were, and then each one began to sink, slowly at first, and then the cold blackness engulfed them.

I pictured my father's countless blows and threats to my young body. I was crying now, allowing myself to hate him for what he did to me.

The pieces from my mother were heavy in my hands. They were filled with disbelief and yearning, and they burned my fingers as I held them at arm's length. I was still searching for her, longing for her protection. I bent over the green railing and threw them with sadness as far as I could. I whispered, "I wish you had protected me, Mom."

Another piece came to the surface, and I pulled my arms across my chest. "I'm sorry," I said. "I'm sorry I didn't protect you better. I didn't know how." I stared at the little girl inside that shattered piece of me. I saw the beauty I had been born with, and then I saw the slow eclipse of my childhood. I had tried to hate my mom and dad, but I just ended up hating myself; now there was a quieting.

I didn't hear her come up behind me. She laid her hands on my shoulders and leaned into me. "You have been brave long enough; you can let it out." MK's voice was quiet and purposeful, and I just wanted to listen to it as a song. All the voices I created to make myself OK settled, and I could smell my breath; it was warm and saturated, and suddenly I felt alive. I wasn't just surviving.

"I'm fine," I said. My hands were shaking so much. "I'm fine," I said again, so I could hear it and believe it.

MK moved to stand next to me. She put both hands on the railing close to mine. Her hair was down, blowing in my direction, with a light whisper of lilac. I had never seen her hair down, and I wished for a light to illuminate it. It was thick and looked to have a thousand different colors in it.

We stood looking at the lake. I pictured my fear, shame, and sadness reorganizing themselves down on the bottom amongst the algae and darkness, and my body felt lighter. Then she turned to face me. Her eyes were so soft, they drew me in and held me as she guessed all the things that I had been releasing into the water.

"MK, what happened in Liberia?"

She straightened her back and began to twirl her hair into a bun on top of her head.

"Leave it down; it's so pretty," I said.

"I can't get their beautiful faces out of my head; they were so beautiful. Tiny in stature, so strong on the inside, and giggling as they took turns brushing my hair. And they are all dead." She tied the collected mass of hair and memories tight against her skull. "I always wore it down there, even in the heat. They would come from the villages and brush my hair, and I would brush theirs. It became our daily ritual on their way to gather water . . ." She dropped her arms and laid her hands at her sides.

"I hated God when it happened, and I hated Marion for saving me." She looked past the lake and into the forest. "Trees are so precious in Liberia."

We walked back to St. Germain's in silence.

Before going to sleep, I looked across the two middle rows of beds and saw MK on the opposite side of the room, sitting on her bed with her head in her hands, crying. Her hair was cascading down her back, with round curls the color of bronze mixed with gold and sun flecks. I thought of the little girls in Liberia brushing it. I pulled my hairbrush out of my orange crate and walked to her bed.

"May I?" I said. I kept the brush by my knees until she nodded. I moved behind her and brushed the kaleidoscope of hair that was her past as her tears fell to the cold floor.

CHAPTER 26

The next morning, as slumber wore off, I remembered Marion leaving through the kitchen while the rest of us stayed in the dining room, angelic voices carrying her out the door to God knows where. I thought of the different eyes I had seen, the fear in so many. They had bet their lives on God—or maybe they had bet their lives on Marion—and now they had to look deeper.

I walked to church and breakfast alone, wondering who was holding Marion's hand right now. She wasn't in church. She wasn't at breakfast either, which made it a somber event. Even the homemade jam that usually came out only on Sundays tasted sour.

Father Jim and I sat in the little library after the dishes were finished. I wanted to meet for spiritual direction about as much as I wanted to bury my face in a beehive.

"What do you think about what Marion said at dinner last night?" he asked, not making eye contact with me.

I sat tall, not leaning on the bookshelf behind me, and replied, "I thought it was beautiful—I mean sad, but it was beautiful too. I have so much respect for her telling her truth and being so vulnerable."

He raised his head and looked at me. "Say more."

"I felt as if I were watching parents fight—not my parents but other parents—and I was the kid, watching and learning how to argue, hate . . . I don't know. In a way, I feel bad saying this, but I want more of that sincerity and questioning in my life. I don't want more suffering for her; I just want more honesty."

I hadn't meant to say that much. "Do you know where she is?" I asked.

"Yes. She met with some of the staff this morning, and I was there. She leaves this afternoon to go take care of her brother's affairs. She will likely be gone for a few weeks."

"Did she apologize for what she said last night?" I looked out the window to my bridge in the distance, took a big breath in, and held it.

"She didn't."

I let my breath out. "Good."

He cocked his head to the side. "Good?"

"Yes, good. I have to go; MK said she's taking me to a different *poustinia*, and we need to get going."

"Do you two beauties need an escort?"

I got up without replying and walked into the kitchen to find MK.

MK and I had been hiking for over an hour. It was absolutely frigid out, but walking up the hill was moving some warmth through my body. Whenever the sun popped out from behind the clouds, we quickly moved to wherever it was and grabbed every ray we could. I liked the sound of my boots crunching on the freshly fallen snow; I felt part of something instead of separate.

So often my mind wandered to Marion, and in my own way I prayed for her. I asked that she be surrounded with peace even though I knew that would be impossible. I longed to have her ability to be real, to impart to herself and the community what she was feeling inside. I was still terrified of the silence and of being alone.

There had been a few moments in the last months when I'd felt something different, something vast and unexplored inside myself, something peaceful. The moments would come at odd times: during a walk when the sun was out, while staring at a beautiful array of vegetables, or while sipping tea at night. I wondered if it was my spirit trying to introduce itself to me. Whatever those moments were, I began to crave them, look for them around a peaceful corner or in a quiet conversation.

I could feel one of those moments trying to break through as I hiked behind MK. I appreciated the cool air in my lungs, the delicate white drifts of snow that fell from the trees and glistened in the sun before hitting the earth. I could see a tiny cabin ahead of us; it looked only a smidgen bigger than an outhouse. MK led us onto the pocket-size front porch, and we turned and faced the little river we had just crossed. I had no idea where I was or how to get back, and I felt gratitude for MK.

I was looking down and brushing the snow off my hood. "It's beautiful here."

MK was staid. Her eyes were fixed on mine, and she took my hands and held them with hers. I surveyed our surroundings, aware that the energy had just shifted.

"This is *your poustinia. Your* desert."

I did a double take and met her eyes again. "Way out here? Absolutely not," I said. Panic rose to my throat. *I will not stay here alone. I will not. I would rather die. We haven't seen another person in over an hour.*

"This is a holy place of discovery and healing," she said as she held both my hands in hers.

"No, *pleeease*, I can't stay here alone. There is nothing here, no one. Please, stay with me. I can't . . ."

"Be here. Heal. Allow yourself to go into the depths of your being. Without God, without knowing. Just you."

She handed me a small paper bag and walked off the porch. I watched her walk over a small bridge and disappear into the thick evergreen trees just as the sky started to dump snow.

The only food I had was the three pieces of brown bread—which tasted of the outdoor oven where they had been made—and a cookie I'd stolen.

I had twenty-two hours before I could leave, and I needed to make one stolen cookie, two cigarettes, some stale brown bread, and a half gallon of water go the distance with me. I had to get the woodstove going, which meant I needed to force myself outside into the blizzard to collect wood before it got dark, so I wouldn't freeze to death.

White was all I could see outside, but somehow it began to emulate every color of the rainbow as I stared out the old wood-framed window. Even the thousands of evergreens that surrounded my cabin were shades of white.

I looked at the Bible sitting on the tiny nightstand by the twin bed. It was the only book in the cabin, and all I could think of was how much I wanted to use it for kindling. I asked myself if it would be just to spite my father or to test God, to see if He really would strike me down as I had been taught He would.

My father's gun snuck into my consciousness, as it had a thousand times before, and it was as if it had happened yesterday. I felt myself physically cower inside the forgotten cabin. I was that little girl in a grown-up body. I thought of the night I was raped, and afterward sitting in the bathtub. I wondered now if I should have taken my own life, there in the lukewarm water. Let my life slip away in that cold porcelain vat.

I felt the memories breathing inside me. Dark, spitting, unforgiving. I moved toward the cigarettes that were on the other side of the room, just five steps away. I picked up a cigarette and placed it between my lips before rubbing my fingers up and down my black corduroy pants to stimulate some warmth inside that living hell.

I slid down the wall next to the wood-burning stove, unable to stop the show that I knew would begin any moment. One by one, the memories came. They flashed against the backdrop of the tiny knotted wall as if in a silent movie. The memories now demanded a voice; I had always seen them from a distance, watching from above, never surrendering to the reality that this was my childhood, my journey, that I was watching.

My body swayed left to right, and my own blood was burning my insides. The energy was being forced to my throat and begging my voice to come to the surface and scream out against the injustice.

"I WILL NOT! No. NO. NO! Please," I screamed at the blank wall, trying to bargain for my own release.

I struck a match and fitted it against the precious cigarette. The smoke burned deep inside my already dirtied lungs, and I was grateful for the rush it ignited inside me.

These memories had existed as terrors that had become horribly comfortable.

The ash fell onto my corduroys and startled my flesh beneath.

"What time is it? Where did MK go?" I said aloud.

My body was slumped and stiff, and somehow I had stuffed myself into the corner behind the wood-burning stove. I moved my fingers and toes to alleviate the tingling, and my legs began to shake.

"MK! Where did MK go? She was here, wasn't she?" I stood and ran to the only door out of this nightmare. "I need to get it together. OK, open the door," I commanded, and my hand moved toward the door handle.

The cabin was closing in, and I couldn't take a breath. I put my right hand in my mouth and pulled down to make sure it was open, and I could feel the pressure of my teeth making indentations on my fingers. The pain it produced made me feel less afraid, and I pulled harder. My eyes darted around the cabin. How could it be that the cabin was getting smaller when nothing was moving?

My left hand was on the wrought-iron door handle, and I could feel its metallic coldness. I pulled on the door in hopes of ripping it off its hinges to give me more space to breathe, but it wouldn't open.

The pulsing in my body had its own rhythm. There was a soft humming in my ears, and my legs were taking turns carrying the weight of my body. I planted my feet, put the cigarette between my teeth, and repeatedly pulled on the door handle with both hands.

I spit the cigarette butt on the floor and screamed, "Let me out, goddammit! LET ME OUT!"

My fingers felt raw from pulling, and I yanked again. The door flew open and slammed against the wall. I landed flat on my back. I shot up and ran out the door.

The snow hit my exposed arms and face like a million mosquitoes pricking my skin. I ran into the nothingness, screaming my mother's mantra of "Jesus, Jesus, Jesus" in hopes that it would somehow keep me safe, the way it had not in my youth.

My breath was shallow and labored, and I could see it billowing in front of me from the cold. My body was on high alert, and I had no escape plan. I began to run through the forest as the sun started its decline for the day. I ran. I ran faster. The freezing bits of ice hitting my body were desperately trying to slow me down.

My body began to itch from the cold. My arms were purple, and the ice that had formed in my hair was freezing my brain. My pace was slowing; the more I told my feet to run, the slower they moved. My thoughts were blurry, wandering from the pain on the inside of my body that could give no voice to the physical pain of being in the cold. I thought of my mother, her beauty and her viciousness. My father, his thundering presence and narcissism. And me: *What would I say that I am? Nothing. Nothing but cold and exhausted to my core.* I was alone.

If I lay down there in the snow, it could be over. I could go to sleep and never wake up; the pain would finally be gone. I looked around for a soft spot.

"I will walk," I said out loud. I walked, frozen and broken, and tried to find my way back to the cabin. I recognized the enormous maple tree that was surrounded by evergreens and thought I might be on the right path.

It was almost dark now; the sounds of the forest were somehow quieter, the wind still whistling through the canopy of the trees but with a gentler presence. I listened as the snow crunched under my boots and the dusk gave way to night. I looked up, and the first star glistened against the black backdrop. I wanted to hold it, or at least steal some of its brilliance. I was alone, but maybe I was enough.

I scrounged for sticks for the fire along the way. The door was still open when I got to the cabin. I put the sticks in the stove and headed out for some logs that I had spotted just a few feet from the cabin.

I built the fire the way Shirley had taught me: a teepee of sticks, smaller ones on the inside and getting progressively bigger on the outside. It was working, and I sent a small smile to her across the miles through my chattering teeth. I took off all my clothes, spread them out on the small stove, and stood close to the fire, begging for warmth.

The fire was ready for its first log, and I gingerly placed it, wanting to touch the flames. The heat began to swell and warm the tiny room. I turned and saw the forgotten paper bag that MK had left on the bed and practically ran the five steps from one side of the cabin to the other. I grabbed the bag and ran back to the fire. My fingers moved slowly from the cold. I pulled out one large piece of white paper and a pen. There were three words on it with three dots next to them: "I AM KATHLEEN . . ."

I stared at the empty white space on the page, wanting to fill it in but knowing the ink would spill a tragic story of my identity. I wanted it to be different. I had caught some short, beautiful glimpses of myself in the months I had been here, but they seemed and felt like glimpses of someone else, someone with power and worthiness.

I stood naked, holding the pen, and realized that I had begun to share some gentle and loving moments with myself in the quiet confines of my soul. I felt a pendulum inside that was swinging from self-harm to belief in myself.

I had walked into this community carrying more than I could handle. I had had no pendulum, just self-doubt, confusion, and a façade to introduce people to so they would not scratch the surface to find me. Now I was looking at a piece of paper with three words on it, and there was a desire to define myself differently.

What if I filled it in with the truth, in black and white, and owned my journey? What if I stopped wanting to change my childhood? What if I could find a mirror, look into it, and say out loud that I was raped, that my mother knew it and did nothing, and that I was scared to eat now because of it somehow? What if I could say the number of times my father had threatened me, the number of times he had hit me with force? What if I could tell myself how different I felt from every other person on the planet because of it? What if I could say I hated them for what they did?

Maybe, if I could say all of it out loud, then somehow, I wouldn't be afraid of myself anymore. I wouldn't need to run so hard. I wouldn't need the adrenaline. *I* would love me. *I* would fill me. I would connect myself to the rest of the world, even if it was with pain as the common denominator amongst us all. I would connect to people at their core because I would be connected to myself.

I couldn't stop staring at the three words and the blankness surrounding them. I felt the weight of the pen and dropped it back into the bag. I put on my almost-dry clothes and stoked the fire again, watching the embers suck the oxygen.

"Just write one word. One word from the inside out. What is my essence?" I said to the fire.

I had cried until there was no sound. I had experienced the unforgivable darkness. But all along, in the deepest part of me, I had known that I was strong. Strong enough to look my father in the eye when he hurt me. Now I had to walk beyond, one step past where I thought I could go—that would be where I would find my breath, my voice, my life. I would not be able to return to who I was, and I did not want to.

I am Kathleen . . . I felt the pen in my right hand, ready to make its mark. I was finally holding the instrument; it was my life in my hand. I stared at its strangeness and felt what it was capable of revealing.

I am Kathleen . . . I sat on the bed and began to reveal who I was.

"I am Kathleen . . . I am Worthy, Powerful, Connected, and Sensual."

I started to laugh inside of what used to be my cabin of terror. The words were sitting in me, wiggling their way to the forefront and watching other untrue, exhausted words be dismissed from their posts. The first rays of sun were poking through the wood-framed window, and I kept writing my essence.

I said those beautiful words aloud for my being to hear.

"I am Kathleen . . . I am Worthy, Powerful, Connected, and Sensual, experiencing life with Abundance, Laughter, and Vulnerability."

I had known tears of pain, tears of denial, and tears of fear. These were different: they were tears of release, and they were running down my face more impertinently than any other tears before. These simple drops touched my skin with forgiveness. Only now they could give me worth instead of emptiness, power from survival, and connection instead of dark separation. I gave myself permission to be me. Whoever that would be, I promised to live by my essence instead of my past.

For the first time, I loved myself.

CHAPTER 27

We were down to onions, beets, and carrots in the root cellar; that was it. I filled the wheelbarrow and made my way back to the farmhouse. The sun warmed the snow, and I wanted to stay outside all day. It was the first day I could remember when I wasn't absolutely freezing.

MK was waiting for me at the back door. "Here, let me help . . ."

She took the basket of frozen carrots out of my hands.

"Um, I know there's a phone in the study. Can I make a call? I definitely won't take long."

"Yes, that phone call is way overdue. Can I sit with you?" Of course she knew I was calling my dad.

I stood up straight to remind myself that I was a grown-up and said, "I'm scared."

"Of course you are, but more important is that you're ready. Now, let's go: we have a busy day ahead of us. Don't dawdle; come on."

I led the way to the study off the kitchen, paused just slightly, then walked to the recliner, sat down, and looked at MK, who was sitting on the couch diagonal from me. I locked on her eyes and didn't need any words. I picked up the green handle and dialed my childhood phone number.

Ring.

Ring.

Ring.

On the fourth ring, I heard his voice.

"Hello." It hadn't changed: it was demanding and powerful. I froze. "Hello," he said again. I didn't want to call him "Dad" or "Father," but I didn't know what else to call him.

"Um, hi. It's me, Kathleen . . ."

He cut me off before I could say anything more. "It's about time."

"I know," I said as my voice got louder. I didn't sound like a young girl; I sounded older, wiser, and grown-up. "I'm not coming home tomorrow." I smiled at the phone and said it again: "I'm not coming home."

"You *are* coming home, Kathleen." His voice was less scary.

"No. I'm not. Good-bye, D . . . Good-bye." I gently put the receiver back on the hook and looked out the window. The sun was shining bright against the snow.

"Well, that's that. Let's get going." MK was up and ready. I joined in behind her with a kick in my step.

"Your hair has grown a lot." She tossed the words over her shoulder at me. "You are taking care of yourself," MK said.

"You mean I'm getting fat," I said.

"I gave the scale from our bathroom to St. Joseph's," she said, her eyes straight ahead.

"You did *not*. MK . . ."

"You weren't being healthy," she said. "I'm really proud of you, not just for today, but for looking at yourself and doing the work. And wearing size sixes." She looked back at me and smiled.

"How do you . . . Never mind," I said. *Of course* she knew my obsession with the scale and my trips up the rickety stairs to find clothes. I could put only one finger between my skin and my jeans. "My heart feels lighter," I said, and as I walked up beside her, MK took my hand in hers.

"Today is one of my favorite 'B's' of the year," she said as we walked to a faraway barn with about a dozen other people headed in the same direction. The term "B" came from "the Baroness," Catherine Doherty, the founder of Madonna House. The residents used to call her "the B."

Somehow, over time, it had morphed into the name for tasks that weren't regular everyday ones.

I hadn't paid much attention to the dark-colored barn we were approaching before; it had blended into the backdrop of the farm.

"What kind of a 'B' is it?"

MK's bun was loose today, and her arms were moving like spokes in a wheel, quickly pulling her up the hill to our destination. "It is a chicken 'B.'"

I immediately hoped it wasn't like the sheep "B." I had spent three full days taking the freshly cut wool and banging it against barbed wire set on top of two step stools to get the feces off. It was disgusting, and it took forever to get the lanolin out of my hair. Wink had called me "Slick" for a month.

"This 'B' is only one day, and it is beautiful to see our community honor life in every cycle. Even death."

"What?" I said.

We were at the door of the barn, and people were filing in one by one. I was hoping it would be warm when we got inside. I looked at MK. She looked happy today. I realized how grateful I was to be with her.

The barn smelled like damp hay and uncertainty. There were five lightbulbs throughout the building, and it was cloudy and ill lit. There was one station for eight people with empty buckets on a table; the other station had contraptions set in a straight line with a handle on the end and what looked to be sharp knives on a wheel in the middle.

MK took my hand and led me to one of the paint bucket stations, where she was going to be in charge. Her hand was so calming to my heart that I didn't want her to let go. People settled into their stations, and then Father Jim began with a prayer.

His voice was loud, and he had his back to countless chickens that were busily looking for grain. "Heavenly Father, we gather here today and ask You to bless Your creations. May they nourish our bodies and fill us with Your goodness. Keep us safe and guide us closer to You."

I leaned over and too loudly said, "Shit, MK, are we going to kill those chickens? Please say no. Shit."

"*You're* not going to; they are. No cursing and no talking," she said as she pointed at five farmers and Wink, who were standing by the pen, most in overalls.

Once everyone was settled in front of an empty paint bucket, MK took her place in front of us and began. "One of the farmers will hand you a chicken. The head will have just been cut off . . ."

Had she just said what I thought she'd said? *Please don't continue,* I begged silently.

". . . the body is going to be warm, and you may still feel some movement inside the chicken, which is normal."

OK, I can't even get a paper cut without having to put my head between my legs; the sight of blood is too much. What the hell do I do with the dead chicken when it's handed over from its beheader? I knew better than to interrupt MK when she was in this role. At least there was an empty bucket in case I needed to throw up.

MK's head was slowly rotating to look at each of us. Her shoulder blades glided down her back, and her neck was long. Even delivering this news, MK looked regal, as if she were holding court.

"Open the gullet of the chicken and stick your arm down into the open area and retrieve any unlaid eggs. They almost feel like a soft-boiled egg without the shell. Just root around until you find it; we don't want any to go to waste." She made a scooping motion with her right hand.

"Take the shell-less egg or eggs out of the chicken and put them in the bucket in front of you. Periodically, I will ask one of you to gather the eggs from all buckets into one. The first bucket will go to Laura in the kitchen for lunch today. The others will go to the root cellar until we load them up to be taken to the main house. Here, watch," she said as Wink approached.

Wink was walking toward us with a decapitated chicken in his hand. The feathers were wilted, but the feet still had life in them. MK took the chicken from Wink and came and stood in front of me. She took my hand, pushed my sleeve up to my underarm, and stuck both of our hands down the gullet, wiggling my fingers with hers to find the unready egg.

"Feel for it with me . . . There—feel that? That is the egg. Cup it with your palm and bring it up."

"Oh my God . . . this gives 'fowl' a whole new meaning." Everybody chuckled except for MK, who tilted her head to the side and opened her eyes wide in my direction.

"Sorry." I laughed, which was better than throwing up. "It looks like a real egg. It is disgusting and amazing at the same time," I said.

"C'est la vie," MK said, and turned to teach the other group how to defeather the chickens using the primitive contraption with the handle.

I put the egg in the bucket with a loud *schlup*.

"Welcome to the Easter egg hunt," Wink said, and smiled as he handed me another dead chicken.

"What did the chicken say to the farmer?" Wink said to the people sitting and eating at the wooden table in the farm kitchen.

"OK, enough with the chicken jokes while we're eating," Betsy said.

Father Jim walked up to our table. He was wearing painter's pants and a black T-shirt, and he had tiny specks of white paint in his hair.

"Ready for a chat?" he said to me. He walked toward the kitchen, and I followed, leaving very little on my lunch plate. I looked at it and smiled as I left.

We went into the study, and Father Jim closed the door behind him. I hadn't noticed what the study looked like before this morning, and I took a moment to look around. It had a door to the outside on the far side of the room. There was wood paneling from the 1970s and a green shag carpet. It was cozy and warm. Father Jim had seated himself in the recliner next to the couch. I looked out the window and saw people starting to filter back into the barn for the afternoon session of the chicken "B."

"Let's begin with a prayer," he said. I took my seat on the couch. "Almighty Father, Kathleen comes here to seek guidance from You. May I be Your humble servant and relay Your words to her." Father Jim's eyes opened and he looked around the room.

"My heart feels great today. I feel happy," I told him.

I'd been thinking about sharing more deeply with Father Jim—test the waters, maybe. So much had happened to me since I got there. I had spent my life living in terror, and now I had real moments, sometimes whole days, of peace.

Father Jim interrupted my thoughts. "God wants your heart to be heavy so you will let Him in to help you."

"Heavy?" I said. "I just said I was happy."

"What is heavy for you? Tell me something heavy."

I looked at him and spit the words out. "I was raped." I immediately wanted to get the words back.

Father Jim sat farther back in his chair. He looked at me and nodded his head in silence. I wanted to get up and run, but I just sat there. My chest and neck were vibrating, and I put my hand to my heart.

I took a very deep breath. "His name was Robert." My eyes searched around the room, looking for him. As if saying his name out loud could make him manifest.

"My parents knew but didn't do anything, so they must have believed it was my fault. Maybe it *was* my fault. I have never told a single person. I have never talked about it." I put my hands on my knees to make them stop shaking, and I looked at Father Jim.

"Please don't tell anyone." I was foggy and light-headed. I intertwined my fingers and pulled them apart. They were wet with fear.

I put one hand on the back of my head. Pain was ripping across the back of my skull. I clutched my belly, holding down the vomit that was trying to escape through my narrowing esophagus.

I looked at Father Jim, who shifted to the front of the recliner, cleared his throat, and looked at me.

"It would be hard to count the number of confessions I've heard from the men in this community because of you," Father Jim said. "I don't know if a day has gone by . . ." He was speaking as if in a tunnel, the words losing their form in the short distance from his mouth to my ears.

"What?"

"At first it was just because you were a new face for them to fantasize about—happens all the time when new girls get here. You were pretty put together, if I remember right, in the beginning. I understood what they were talking about: you really got under some skin here with the males."

He paused and looked out the window. I was staring at him, unable to move.

"Then you started gaining weight and your attractive quotient went up; men like a little meat on a girl's bones, ya know. I remember that red shirt you used to wear a lot when you first got here. I liked when you wore that . . ."

I squeezed my knees tightly together, my chest was so heavy. I gasped, trying to get oxygen to my lungs. I swallowed excessively and stared at him. He wasn't looking at me; he was still looking out the window and smiling. I raised my right hand off my knee just slightly and waved it back and forth, wanting his attention. My whole torso was moving with the wave of my hand.

From a faraway place, I heard Father Jim say, "I absolve you of your sins. For your penance, say one Hail Mary and one Our Father. I absolve you in the name of the Father, the Son, and the Holy Spirit."

There was a roiling heat in my blood. I could feel it begin to pulse like water before a boil.

"What exactly did you just absolve me from?" It came out as a whisper, so I stood, tried to plant my feet, and said it again. Much louder. "What exactly did you just absolve me from?"

Keele Burgin

Father Jim pushed his arms into the seat of the recliner and pushed himself up in his chair. "Oh," he said.

"'OH'? Did you just say 'Oh' like you didn't even remember that I was here? Oh?" My tone was certain. I fumbled with my shirtsleeve, pushing it up my arm and down again. I walked to the window, turned, and looked him dead in the eye. My body was still trembling, but I was sturdy on the inside.

"Sit down and we can talk about something else," Father Jim said as he settled into his chair again.

I heard a faint buzzing in my ears, and then something snapped and the buzzing was gone. The air was cold going into my lungs, and I could taste salt on my tongue. I took a deep breath, held it tight inside of me. I narrowed my eyes to meet his and stood straight.

"I was fifteen. I was only fifteen!" I sat on the couch and looked down at my feet. My shoulders were so heavy, I let them slump toward the floor. "No, I won't do this." I stood up and faced Father Jim again. "Look me in the eye," I demanded, and continued.

"How dare you . . ." My voice was loud again. I was fighting to find the words, translating them as if from a different language. The heat in my body was rising up my neck, and I took two steps closer to him.

"You just absolved the wrong person!" My breath was noisy, and heat flushed through my body.

Father Jim looked at me.

His body slouched against the back of his chair, and he cast his eyes to the floor. He looked bored. I stepped in front of him, bent my head to look in his eyes, and said, "You and my dad are the same." Then I opened the wooden door and walked into the kitchen, shaking from head to toe.

"Well, well . . ." MK walked to me from the stove.

"I think I am going to throw up." I had no idea why MK wasn't at the chicken "B," but I was grateful for her presence. I later wondered if she had had some sort of intuition or wanted to protect me.

"You're going to be just fine. Come here." She took my hand and led me into the privacy of the greenhouse. The stillness and the smell of herbs were so different from the boiling anger I felt inside. I was stiff, and I gasped for breath.

We sat on the rock ledge and she pulled me close to her. I smelled the soap from the laundry on her shirt. I let myself relax against her chest.

"No one is going to hurt you again. It wasn't your fault." She rocked me back and forth until I could feel my muscles loosen, and I went limp in her arms. My eyes were so tired; I finally blinked and the burn sent tears down both cheeks.

"You are unpacking some tricky stuff. Just breathe," she said. "You talked, you turned the light on. You are so brave." She combed my hair down my back with her fingers, and I cried until there was nothing left. Finally, the thousand-pound sack of shame I had been carrying around since childhood lay in a puddle on the greenhouse floor.

"MK?" I said.

"Yes."

"I feel better. I mean, my whole body feels . . . different. It's hard to explain, but I feel like . . . um . . . I feel . . . whole." I sat up straight and looked at her. "Thank you."

"You are so deserving." Her eyes were a deep well of pain and acceptance and love. "No one has power over you anymore. You are in charge of your life."

"I've been buried alive all my life. All I could do was keep digging," I said.

"Not anymore: you are out in the bright, shiny light where you belong," she said, hugging me.

"No more spiritual direction for me," I said.

"OK. No more spiritual direction for you."

"I'm sorry you missed your favorite 'B' this afternoon," I said.

CHAPTER 28

Summer, 1994

It was afternoon teatime, and I was in the little library behind the main dining room, writing to Shirley. I missed her, and I felt more connected to her than ever. I had accepted my past, and it allowed me to love Shirley even more. The miles didn't matter: I could reach out and touch her hand, picture cooking with her, and almost hear her crackling whisper of a voice as I finished the letter.

I folded it up, put a stamp on it, and placed it in the mail drop.

I walked to the back of the dining room and hid myself in a corner to experience the community for the last time. The thousands of moments were coming to a close . . . the learnings, duties of the moment. I felt my cells had been renewed and repurposed and were now taking their bow.

Wink would tell everyone when I was gone; I wanted it that way. "Good-bye" means forever, and since these people would be traveling with me in my heart, there was no need to utter a word. This was not a place where you said good-bye; you just passed through, took a piece of each one of them with you, intertwined it with the very fabric of your being, and kept moving and hopefully growing. These people had embraced my brokenness, put up with the defiance that masked my fear, and helped me replace it with stillness, acceptance, and self-love. They had allowed me to heal myself, in my own time. Their love had given me what I hoped to be lasting repair. A gift I hoped to give others.

I caught Wink's eye and smiled. He was a big brother watching me grow and change and fall in love with myself over time. He was completely himself, with humble confidence, and never took anything too seriously. He was a lovely man, and I would miss him greatly.

I looked around the room for Father Jim. He was sitting with a newly arrived guest. I was grateful to him in a way that was hard to explain to my heart. He had helped me grow in a profound and lasting way; because of him, I had stood up for myself and realized my truth. He was the first person in my life that I had fully let myself be angry at; I had let the emotions out even when they didn't look pretty.

He was there to remind me to speak louder and have conviction about who I was as a woman. He was there to remind me that some people would only see my outside and that they would be missing the best part of me.

Oh, MK. I heard her laugh before I spotted her on the opposite side of the dining room. She was wearing her Christmas sweater, and her hair was as frenetic as ever, still trying to escape the bun on top of her head. Maybe her laugh was better than most because I knew the sadness of what had happened in Liberia would return and dissolve her laughter into tears.

She had taught me to put down my angry façade and actually *be* angry. She had taught me that tears have a place in my life—that they could help me understand myself better and cleanse my shame. What a gift that we spilled them together in our cozy farm kitchen. I had never seen so many tears flow into a recipe.

I saw Marion Scott sitting at a table reading, and I felt tears of gratitude behind my eyes. She had led me, ever so gently, along this path of the unknown. I would never be able to pay her back for the permission she gave me to test my God, my beliefs, and my worst fears. She had taught me that this was *my* journey with my God, whoever I deemed Her to be. She had taught me that showing my unfiltered emotions, regardless of how dark they felt, was a much-needed release. She had taught me to be honest.

There was no shortage of people to observe and hold close that afternoon. I wanted them all to have a part of me; I finally felt I had something substantial and worthy to give. Instead of closing my eyes in prayer, I opened them fully and silently thanked this crowd of healers for walking beside me for the last year.

"Ready to go, City?" Wink stood next to me.

"Ready." I stood up, grabbed my backpack, and headed out the door to the van with Wink.

We drove in calm silence to the café. Standing outside, leaning against the van, I could feel his peace and his protectiveness as we waited for the bus.

"Thank you, Wink." My heart was full as I listened to the whistling of spring sounds swirling around us. I slid a whole pack of Marlboro Lights into his pocket.

The bus pulled up to the café, and we watched as a skinny blond girl walked off and began unloading her suitcases from the underbelly of the bus. I watched her eyes darting around, trying to find a place to land as she tried to take in the lay of the land.

Wink pulled me close and hugged me.

"You've got this, City."

I walked toward the bus, and as I hopped onto the first step, I turned to watch him walk to the blond girl, who was sitting on top of her suitcases.

"Howdy," he said.

"Um, hi. Do you know how to get to Madonna House?" she asked.

ACKNOWLEDGMENTS

It is a miracle any book makes it into the world. The sheer terror of it not being good enough to get published, followed by an equal amount of fright that it will get published, is not for the faint of heart. For that, I thank Erin Calligan Mooney at Little A; her guidance and mind meld about what this book needed to be in the world was intensely comforting to me.

I wrote this book because I want all women to tell their stories. The story, with all the truth, vulnerability, guilt, shame, and knowing, that occupies every life. I want to hear the ones that spill from the deepest places inside, the places that haven't been given a voice yet, the things they don't want to say out loud. In the end, when mine was finally written, it washed me with self-love, worthiness, and acceptance of my passage thus far. I am proud of my journey and all the scars that came with it. I want to pay that feeling forward in every way I am able, for as long as I am here.

If I have learned one thing about myself, it is that I am resilient. I am resilient because I know the following people will carry me if I can't get up. And they have. I have no contact with my family of origin, so the people below and their families are my chosen family and always will be.

Helena, you are my sister for life. We've come a long way, babe, from "I like your bangs," to raising our amazing children together. I'm pretty sure our kiddos don't know that they aren't blood related. I can't help but love that! Thank you for being Noah's godmother, for lending your wisdom in challenging (and completely insane) life situations, for your true listening ear, and for your hilarious and contagious sense of humor. Our ability to laugh, self-deprecate, and support each other through our trying roads has been such a source of love in my life. In so many ways, we have grown up together, and I am thrilled to see what's in the cards for us moving forward. I love you.

Meeshie, thank you for your unswerving love. We have walked through a lot in our decades together. I will never forget telling you that Noah was in my belly; what a magical moment. Thank you for coming to Boulder every week when my twins were born and jumping in with both feet when I was so overwhelmed. Thank you for being L's and G's godmom, for same/sames, for Thailand (oh the memories), for dealing with my lack of planning, and for loving who I love without judgment. We kid that we take turns picking each other up, and I honestly don't know what would have happened if you weren't there for the last round. I needed you like breath, and there you were. Thank you.

Alio, wow, what a journey we have been on together. Thank you for teaching me that family can be chosen and women are trustable. I love our decades, our story (the ups and downs), our late-night dance parties, our spectacular rendition of "Total Eclipse of the Heart," our collective craziness with raising our kiddos, and I love our honesty and ability to call each other out, because we know all of our patterns inside and out. You are so blessed to have Judy and Birdy, and I am so grateful you have shared them with me. I love being counted as one of your family. Our daily touch points have been a lifeline for me and our commitment to not be in crisis at the same time has proved to be essential. I love our laughter. Being able to tell you all the things I don't want to say out loud has been intensely freeing. It has been an honor to grow with you.

Colette, ahhhh, Colette . . . our hours of talking, laughing, eating at our favorite dives, and allowing the world to ebb and flow around us has been a pure gift. I am so grateful for the way we pick each other up out of the muck. And my favorite line of yours, "I am grateful for your dad, 'cause he made you the badass, resilient woman you are." I so appreciate your candor, your contagious laughter, and your ability to be exactly who you are no matter who's around. Even when you drop the f-bombs in front of my boys. (Keep doing it; they love it.)

Emily, you are steadfast, and you give from the most generous place. I am so grateful that our worlds came together. Thank you for allowing me to see your world up close; I am so proud of the woman you are and the commitment you inspire in others. It is delicious to see you happy; you are so deserving!

Bob, our childhoods collided, but we gave each other our greatest gifts: our three boys. Thank you for nurturing me as a writer, for the nights at Laudisio's where I was scared to read my words out loud, and for helping me get ready to soar.

BrookieJi, my amazing sister. Thank you for being a rock; you never wavered when I wasn't quite ready to see the truth. Thank you for your part in getting me here. Your unique outlook on life has given me more freedom to be who I am meant to be in the world. I admire your loyalty, your undeniable intuition, the way you pour love on your people, and your sheer strength. I love the way we just get each other, whether it be on a trip (ahhhh, Bali, Tulum . . .), an impromptu late-night get-together, or a magical night out in Boulder, I can look over at you and know that you are in my life forever, and I am so grateful.

And now for the heartbeats that beat with mine.

Noah, my Bu. Thank you for being my protector; I promise I am OK, so you can relax; and if I am not, I know I can lean on you. Your trust and confidence in me has allowed me to step deep into the woman

I am. Thank you for teaching me how to be a mom, for calling me Mama in only the way you know how to do, for allowing me to make mistakes, and for helping me learn that this is your journey. I get the distinct privilege of watching you grow into the amazing young man you are with all the bumps and bruises that it should and does come with. You have been through ten lifetimes of experiences in your short journey thus far, and I know in my heart of hearts that you will use them for the betterment of others. Your sensitive, amazing, full-of-life heart has the ability to change all those that come in contact with you.

Liam, my sting bee, my LBK, my poet. You are wise beyond the years you have logged here. Thank you for always catching me and saying the one thing I need to hear to get my writing back on track. Thank you for calling me out on my fear about completing my book, for telling me to "jump" (that poem you wrote for me is etched in my heart), and for always finding me right when I need a hug and an "I love you, Mom." When you write, you melt my heart. Please, please write. I love your ability to see a photo and then take it, and the way you tell stories through your films. I am forever grateful for the day we bumped into my father for the first time in years and you held my hand so tight. You were nine, and you were so brave. When he bent down and said, "Do you know who I am?" you spoke with strength and said, "You are my mother's father." He bent down, looked at you, and aggressively said, "I am your grandfather." With your beautiful power, you retorted, "No, you are my mother's father." You are a genuine and intuitive boy; believe in both, they will guide you in your life.

Greyson, my G$, my G, my sweet boy. Thank you for your earnestness, for the way you lead with such grace and kindness. I love your devotion to animals, your love of our family, and your big dreams for your future. You can do absolutely anything you set your mind to. Don't forget that it is OK to make mistakes along the way. I love your drawings and your writing; you know how to capture a moment and add magic. Thank you for breakie in bed and for writing to me. I am grateful for your sensitive, amazing soul. I'll never forget when the doctor told me you didn't have a heartbeat at six weeks and that you were not viable. I never, not for a second, believed her. I knew you were there and that you had big things to do in this world. And here you are doing them. I look forward to watching your journey every single day, and I am so proud to be your mom.

Keith, your intense care, empathy, and intuitive nature has allowed me the safety to spill my traumas. Thank you for being the perfect blend of persistent and gentle and for guiding me to this healing place. I could not have written this book without going back to my childhood and doing the work to identify what happened and internalize that it was not my fault. Our work together gave me that priceless gift. Thank you for showing up the way you have for over ten years, I am beyond grateful to have you in my life.

ABOUT THE AUTHOR

Photo © 2018 Jonathan Caliguire

Keele Burgin is an entrepreneur, activist, mother of three, author, and filmmaker. Her story of survival and self-discovery has inspired a life dedicated to impacting tens of thousands of women across the globe. She has served in leadership roles on the boards of multiple nonprofit organizations that empower women.

Keele made her mark in the business world by cofounding two companies, taking her first one public. Her second, a venture out of her hometown of Boulder, Colorado, is designed to help women rearchitect their lives by relinquishing the patterns of behavior that hold them back.

For more information, visit www.keeleburgin.com.